in New Jersey

Walks, Hikes, and Backpacking Trips from the Kittatinnies into Cape May

BRUCE C. SCOFIELD
STELLA J. GREEN
H. NEIL ZIMMERMAN

Photographs by the authors

Second Edition

Backcountry Publications
Woodstock, Vermont

An Invitation to the Reader

Over time trails can be rerouted and signs and landmarks altered. If you find that changes have occurred on the routes described in this book, please let us know so that corrections may be made in future editions. The author and publisher also welcome other comments and suggestions. Address all correspondence to:

Editor
50 Hikes™ Series
Backcountry Publications
PO Box 748
Woodstock, VT 05091

Library of Congress Cataloging-in-Publication Data

Scofield, Bruce.
50 hikes in New Jersey : walks, hikes, and backpacking trips from the Kittatinnies to Cape May / Bruce Scofield, Stella J. Green, H. Neil Zimmerman ; photographs by the authors. — [2nd ed.]
p. cm.
Rev. ed. of: Fifty hikes in New Jersey. c1988.
Includes bibliographical references (p.) and index.
ISBN 0-88150-357-6
1. Hiking—New Jersey—Guidebooks. 2. Backpacking—New Jersey—Guidebooks. 3. New Jersey—Guidebooks. I. Green, Stella J. II. Zimmerman, H. Neil. III. Scofield, Bruce. Fifty hikes in New Jersey. IV. Title.
GV199.42.N5S27 1997
796.51'09749—dc21
96-48303
CIP

Second Edition

Published by Backcountry Publications
A division of The Countryman Press
PO Box 748
Woodstock, Vermont 05091

Distributed by W.W. Norton & Company, Inc.
500 Fifth Avenue
New York, NY 10110

Series design by Glenn Suokko
Page compositon by Justine Trubey
Trail overlays by Richard Widhu
Cover photograph © Scott Barrow, Inc./StockBarrow (914-424-4441)

Printed in the United States of America

10 9 8 7 6 5 4 3 2

ACKNOWLEDGMENTS

The authors wish to acknowledge and thank the many people who helped us with information, patience, and enthusiasm. We certainly could not have persevered without them. So, thanks to John Auciello, Thomas Berrian, Dick Bittner, Robert Britton Jr., Jane Bullis, Daniel Chazin, Gary Church, Rab Cika, Wayne Clements, Dean S. Cramer, Earl Danley, Howard Dash, Joan Dean, Mary Derstine, Nancy Diekroger, A. Ross Eckler, William Foley, Ken Garty, German Georgieff, John Green, Robert E. Green, Matthew Guuby, Joyce and Warren Hale, Barbara Harding, Lillian Hoey, Holly Hoffman, Bill Holton, Bob Johnson, Tom Keck, Jeanie Levitan, Christopher Lloyd, Ken Lloyd, Bruce Matthews, Richard Maxwell, Jane McGraw, Barbara McMartin, Richard Maxwell, Bob Messerschmidt, Lucy Meyer, Berte and Bill Miles, Ken Negus, Barry Orr, Daisy Orr, Leslie Presser, Bert Prol, Dave Robinson, Charlie Sanders, David Simpson, Robert Sommers, Malcolm Spector, Bob Spillane, Robert Stillman, Harry Swan, Paul Tarlowe, Bob Torres, Bruno Walmesley, Richard Warner, Jerome Wyckoff, and Russ Zito.

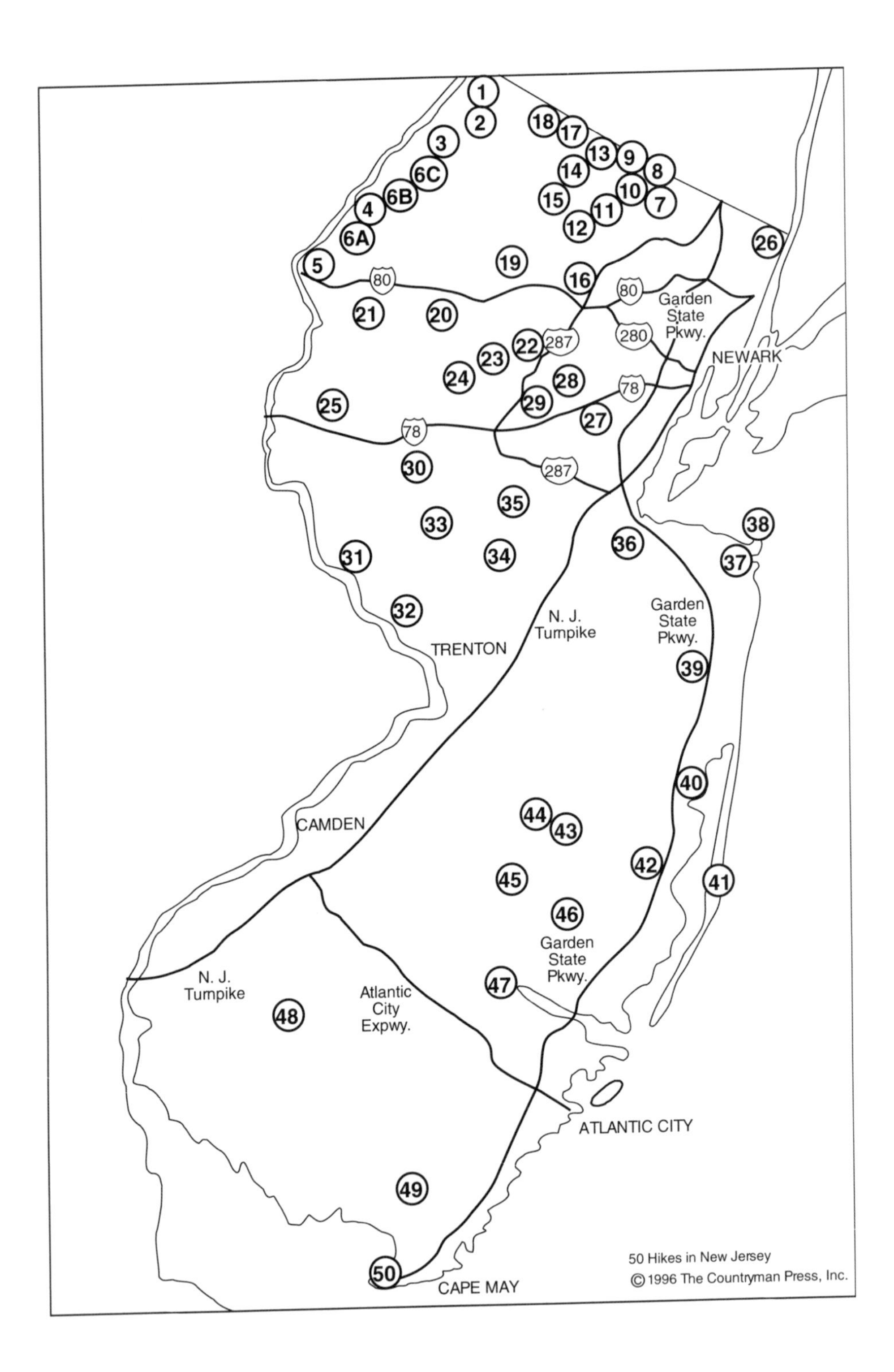
1
2
3
6C
6B
4
6A
5
18
17
13
9
8
14
10
7
15
11
12
26
19
16
80
80
Garden
State
Pkwy.
21
20
22
287
280
23
24
NEWARK
28
78
25
29
27
78
30
287
35
38
33
36
31
34
37
32
Garden
State
Pkwy.
N. J.
Turnpike
TRENTON
39
40
44
43
CAMDEN
42
45
41
46
Garden
State
Pkwy.
47
N. J.
Turnpike
Atlantic
City
Expwy.
48
ATLANTIC CITY
49
50
CAPE MAY
50 Hikes in New Jersey
© 1996 The Countryman Press, Inc.

Contents

COASTAL PLAIN

Introduction

New Jersey boasts an abundance of fine hiking trails. The famous Appalachian Trail crosses the northern part of the state, as does most of the 150-mile Highlands Trail; the 60-mile Delaware and Raritan Canal State Park Trail crosses from New Brunswick to Raven Rock, north of Trenton; the 50-mile Batona Trail traverses the New Jersey Pinelands; and the Long Path commences its journey northward on the Palisades at the George Washington Bridge. Some trails are located on old roads and footpaths that existed prior to the acquisition of the land for public use, and some date back to the Depression and the federally funded Civilian Conservation Corps, whose members built park and recreation facilities still used today. Many trails, including the Appalachian Trail, are maintained by volunteers, whose dedication is evidenced by the fresh paint marks, water bars, and trails cleared of blowdowns and other hazards.

Hiking in the Garden State is varied, from the flat sandy trails in the southern section to the hilly and rocky highlands in the north. There are swamps and beach areas, woods and grasslands. Nine-tenths of New Jersey borders on water; of its 480 miles of boundary, all but 48 are along either the seacoast or a riverbed. Except for the northwest section, the typical New Jersey landscape is a low, flat plain filled with meandering streams; four-fifths of the state is no more than 400 feet above sea level, and most of it is less than 100. The high point, in the northwest corner, is 1803 feet above sea level.

THE GEOLOGY AND TOPOGRAPHY OF NEW JERSEY

Geologists divide New Jersey into four primary provinces. In the northwest, running roughly southwest to northeast, is the Appalachian Ridge and Valley Province, containing the highest elevations in the state. Here, in what was once a major mountain range (since leveled by erosion), is a series of parallel valleys and ridges composed of Silurian and Devonian sandstones and conglomerates 375 to 435 million years old. The Ridge and Valley Province extends for more than 1200 miles from Alabama to Canada and, because of its regularity, is used as a navigational landmark by migrating birds. Hawk sightings along the main ridges are frequent during the fall migration. The Delaware Water Gap National

White-tailed deer in Jockey Hollow (Hike 22)

Recreation Area, Worthington and Stokes State Forests, and High Point State Park together preserve nearly all the mountainous portions of this province. The Appalachian Trail follows the crest of the main ridge, Kittatinny Mountain, for more than 40 miles on its way from Georgia to Maine. The hiking in this province can be challenging because of steep inclines and extremely rocky footing.

Southeast of the Ridge and Valley Province and paralleling it lies the New Jersey Highlands Province. This mountainous area is composed primarily of Precambrian gneisses and schists, which formed 600 to 800 million years ago as the core of mountains even more ancient than those of the Ridge and Valley Province. The elevations of the flat-topped summits characteristic of this province lie only a few hundred feet lower than those in the Kittatinny Mountains. The range extends north into New York State as the Hudson Highlands and south into Pennsylvania as the Reading Prong. (The term "Reading Prong" actually refers to the whole range south of the Hudson in New York, New Jersey, and Pennsylvania.) Hikers will find not only more trails in this province than in any other in the state, but also numerous lakes and reservoirs. The province includes the large Wawayanda State Park and the vast holdings of the Newark Watershed Conservation and Development Corporation, which supplies drinking water to New Jersey's largest city. A number of other state and county parks and forests preserve segments of the natural features of the area.

Comprising most of northeastern and central New Jersey, the Piedmont Lowlands Province is a low-lying plain composed mainly of Triassic and Jurassic sandstones and shales dating back 190 to 215 million years. In places, old lava flows from these periods have withstood erosion better than the shales and sandstones and now stand as mountain ridges. Just across the Hudson River from New York stand the Palisades, the eastern edges of a sill of igneous rock that in places rise more than 500 feet above the river. Farther west are the Watchung Hills, roughly parallel ridges made up of the resistant edges of westward-sloping, basaltic lava flows, which also rise about 250 feet above the surrounding plans. Cushetunk Mountain and others near it are somewhat similar features called *dikes,* composed of diabase, not basalt; they are found in the southwestern portion of the province where it extends into central New Jersey.

Extensive development has marred much of the natural aspect of the Piedmont Lowlands Province, though a few parks offer an opportunity to explore what was once the forest frontier of the New York region. Palisades Interstate Park preserves much of the northern portion of the rock ramparts overlooking the Hudson. Several reservations along the crest of the first Watchung Ridge and the Round Valley Recreation Area on Cushetunk Mountain preserve some of the remaining high woodlands. In this province are also found several tracts of land that, although low and flat, offer some interesting hiking possibilities. The federally owned Great Swamp Wildlife Refuge and neighboring county parks have miles of trails, some on boardwalk, that penetrate the wetlands of a former glacial lake of immense proportions. From Raven Rock on the Delaware River to New Brunswick on the Raritan, the towpath of the old Delaware and Raritan Canal (now a state park) offers the hiker 66 miles of wooded walkway along a quiet but very alive body of water. During its heyday, the canal was the scene of intense activity. In fact, for a while, the Delaware and Raritan Canal did more business than the much better known Erie Canal in New York State.

Encompassing nearly all of New Jersey south of a line drawn between New Brunswick and Trenton is the Coastal Plain, the largest geomorphic province in the state. This entire area is composed of ocean and stream deposits of sands, silts, and clays laid down during late Cretaceous and early Tertiary times, 50 to 80 million years ago. The lowest elevations in the state are here, ranging from only a few hundred feet inland to water level on the seashore. From the gently rolling topography of the Pine Barrens to the sandy beaches along New Jersey's 127-mile coast, this province offers the hiker an environment very different from that in the rest of the state. The Pine Barrens, a sparse pine and scrub oak forest of about 1 million acres, has been saved in large measure from the pressures of development. The heart of the Pinelands is preserved in several state forests, the largest of which is Wharton, headquartered at the old bog-iron-mining town of Batsto. The Batona Trail (named for the BAck TO NAture Club of Philadelphia) penetrates the forest for some 50 miles from Lake Absegami to Ong's Hat. This marked footpath passes deep cedar swamps, parallels rivers of cedar water, and climbs Apple Pie Hill, the highest "summit" in the Pine Barrens. Throughout the Pinelands are sand roads, some more than 200 years old, that make for excellent walking through this wilderness of pines.

Several areas along the Jersey coast have been preserved in their original state in tremendous contrast to the overdevelopment that has occurred elsewhere. Here dunes, marshes, and moving sands pushed by the ocean currents present interesting walking opportunities. The New Jersey coast lies along the Atlantic Flyway, the route taken by migrating birds as they wing their way toward warmer climates. To avoid crowds, we recommend that the coast be hiked during the off-season.

LONG-DISTANCE TRAILS

Two long-distance trails pass through New Jersey, and a third is under construction. The Appalachian Trail (AT), a National Scenic Trail, enters from Pennsylvania at the Delaware Water Gap on its 2152-mile journey from Georgia to Maine. It runs across the northwest corner of the state for approximately 80 miles and exits just east of High Point. Through-hikers are those hiking the AT's entire length; most require about 6 months on the trail and adopt trail names for the journey. Marked with white rectangles, the AT is administered by the Appalachian Trail Conference headquarters in Harpers Ferry, West Virginia.

The Long Path, marked in parakeet aqua, begins its northward journey at the George Washington Bridge. For years, its northern terminus was at Windham in the Catskills, but it has now been extended as far north as the Mohawk Valley. It is administered by the New York–New Jersey Trail Conference; the plan is to extend the trail into the Adirondacks. Both the AT and the Long Path are maintained by volunteers.

In addition, the new 150-mile Highlands Trail will link the Delaware and Hudson Rivers. It uses established trails, and some new footway is being constructed for it; where necessary, connections are made by short sections of paved road. As this book went to press, approximately 75 miles of trail were in place. When finished, the system will link 26 county, state, and federal parks; forests; and open spaces. It is the result of cooperation among the New York–New Jersey Trail Conference, the New Jersey Conservation Foundation, and the National Park Service.

THE NATURE OF HIKING

Being out in the woods does carry a certain element of risk. All hikers should be prepared with emergency gear and be able to look after themselves. Taking minimum precautions will ensure that your trip is pleasant. Enjoy your hobby.

The hikes here have been assigned a hiking time based on an average pace—perhaps with an edge toward a slow one. Every hiker develops a pace at which he or she feels most comfortable. The slow amble with frequent stops that most beginning hikers adopt soon gives way to a more rhythmic stride. It is usually best to adopt a pace that can be maintained whether the trail ascends, descends, or is level. Begin with short walks on a regular basis and, as skills and muscle power build, move on to more challenging hikes. In addition to the physical elation of exercising in the outdoors, hobbies such as bird-watching, tree and flower identification, wildlife observation, photography, and local history can be made a part of almost any hike.

To enjoy the outdoors requires a certain amount of planning. Study the route and allow sufficient time to complete the trip before darkness falls. It is not sensible to hike alone. A group of four people is safe and enjoyable. If someone is injured, two of the hikers can go for help while one stays with the injured party. However, large groups tend to destroy the feeling of isolation obtainable in wildlands. If you are going to hike alone, tell someone dependable where you are hiking and when you expect to return, and do not deviate from the established plan.

As a hiker, your body is your resource. It needs enough food to keep energy levels high; it needs water; above all, it should not be pushed to the point of exhaustion. Hiking is pleasurable if adequate preparations are taken to make it so. Keep your body at a comfortable temperature—neither so warm that excessive perspiration occurs, nor so cold or wet that hypothermia becomes a problem. Getting wet, whether from rain or sweat, should be avoided. Hypothermia (once called exposure) can creep up unawares. The outdoor temperature does not have to be very low. You can become hypothermic in 50-degree weather if there is rain or wind and you are unprepared. Watch your companions for signs of poor reflex actions—excessive stumbling, the need for frequent rest stops, or a careless attitude toward clothing and equipment. Once uncontrollable shivering has started, it may only be a matter of minutes before the body temperature has cooled beyond the point of recovery. Immediate warmth for the afflicted person is the only solution.

Suitable clothing and equipment are essential as safeguards against emergencies. It is assumed—and highly recommended—that new hikers will start their hiking career during the warmer months, so the pieces of equipment discussed here are only the basics. Winter hiking is superb, with fewer people in the woods, no bugs, and a completely different feeling from summertime hiking, but remember: Rocks may be icy, wet leaves and lichen make rocks slippery, and clothing and equipment must be adjusted to fit the conditions.

Clothing: This is largely a matter of personal choice and the temperature of the day. We do not recommend jeans or other all-cotton pants. When cotton becomes wet, it is heavy, dries slowly, and does not retain warmth. Your breathing will be impaired if your waistband or belt is too tight. Some hikers prefer suspenders to a belt for this reason. We prefer layering as the method of dress—possibly a long-sleeved shirt over a short-sleeved T-shirt for the upper body. Be certain that clothing is loose enough not to chafe. Whatever you wear, though, avoid becoming wet with perspiration; remove layers as needed. You should also add a layer at rest stops to prevent getting chilled. For emergency use we recommend you carry a wool shirt or sweater, wool or polypropylene hat and gloves, a small flashlight, a simple first-aid kit, a pocket knife, toilet paper, and (in summer) bug repellent. In winter, you should also bring instep crampons for icy portions of the trail.

If you would be helpless without your eyeglasses, carry an extra pair.

Boots: First of all, feet must be comfortable. A few hikes in New Jersey can be walked easily in running shoes or sneakers; these may be the preferred footwear of young people for all hiking in the Garden State. However, we strongly recommend that you wear a lightweight hiking boot with effective ankle support. If you need new boots, to ensure a good fit take with you to the store the socks you plan to wear on the trail (see below). There should be ample room in the boots so your toes are not cramped, and there should not be much forward movement of your feet in them. Most good outdoor stores have salespeople on their staff experienced enough to advise on boot choice. If possible, walk around in your home or office for several days before deciding that this is the pair. Your first hike in new boots should be a short one, and should a "hot spot" develop, stop immediately and apply moleskin or molefoam to protect the area against developing a blister.

Socks: Wear two pairs to prevent blisters: an inner pair of lightweight polypropylene or wool and an outer of thicker wool.

Rain/wind protection: Ideally, your coat should have a hood and be waterproof. The hood will prevent cold wind from penetrating between your collar and neck. There are many varieties in the stores. Remember, though, that hiking will generate perspiration, and some parkas will generate rain inside a garment even if it is not raining outside. Waterproof, breathable fabric such as Gore-Tex® is favored by many hikers.

Pack: A lightweight day pack is indispensable for carrying those pieces of equipment essential to happiness on the trail. Most day packs are basically small backpacks that ride high on the back. Some of the newer fanny packs, as well as a hybrid called a lumbar pack, will hold nearly as much as a small backpack and may be more comfortable.

The following items are always in our packs, even for a short hike:

Water: The time has passed when you could be refreshed at that beautiful stream by drinking the pure, cold water. *Giardia lamblia* and other bacteria have destroyed that pleasure. Always carry a minimum of a quart of water per person, and drink it, even if you are not aware of feeling thirsty. Monitor your urine, and if it is dark, increase your water intake, particularly in colder weather when thirst is not as apparent as it is in hot.

Lunch: Even if lunch is not planned on the trail, take an emergency ration—fruit (hard fruits like apples don't bruise easily), some trail mix, a chocolate bar, or gorp (Good Old Raisins and Peanuts—with M&Ms, if you wish).

Maps: The maps in this guide, along with the text, are all you really need for these hikes. As you become experienced, though, you may want to explore areas in more depth. Each hike refers you to other maps, as keyed at the end of this introduction. For hiking in New Jersey, it is not usually necessary to carry a compass, particularly if you are on a described hike; however, if you stray from the trail, having a map and compass—and knowing how to use them—can return you to the path or to civilization. You will need a good New Jersey road map to find your way to the trailheads. Each hike tells you how to reach the trailhead itself, but getting to the nearby town is often up to you. New Jersey, like most states, issues an official highway map, and it is free. Write to the New Jersey Division of Travel and Tourism, CN 826, Trenton, NJ 08625; 609-292-2470.

FACTS FOR HIKERS

Trail markers: The trails in the Garden State are mostly color coded with paint blazes on convenient trees. Sometimes metal tags held on by nails substitute for paint. Three blazes in a triangle indicate the beginning or the end of a trail, and major turns are indicated by two blazes with the turn direction indicated by the upper blaze. A trail is a dynamic entity and rerouting takes place frequently; the original paint blazes are then painted out, but are often still visible for some years.

Ideally, markers are spaced so that you can easily see the next as you move along the trail. At times, markers become obscured by new growth or blowdowns, and their clarity also varies from time to time. The hikes described in this book are mostly on marked trails, and a notation has been made where markers are indistinct or missing. Markers tend to be prolific where you need to be alert.

Ticks: These are a problem in New Jersey and other nearby states. Lyme disease is not to be trifled with. The deer tick that carries Lyme disease is very small (the size of a period in this text); do not confuse it with the common wood tick, which is the size of a match head or—when engorged with blood—the size of a pea. Deer ticks are more abundant in shore areas where deer are common. A bite from an infected deer tick will result in a circular rash, which should be immediately treated by a doctor. Learn to look for and remove ticks after hiking in an infested area. Long-sleeved shirts and pants with the legs tucked into socks are a must in these areas. Spray your feet and legs with a tick repellent containing DEET. A flyer on Lyme disease is available from the New Jersey State Department of Health, CN 360, Trenton, NJ 08625 or from the New York–New Jersey Trail Conference.

Mountain bikes: When this book was published in 1987, there were no bicycles on New Jersey trails. But modern technology has produced a rugged bicycle that can withstand trail use, and today's mountain bikes can traverse terrain once reserved for the hiker alone. The popularity of these new bicycles with a younger generation (most younger than 35) has been phenomenal, and by the early 1990s many New Jersey trails had experienced sharp increases in use. User conflicts naturally arose, and they continue to be a problem in some places. Mountain bikers assumed the trails made and maintained by hikers were there for them to share. Hikers resented encroachment and trail destruction (mountain bikes create many erosion problems and intrude on the natural setting many hikers seek) and fought to have them banned from parks and forests. Equestrians resented the speed at which some bikers travel along trails, speeds that scare their horses. These problems are still with us, and policies are constantly being shaped and reshaped—mostly on a case-by-case basis—by the various agencies that administer the public land on which trails are located. If mountain biking is of concern to you, you may wish to contact the park or forest in which you will be hiking for information on policies or to express your opinion.

Parking fees: Many state parks and forests charge moderate fees for parking, normally between Memorial Day weekend and Labor Day weekend. Weekday rates are lower than weekend, and Tuesdays are free. A New Jersey State Park pass is available that provides free entry to all parks for one year. State residents older than age 62 can obtain a free parking pass, good at any time. Apply at any park or forest office.

Hunting: New Jersey has a short deer-hunting season, usually in December. Avoid hiking in hunting areas during firearms season. Check with the local park office, the New Jersey Department of Environmental Protection, or the New York–New Jersey Trail Conference for specific dates. There is no hunting in New Jersey on Sundays.

TRAIL ETIQUETTE

There is a certain etiquette to hiking. Two of the most important phrases to remember are the familiar "take only photographs, leave only footprints" and "carry out what you carry in." If every user of our woods followed these guidelines, litter would not be a problem. Many concerned hikers carry empty garbage bags in their packs and toward the end of the hike pick up litter and carry it out.

Some trails border or actually cross private property. NO TRESPASSING signs should be honored and care taken to respect private landowners by not damaging fences or trees and by not littering. A few thoughtless walkers can damage good relations built up over the years with trail neighbors.

On the trail, give way to the person walking uphill. If there are trail registers, carefully fill out the first register on your hike, and sign out at the last.

On overnights at existing shelters, remember that lean-tos should be available for all who need to use them. On those wet and windy nights, make room cheerfully for latecomers. Pack away all evidence that you have been there and leave the shelter exactly as you would wish to find it on arrival.

Check before beginning your backpack whether fires are permitted in the area. Rules are changing, mostly in the direction of banning them. When fires are permitted, no live trees should be cut for firewood, and the fire should be contained in a fireplace (provided at many shelters). It is courteous to gather enough dead wood so that the next occupant can at least get another fire started. Wood is in short supply in frequently camped areas. Whether you build them for atmosphere or smudge (keeping mosquitoes away), keep fires small and safe. A small, lightweight backpacking stove is preferable for cooking. These are inexpensive, cook quickly, and keep pots unblackened.

There are certain areas in the United States—on the beaches of the Colorado River in the Grand Canyon, for instance—where human body waste has become such a problem that now it is required for all such matter to be carried out. With the increasing number of people using New Jersey trails, it is not unthinkable that in the future we might all be required to carry out our personal waste. To avoid this inconvenience, use the outhouse where one is provided, and otherwise be a "copy cat"—act as a feline does. Choose a spot far away from any water and the trail, remove the layer of leaves and twigs, dig a hole at least 3 inches deep in the soil, with either a rock or a sturdy stick (some hikers carry a special trowel for this purpose), take care of your business, cover the whole mess over so that no disturbance is apparent, and take out the used toilet paper. Double Baggies work well.

HIKING ORGANIZATIONS

The umbrella organization for hiking in New Jersey is the New York–New Jersey Trail Conference, a nonprofit federation of 10,000 individuals and 85 hiking and environmental organizations working to build and maintain trails and to preserve open space. Its trail network is 1300 miles of foot trail. Formed in 1920, the Conference built the first section of the Appalachian Trail in 1923.

The Conference is supported by dues, publication sales, and donations—along with thousands of hours of volunteer time. Members receive the bimonthly *Trail Walker*, can purchase maps and guides at a discount, and can avail themselves of the Conference library. Dues start at $18 for an individual ($12.50 for students and retirees); $23 for a family. A single life membership is $300.

We encourage you to support the

people who support the trails. The Conference can be reached at GPO Box 2250, New York, NY 10116 (or access it on the Internet at www.-nynjtc.org/).

There are also many fine hiking clubs in New Jersey, catering to all grades of hikers in many areas of the state. These clubs are an excellent way to meet people who share your love of the outdoors. The clubs are your ticket to the special natural sections of your area and will help you learn the ins and outs of hiking in the Northeast. For a listing, send a self-addressed stamped envelope to the Trail Conference at the address above.

Many of the trails in this book are maintained by volunteers. Respect their work and their tender loving care, and do not cut corners on switchbacks or otherwise erode the trail unnecessarily. If you'd like to help maintain a trail, contact the New York–New Jersey Trail Conference.

MAP KEY

USGS: Topographic quadrangle maps are available for all parts of the United States. For a New Jersey index, write to United States Geological Survey, Branch of Information Services, Box 25286, Denver Federal Center, Denver, CO 80225; 303-202-4700. The maps used in this guidebook are all 7½'. They were not designed with hikers in mind and often do not show the trails—or show them incorrectly. (The exception to this generalization is the Pinelands, where USGS topos clearly show nearly all the sand roads of the area.) Despite the drawbacks, USGS maps depict general topography superbly, which is why we have used them as the base maps for the hikes in this book. The New Jersey index also lists retail stores throughout the state that sell these maps over the counter, and they are available from the New Jersey Geological Survey, Bureau of Revenue, New Jersey Department of Environmental Protection, CN 417, Trenton, NJ 08625-0417; 609-777-1038. A catalog is available.

NYNJTC: Waterproof, color topographic maps, usually sold in sets, published by the New York–New Jersey Trail Conference, GPO Box 2250, New York, NY 10116; 212-685-9699.

WB: Topographic color maps printed in the rear of the *New York Walk Book,* 5th edition, by the New York–New Jersey Trail Conference and published by Doubleday in December 1984; available in many bookstores or directly from the Conference. Regarded by many as the hiker's bible. A new edition of the *Walk Book* will be available in 1997.

HRM: Topographic Hiker's Region Maps published by Walking News, PO Box 352, New York, NY 10013.

DEP: Sketch maps, usually free, from the various state park and forest offices; or write to the New Jersey Department of Environmental Protection, Division of Parks and Forestry, CN 404, Trenton, NJ 08625; 609-292-2797 or 1-800-843-6420.

National Park Service: Park maps, usually free, from individual park offices. Addresses in hike text.

RECOMMENDED BOOKS

Bennett, D.W. *New Jersey Coastwalks.* Highlands, N.J.: American Littoral Society, 1981.

Dann, Kevin. *Twenty-five Walks in New Jersey*. New Brunswick, N.J.: Rutgers University Press, 1982.

Kjellstrom, Bjorn. *Be Expert with Map and Compass.* New York: Collier Books, 1994.

Kobbe, Gustav. *The New Jersey Coast and Pines.* New York: Walking News, 1982.

Lenik, Edward J. *Iron Mine Trails.* New York: New York–New Jersey Trail Conference, 1996.

Mack, Arthur C. *The Palisades of the Hudson.* Edgewater, N.J.: The Palisades Press, 1990.

McClelland, Robert J. *The Delaware Canal.* New Brunswick, N.J.: Rutgers University Press, 1967.

McPhee, John. *The Pine Barrens.* New York: Farrar, Straus and Giroux, 1968.

New York–New Jersey Trail Conference. *The Daywalker.* New York: Doubleday, 1983 (being revised).

———. *Guide to the Appalachian Trail in New York and New Jersey.* 13th ed. Appalachian Trail Conference, 1994.

———. *Guide to the Long Path.* 4th ed. New York: New York–New Jersey Trail Conference, 1996.

———. *The New York Walk Book.* 5th ed. New York: Doubleday, 1984 (being revised).

Ransom, James M. *Vanishing Ironworks of the Ramapos.* New Brunswick, N.J.: Rutgers University Press, 1966.

Scheller, William B. *Country Walks Near New York.* 2nd ed. Boston: Appalachian Mountain Club, 1986.

Scofield, Bruce. *Circuit Hikes in Northern New Jersey.* 4th ed. New York: New York–New Jersey Trail Conference, 1995.

Thomas, Lester S. *The Pine Barrens of New Jersey.* New Jersey Department of Environmental Protection, 1983.

Wyckoff, Jerome. *Rock Scenery of the Hudson Highlands and Palisades.* Glens Falls, N.Y.: Adirondack Mountain Club, 1971.

Zatz, Arline and Joel Zatz. *Best Hikes with Children in New Jersey.* Seattle, Wash.: The Mountaineers, 1992.

KEY TO MAPS

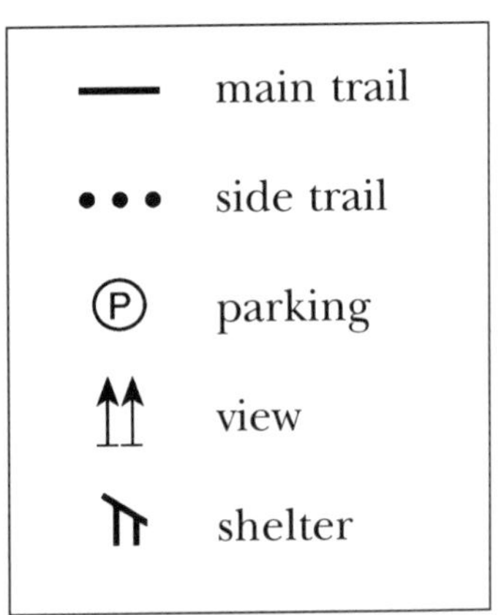

RIDGE AND VALLEY PROVINCE

1

Cedar Swamp and High Point

Total distance: 4 miles

Hiking time: 2½ hours

Vertical rise: 300 feet

Rating: Moderate

Maps: USGS Port Jervis South; NYNJTC North Kittatinny Trails #18; WB #18; HRM #52A; DEP High Point State Park

In the far northwestern part of New Jersey is High Point State Park (1480 State Route 23, Sussex, NJ 07461; 201-875-4800), where the highest elevations in the state are found. The entire park is quite large—14,000 acres—and offers good hiking along the Appalachian Trail and on a number of other marked trails and woods roads. The hike described here is in the section of the park north of NJ 23. This part contains the highest elevation in the state at 1803 feet; the High Point monument; and Cedar Swamp, New Jersey's first natural area. The area is the most visited and used section of the park, and an off-season or midweek hike is suggested if you desire solitude. Plastic post markers throughout the park show permitted activities on the trails. Mountain bikes are not allowed on either trail used for this hike (the Appalachian and the Cedar Swamp Trails).

The land making up High Point State Park was donated to the public by Colonel and Mrs. Anthony R. Kuser and Bernardsville, New Jersey. The park itself was created in 1923 and has long been a favorite mountain retreat for native New Jerseyites. The most obvious feature of the park is the monument itself, an obelisk that towers 220 feet above the highest piece of ground in the entire state. The views from the mountaintop around the tower and from the tower itself are without a doubt the most expansive in the state. The general design plan for High Point State Park was created by the sons of the great landscape architect Frederick Law Olmsted.

On October 12, 1965, the Dryden Kuser Natural Area was dedicated in memory of the late Senator Dryden and Colonel Kuser. This area contains a unique cedar swamp, the present-day remains of an earlier glacial lake.

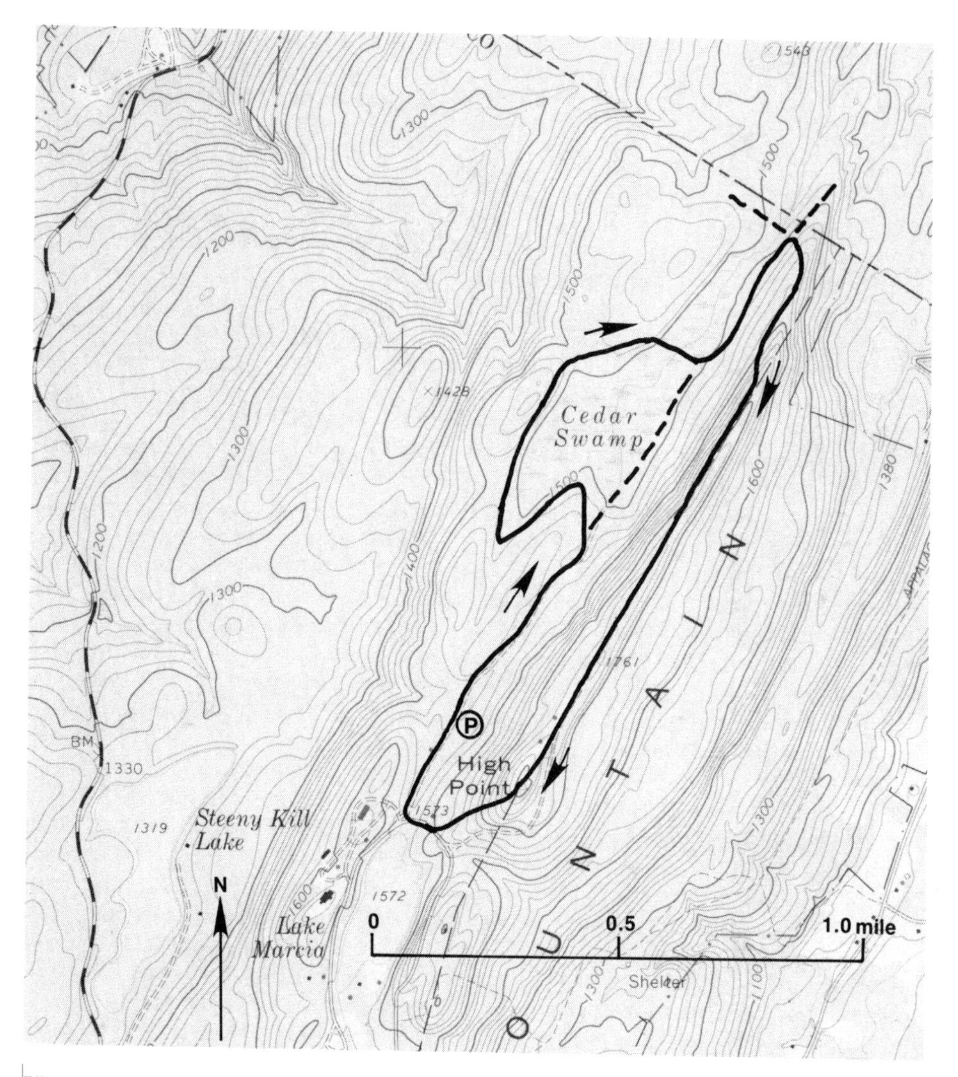

Here are found hemlock, rhododendron, and even Atlantic white cedars far from their usual habitats in southern New Jersey.

How to Get There

From NJ 23, turn north on the park road opposite the park headquarters and office. An entrance fee ($5 daily, $7 weekends) is charged between Memorial Day and Labor Day. Proceed straight into the park following signs to the Dryden Kuser Natural Area. Pass Lake Marcia on the right, and after 1 mile, turn left to go to the natural area. Travel down this road for 0.25 mile and park on the right side, just after a DEAD END sign and just before a gate that closes off the road to vehicles. (Hikers who don't mind walking an additional 2.5 miles can avoid the entrance fee. Park in the large parking area near the park office—see Hike 2—and walk north on the Appalachian

Trail. After 1 mile, turn left onto the red/green-marked Monument Trail, and then turn right onto the road to the natural area.)

The Trail

Walk north past the gate on a paved road. After about 10 minutes, you'll pass two stone pillars next to a park bench, one of several on this hike. Continue on the road, which gradually heads downhill toward the swamp. At the dedication plaque set in stone, bear left on a walkway of slate chips onto the perimeter path encircling the swamp. The walking here is very pleasant and easy. The heart of the swamp will always be on your right, and soon pines, hemlocks, and cedars appear above rhododendron groves. The swamp is deep and dark and supports mosses, ferns, and even the carnivorous pitcher plant and sundew.

Soon after entering the swamp area itself, the path swings sharply left and temporarily heads south. The trail rises slightly now, allowing a few views over a somewhat drier section of the swamp. Here there are standing dead trees and occasional pines. Soon the trail curves to the right and begins to head northward again, returning to the wetter section of the swamp. Just after a sharp right turn, you'll pass a bench located near where a footpath, the Shawangunk Ridge Trail, comes in from the left and joins the route of this hike. The Shawangunk Ridge Trail links the Kittatinny/Shawangunk ridge with the Catskills. Its parakeet aqua markers will now appear at all junctions. Soon after this intersection, cross the swamp itself on boardwalk. The swamp is now on both sides of the trail and, in spite of the boards that provide a dry walkway, the footing may sometimes be slippery. The swamp is intensely green and dense in this section, with an abundance of moss under very large white cedars.

At the end of this wet section, a little more than a mile into the hike, reach a trail junction near another park bench. Turn left here and continue heading north on a much drier path with the swamp on your left. There are a few large hemlocks along this section of the hike. Walk approximately another 10 minutes to a junction with the Monument Trail. There is a circular clearing immediately before this junction, and at the junction itself is a small bridge over a brook on the left. The New York–New Jersey border is very close at this point. Turn right on the Monument Trail, a footpath marked by metal tags painted with a red and green circle. It also has some parakeet aqua markers of the Shawangunk Ridge Trail.

The Monument Trail almost immediately begins to climb and leads to the highest summit in New Jersey. The trail, built by the Civilian Conservation Corps in the 1930s, is well constructed with large blocks of stone placed along the edge. The trail is much steeper, quite a change from the level walking encountered so far. You will reach the ridge after about 10 minutes of continuous climbing, with views to the east and west appearing through the trees. The trail now heads southward on a narrow ridge of Kittatinny Mountain and continues to gain elevation as it wanders through the scrub oak swinging between the eastern and western sides of the ridge. Soon—about 2.5 miles into the hike—a number of viewpoints appear on both sides of the trail, each better than the last. The footing, quite rocky in places, is typical of the higher elevations on Kittatinny Mountain. Just after the trail makes a short jog to the left, there is a good lookout to the

High Point Monument

east out over the Wallkill River Valley, which includes a few farms and much forest. The first big ridge visible beyond the valley is Pochuck Mountain, and beyond that you can see the long Wawayanda Ridge where the Vernon Valley–Great Gorge ski area is located. Ahead, among bare rock outcrops and pitch pines sculpted by the high mountain winds, is an overlook to the west. The bend in the Delaware River, I-84, the Pocono plateau, portions of Port Jervis, and—in the distance to the north—the Catskill Mountains are all visible.

Continuing south on the trail, which now rises gradually, you can see glaciated outcrops of rock topped with pitch pines. This sedimentary rock is known as the Shawangunk conglomerate and was formed by deposits in an ancient sea. After folding, faulting, and uplifting, these erosion-resistant sediments remained as the backbone of the ridge when the weaker surrounding rocks were worn down and washed away. The trail soon levels off and becomes easier to hike. Quite suddenly, it arrives at the huge parking area and the gigantic monument. Here you will also find a white pipe that designates the Monument Trail. Welcome to civilization.

Walk directly toward the monument through the parking area and past the rest rooms. The views are fantastic, particularly at the monument itself or from within it during the summer. The monument is 220 feet high on a base 34 feet square that tapers to 19 feet at the base of the apex. It was built of local quartzite and faced with New Hampshire granite. A plaque on the monument indicates that it was ERECTED BY COLONEL AND MRS. ANTHONY R. KUSER TO THE GLORY AND HONOR AND ETERNAL MEMORY OF NEW JERSEY HEROES BY LAND,AND SEA, AND AIR IN ALL WARS OF OUR COUNTRY. To the south is Lake Marcia and the long spine of the Kittatinnies (40 miles to the Delaware Water Gap). West is the Pocono plateau (some call this eroded plateau "mountains"), and the Catskills are to the north.

From the monument, find a path that begins near the northwest side of the foundation and head downhill. This walkway—marked with green/red, parakeet aqua, and white markers—follows a utility line and provides an easy path downhill as an alternative to the road that it parallels. Turn right onto Monument Drive, which you will reach after only a few minutes. Lake Marcia is to your left. Make a right to pass the rest rooms, and turn right onto the road leading to the Cedar Swamp picnic area. It should take you only 5 or 6 minutes from here to reach your car. (An alternative is to stay with the red/green markers of the Monument Trail, which lead across two roads and then along the northern shore of Lake Marcia. Leave the Monument Trail where it meets the road to the natural area.)

BCS

2

South of High Point

Total distance: 6 miles

Hiking time: 4 hours

Vertical rise: 300 feet

Rating: Moderate to strenuous

Maps: USGS Port Jervis South; NYNJTC North Kittatinny Trails #18; WB #18; HRM #52A; DEP High Point State Park

South of High Point monument and the popular Lake Marcia is a section of High Point State Park (1480 State Route 23, Sussex, NJ 07461; 201-875-4800) that is wild, expansive, scenic, and lightly used. The Appalachian Trail (AT) passes through this area, and the Rutherford shelter, one of the few New Jersey AT trail shelters, is also found here.

A warning is in order. If you have not had any experience with this section of the AT, or if your feet are particularly sensitive, be prepared for a rocky path that will test your boots. The first 2 miles of this hike will be demanding on your feet and on your balance. Most people prefer to do the hike in the direction described below because the second leg of the hike is on a flat woods road. You'll get the worst done first.

How to Get There

Take NJ 23 to the High Point State Park ranger's office at the top of Kittatinny Ridge on the south side of the highway. Stop in at the office for a map or to pick up a permit if you are leaving your car overnight. Park at the AT parking area, which you can reach via a driveway found about 200 feet east of the office on the same side of the road.

The Trail

From the back of the parking area, enter the woods on a path marked by two large granite blocks. This trail, marked with both the white markers of the AT and the yellow markers of the Mashipacong Trail, quickly turns left and heads south. In another 200 yards you will arrive at a trail junction that is marked by a painted, vertically placed drain pipe. At this four-way junction, where the yellow trail turns right and the Iris trail starts on your left, walk straight ahead, now following only the white markers of the AT.

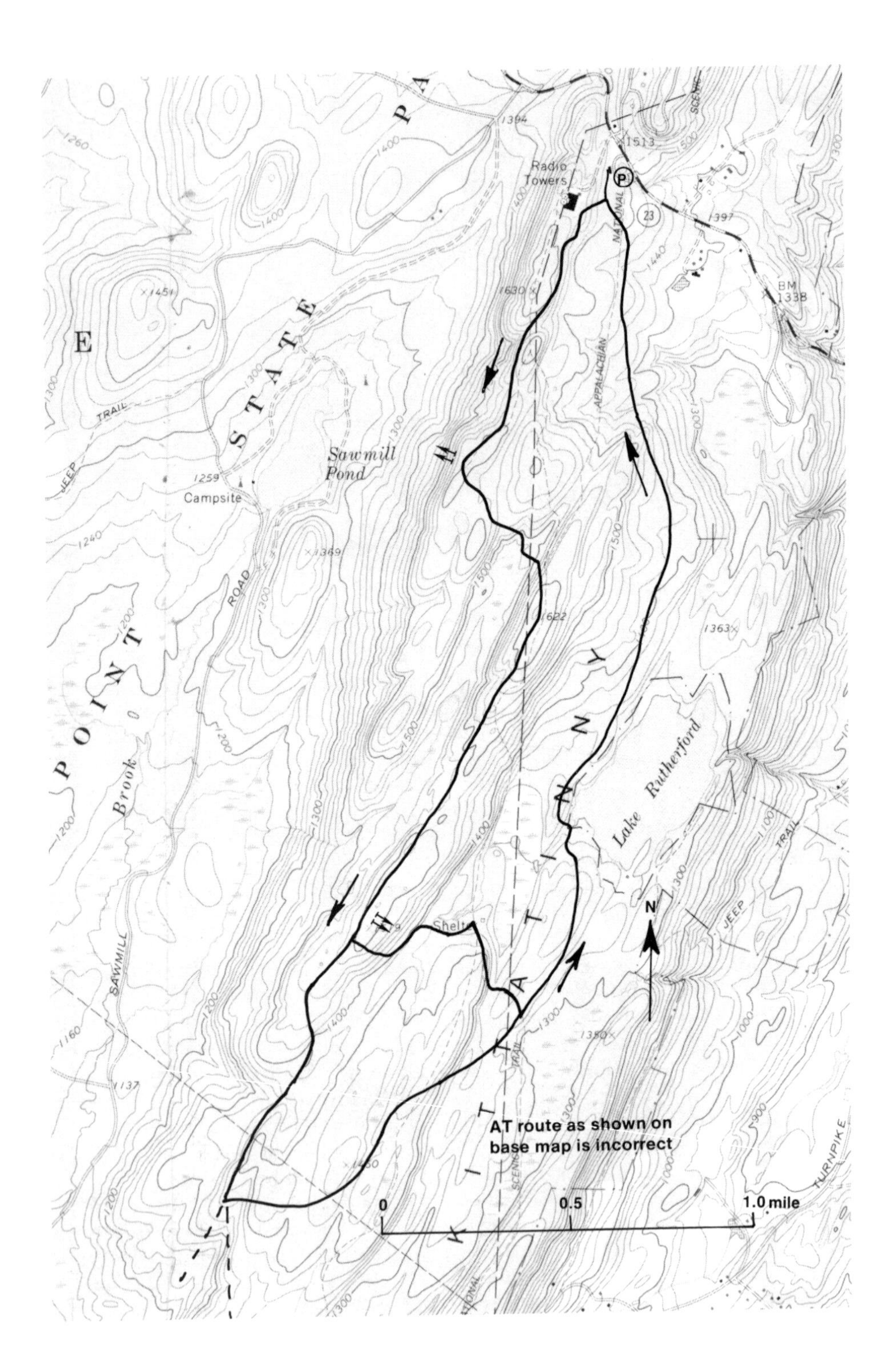
AT route as shown on
base map is incorrect
Radio
Towers
Sawmill
Pond
Campsite
Lake Rutherford
Shelt
N
0
0.5
1.0 mile
BM
1338

After only a short distance, the AT begins to climb. There will be a large cliff (more like a wall) on your right as you ascend along a man-made embankment. The next section of the AT passes through a beautiful stretch of trail and forest. In places pine needles cover the rocky trail, which winds through huge fern fields under oak, maple, and large white pines. The trail follows the eastern side of a ridge for a while, then swings over to the western side. Your feet will notice that the rocks are particularly jagged in this section, a characteristic of the AT in Pennsylvania and New Jersey. You'll pass a junction with the Blue-Dot Trail, which descends steeply and reaches Sawmill Lake below in about 0.5 mile. Vistas along the trail in this section offer good views of this lake and beyond—including the Delaware River and Pennsylvania. The AT next turns away from this ridge and descends steeply over rocks into a valley.

After climbing a parallel ridge to the east, the AT turns south, reaching a series of rocky outcrops vegetated only sparsely with pitch pines and scrub oaks. For the next mile the trail is quite rugged and very rocky in places as it passes through first this raggedy forest and then an oak-and-maple woods. After a long and gradual descent, the trail arrives at a series of cliffs offering some of the best views on this hike.

Here is Dutch Shoe Rock: a large, glacially polished rock slab that offers a tremendous vista to the east. Lake Rutherford and, in front of it, a large marsh near the hidden AT shelter below are just to your left. In the distance are Pochuck Mountain and Wawayanda Mountain, both traversed by the AT farther north. As you walk south on the AT, the vistas continue. The best viewpoint is located about 150 feet north of a trail junction where a blue-blazed trail leads down the slope to the Rutherford AT shelter.

You have two options at this point. The first, which is all on good trail but will add about 0.5 mile to your hike, is to continue following the AT south for another 0.8 mile to its junction with the red-blazed Iris Trail. Turn left here and follow the red markers through a deep woods. The Iris Trail utilizes an old woods road that will feel positively soft after those first few miles on the jagged rocks of the AT. Keep left at a junction, staying with the red markers, and soon you will arrive at the west shore of Lake Rutherford. Trail description from there will follow below.

Your other choice is somewhat more adventurous but definitely worth considering if you are backpacking. You can take the blue trail down to the shelter, then pick up an old woods road that leads east out to the Iris Trail. From the AT, follow the blue markers down the steep slope and onto the eastward-trending footpath to the shelter. You'll cross over a small stream and pass a rock-lined spring that feeds a small brook along the way. The Rutherford shelter is one of the more remote AT shelters in New Jersey. The presence of large lilac bushes around it reveals that it was built on land that was once farmed. In back of the shelter are a number of attractive campsites at the edge of the marsh you saw earlier. This remote area is a good place for lunch or a snack, and of course for primitive camping—except during times when insects are biting.

To continue with this option, leave the shelter following the path that leads past the privy. This path, actually an old woods road, is not heavily used, nor is it maintained. Parts of it are grassy and mossy, parts are quite wet, and there may be a few blowdowns blocking the path. For a ways you'll see the large marsh in back of the shelter off to your left, the remnants of which are shown on older maps as a lake. The path rises gradually, crests a small ridge, descends, and then meets the red-blazed Iris Trail in about 0.5 mile. Turn left here and walk another 0.5 mile or so to the west shore of Lake Rutherford. On the way you will cross over one of the small brooks that feed the lake. Here the bright red cardinal lower, a type of *Lobelia,* blooms during the summer.

Regardless of which option you chose, you are now on the west shore of Lake Rutherford, a reservoir that meets the water needs of the town of Sussex. Where the Iris Trail comes closest to the lake, look for a side trail that will take you to a rocky overlook near the shore of the lake. Lake Rutherford is quite large and, except for one distant building, is uninhabited and quite wild. Unfortunately, swimming is not permitted.

On leaving the lake, continue northward on the Iris Trail through a dark and dense forest. The trail, now covered with a fine gravel, gradually widens in this section and is used in the winter by snowmobiles and cross-country skiers. Low rock outcroppings line the trail in places. Forest birds, such as the rufous-sided towhee, are often seen hopping in the bushes. The seldom seen veery, with its ethereal call, also inhabits this woods. The trail gradually rises through a more open forest that is filled with small blueberry bushes, then descends through a mixed oak forest with an understory of ferns. After crossing a small brook on a footbridge, the trail heads uphill and eventually arrives at the junction where you began the loop. Turn right here and follow the white and yellow markers back to your car.

BCS

3

Stokes State Forest

Total distance: 10 miles

Hiking time: 7 hours

Vertical rise: 750 feet

Rating: Moderately strenuous

Maps: USGS Culvers Gap/Branchville; NYNJTC North Kittatinny Trails #17 and #18; WB #17 and #18; HRM #52A and #52B

Acquisitions of land for Stokes State Forest (1 Courson Road, Branchville, NJ 07826; 201-948-3820) began in 1907, and the state now owns 15,000 acres with more than 75 miles of roads and well-defined trails. The area was named to honor Governor Edward Stokes, who donated the first 500 acres. Some of the early tracts were acquired for $1 per acre. Routes used for this hike will be the Swenson (red), Cartwright (red and brown), Bannon (unmarked), Appalachian (white), and Tower (dark green) Trails, as well as Crigger Road.

How to Get There

The entry to Stokes State Forest is on US 206, 3 miles northwest of Branchville, New Jersey, and 10 miles south of Milford, Pennsylvania. The park sign is on the east side of US 206. Drive to the forest office to pick up literature, then follow the signs to Stony Lake via Courson Road. Courson Road passes Kittle Field on the left. Turn right at the T-junction onto Kittle Road and proceed to the Stony Lake parking area. This area is divided into two lots, but it is immaterial for this hike which one is used.

The Trail

Walk to the signboard between the two lots and, facing the woods, look for a wide gravel road leading uphill past a metal barrier labeled ENTRANCE TO SNOWMOBILE AND DOGSLED TRAILS. This road is marked with light green, dark green, blue, brown, and red markers. Be wary of poison ivy at this point. Walk uphill for 5 minutes until the road crosses a metal drainage pipe, then immediately turn left on the red-marked Swenson Trail. From Stony Lake, the trail meanders up a low ridge through areas of mixed white pine, mountain laurel, hemlock, and oak. Portions of the land here were logged 50 to 60 years ago, and there is evidence of the chestnut forest that covered the area prior to the 1920 blight.

Within about 30 minutes, the forest becomes more open as the trail leads to a low-lying wet area with a seasonal

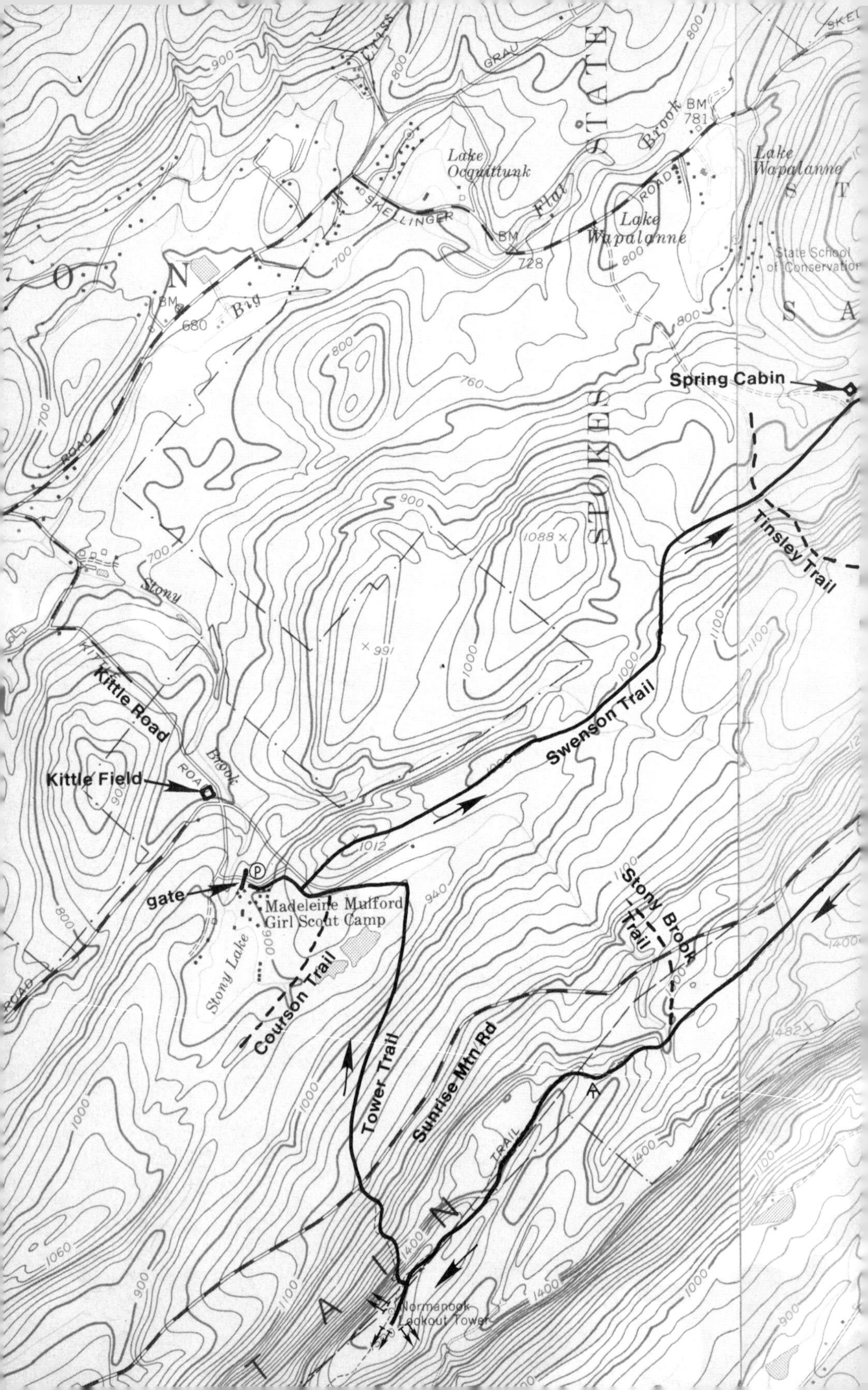

Spring Cabin
Tinsley Trail
Swenson Trail
Kittle Road
Kittle Field
gate
Madeleine Mulford
Girl Scout Camp
Courson Trail
Stony Lake
Tower Trail
Sunrise Mtn Rd
Stony Brook Trail
Normanook
Lookout Tower
Lake Ocquittunk
Lake Wapalanne
State School
of Conservation
Flat Brook
Big Stony Brook
SKELLINGER ROAD
STOKES STATE

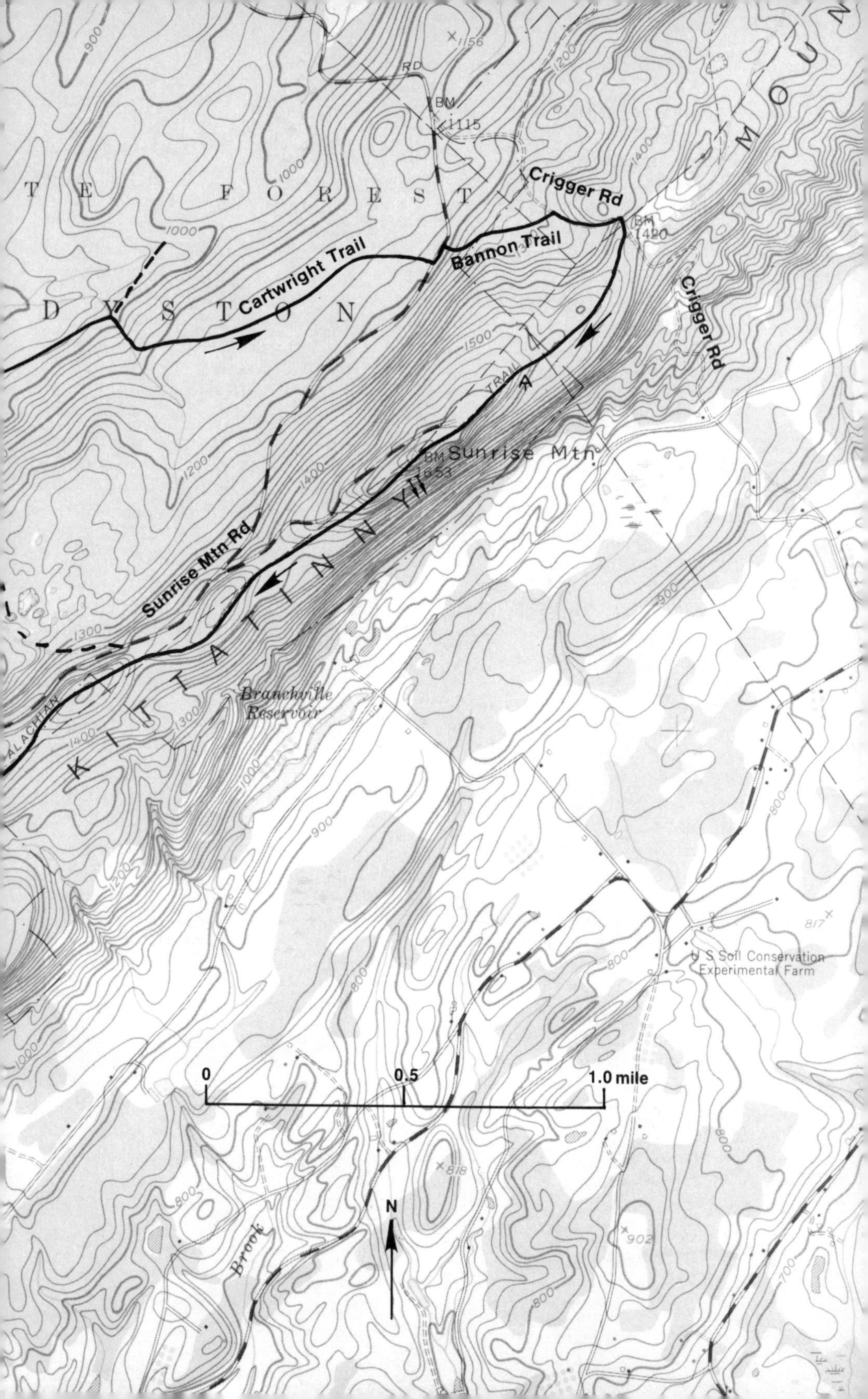
Crigger Rd
Bannon Trail
Cartwright Trail
Crigger Rd
Sunrise Mtn
Sunrise Mtn Rd
Branchville Reservoir
U S Soil Conservation Experimental Farm
Brook
0
0.5
1.0 mile
N
K I T T A T I N N Y
D V S T O N
T E F O R E S T
M O U N

stream. After crossing a brook, the trail parallels the stream for a short distance and gradually climbs to an area of blue markers. These indicate the boundary of a forest management study area, which may eventually lead to a harvesting operation. In spring the woods are crowded with many species of birds on their way north after the winter migration.

Stay on the red trail as it moves through the woods to reach the junction of the Tinsley Trail, which goes steeply uphill to the right. Yellow markers indicate the intersection. They have been considerably damaged by porcupines chewing around the painted edges; the teethmarks can be clearly seen.

The red trail continues steeply down to the left. When the leaves are off the trees, the ridge to the left is clearly visible. The red markers of the Swenson Trail and the yellow of the Tinsley Trail are both used in this short section. The red markers soon indicate that the Swenson Trail travels off downhill to the right, leaving the yellow marker for the Tinsley Trail visible straight ahead. Turn right onto the Swenson Trail, which first descends then climbs over a minor rise to Spring Brook cabin. The trail is now narrower and much rockier and care is needed to walk safely on the rocky footing.

The attractive Spring Brook cabin takes about an hour to reach. It is located near a small pond embellished by a large white dogwood. Spring Brook is often dry here; it appears almost as though the pond has no inlet. There are remnants of old walls in the area, and the trail goes past a substantial woodpile to the right of the cabin. The cabin is used mostly in summer for recreational purposes by employees of the Department of Environmental Protection.

Walking becomes easier after you leave Spring Brook cabin. The trail here is located on a shelf, with the Appalachian Trail ridge visible through the trees on the right. There are numbers of young beech and black birch trees here, and it is interesting to note the similarity between the leaves of these two trees. There are tiny serrations on the edges of the black birch leaf, while the edges of the beech leaves are less ragged with larger serrations.

About 10 minutes from the cabin, the path dips to a low-lying area with higher ground on the left side. It passes through a wide wet area with several small streams and a round mudflat area to the left. One of the last stream crossings is easily identified by an 8-inch-diameter tree bearing a red marker immediately at the point of crossing. Negotiate the stream on rocks behind this marked tree. Twenty yards beyond, find the beginning of the Cartwright Trail, which you will take, indicated by three distinct red and brown markers on the right. The junction is also emphasized by a small cairn on the right side of the trail. Walking from the beginning of the wet area to the trail junction takes approximately 3 minutes, and you've missed the turn if you encounter in the trail a large, felled tree about 2 feet off the ground.

At first the trail seems to ascend a streambed, and the path is indistinct. The markers are easy to follow, however, and after a level start, the trail climbs moderately. Seventy-five years ago, old farmlands were abandoned here. The stumps of chestnut trees, victims of the blight, are numerous, but Solomon's seal, white violets, and many varieties of ferns, together with tall trees, now make this trail very pretty. After leveling out and crossing a stream, the trail widens, then narrows again before emerging onto Sunrise Mountain Road. The end of the Cartwright Trail is indicated by three red and brown markers on a tree by the roadside.

Turn left onto Sunrise Mountain Road and walk 3 minutes to where the road bends sharply to the left, just after an unpaved pullout on the left. On the right, the unmarked Bannon Trail starts at a road sign indicating PARKING PERMITTED ON RIGHT SHOULDER. Look for a yellow paint blob on the first large tree a few yards into the woods and follow a narrow uphill trail until it shortly opens into a wide woods road. After the uphill section, the trail enters a marshy area. Halfway across on the right, look for a tree growing over a rock slab and forming an interesting spring. The marshy area continues for several yards, and the trail reaches a T-junction with Crigger Road about 7 minutes from Sunrise Mountain Road. Confirm your location by looking to the left to see the wooden sign for BANNON TRAIL.

Turn right onto Crigger Road, which is unpaved and unused by motor vehicles. It bends slightly uphill to the left and ascends toward the ridge. Near the top of the hill there are some large boulders blocking the road. Soon after this obstacle, climb over a large pile of slate and rocks to reach the white rectangular markers of the Appalachian Trail (AT). Exceptionally large wild strawberries are rampant here in season, and there is also a patch of May apple with its attractive white flowers, which curiously appear only at the junction of two leaves. Only the fruit of the May apple is edible; all other parts are poisonous.

Turn right onto the AT, which is narrow and rocky here and parallels an old stone wall for a short way. There is a good rest stop within about 5 minutes. Leave the main trail and head up a path to the right to a pleasant, rocky outcrop. Back on the AT, a view to the left becomes more apparent as you climb. Within about 10 minutes, reach a junction on the right with a trail leading uphill toward wooden steps. This side trail accesses the Sunrise Mountain parking lot, which has rest rooms and garbage cans. Ignore it and walk straight ahead up rock steps to a man-made scenic overlook with wooden benches. Reach the rain shelter and cairn at the top of Sunrise Mountain by walking another few minutes along the ridge. Sunrise Mountain is 1653 feet above sea level. High Point monument is visible 8 miles to the north, and on a clear day you can see the Catskills just to the left of the monument.

Turn left and walk downhill from the rain shelter, ignoring a turnoff to the right that appears within a few minutes. The rocky trail undulates and, at one point, other white rectangular markers appear. This path may be the remains of a temporary reroute. Follow the correct trail uphill to the right. It will bring you to the junction of the Tinsley Trail in approximately 30 minutes. Shortly afterward, a viewpoint to the west is just to the right of the trail. High Point is again visible, and Sunrise Mountain Road is startlingly close at the bottom of the hill.

The trail detours slightly to avoid a wet area, passes by two flat depressions to the left (which are sometimes quite full of water), and arrives at a shelter sign with three blue markers on a tree to the left. The shelter is 0.3 mile distant. This wide junction is also that of the brown-marked Stony Brook Trail, which could be used to shorten the hike by about 30 minutes.

Proceed south on the AT across a stream and uphill, very soon looking down onto a 1986 clear-cut that removed diseased and weakened trees in an attempt to improve the growing conditions for those that remained.

Thirty minutes from the Stony Brook Trail junction there is a definite trail to the left. The white-marked AT is routed to the right and climbs uphill on a rocky path. The alternative trail rejoins the correct route farther on and offers an easier path to the same point. Fifteen minutes later you will get your first sighting of the Normanook Fire Tower. The tower is reached by a short climb on some rock slabs. A few yards after beginning the ascent, look to the right to find a green marker on a tree (sometimes obscured by new leaf growth). This spot marks the beginning of the Tower Trail, which you will follow on the way out.

Normanook Fire Tower is manned during times of greatest fire hazard, although the range of visibility is only about 30 miles. It is well worth climbing the six flights of steps (at your own risk) to the top of the tower, though the sight of New York City is blocked by distant hills. There is an exceptionally long picnic table at Normanook where the weary traveler can rest.

Backtrack to the beginning of the Tower Trail (sometimes difficult to find), turn left, and then turn immediately right across a large rock slab to the footway on the opposite side. There are no markers on the rock. Exercise caution, for this trail travels downhill over highly polished boulders that are slippery even when dry. The path switchbacks steeply downhill to the left, levels out on a dirt section for a while, and continues to descend until it reaches Sunrise Mountain Road about 15 minutes beyond the fire tower. Go straight across Sunrise Mountain Road, angling slightly to the right, and reenter the woods. For a short way, the trail descends, then it immediately enters a low-lying area with many wet sections, some of them requiring lengthy detours or stepping-stone stream crossings. In spring, this part of the woods is carpeted with the common blue violet. In addition, keep a lookout for the tiny, magenta-colored flowers of the fringed polygala; the flowers resemble a tiny, tailless airplane and flourish in rich, moist woodlands. If the leaves are off the trees, it is possible to see a magnificent stand of red pines to the left of the trail. The next stream you encounter is deep and must be crossed on stepping-stones. Shortly after passing an old wall, reach a wide T-junction where brown, dark green, and light green markers can be seen on a large tree opposite the emergence of the Tower Trail, along with brown and light green markers on a tree to the left and dark green markers on a tree to the right.

Turn left onto this wide woods road, following the mixture of markers. After a short distance are two enormous lilac trees on the right. This square, grassy area is the site of the old Courson subsistence farm, abandoned in the late 1920s or early 1930s and used as a ranger station until the late 1950s when it was demolished. A few steps down the road on the opposite side of the clearing, where the brook is running, look for the foundations of an old milk house where milk and other perishables were kept cold. All that remains is a square hole supported on one side by a cement slab.

Shortly after you pass the site of the old farmhouse is a junction with the Courson Trail. Do not go straight ahead; turn right, noting that the blue markers of the Courson Trail have been added to the existing dark green, light green, and brown ones. Stay on the wide road up the slight incline on the right, passing first the light green loop and then the red trail on which you began the hike. Walk back down to your car.

Stokes State Forest has cabins available for rent in addition to campsites. An admirable follow-up to this hike might be Tillman Ravine. The spectacular ravine is short and gentle enough to be walked in sneakers.

SJG

4

Rattlesnake Swamp to Catfish Pond

Total distance: 5 miles

Hiking time: 3½ hours

Vertical rise: 500 feet

Rating: Moderate

Maps: USGS Flatbrookville; NYNJTC South Kittatinny Trails #16; WB #16; HRM #43; NPS Millbrook Area Trails map

This loop hike in the heart of the Kittatinnies skirts the edge of a swamp, passes a lake, and then climbs to an excellent ridge overlook. The area is underused, if anything, and if you are hiking during the week, your chance of encountering others is minimal. Though you probably will not see any rattlesnakes (which are on the endangered species list and very rare), prepare for a very rocky trail by wearing sturdy boots.

How to Get There

From exit 12 on I-80, take County Road 521 (CR 521) north to Blairstown. After about 5 miles, you'll come to a junction with NJ 94. Make a left here and, after another 0.2 mile, turn right at the light. Drive through part of Blairstown on Bridge Street. Do *not* make the sharp right on CR 521. When you come to the end of Bridge Street at the top of a sharp rise, bear right and then make the next left. This road, Millbrook-Blairstown Road (CR 602), will take you in 6.2 miles to a trailhead for the Appalachian Trail (AT), which is at the top of the ridge. You'll see the ridge and the fire tower looming in front of you as you approach the area. Parking for a few cars can be found near the gate on the left side of the road. Additional parking is located on the right about 150 yards west in a small area just off the road.

The Trail

Begin hiking south from the gate on a gravel road, following the white markers of the AT. Pass an AT trail sign and register, then cross a small brook. In an area of many clearings (no camping), the gravel road veers to the right, entering a corridor through a jungle of immense rhododendrons. Rattlesnake Swamp appears on your right with its hemlock, mosses, and skunk cabbage. Take note where the AT turns

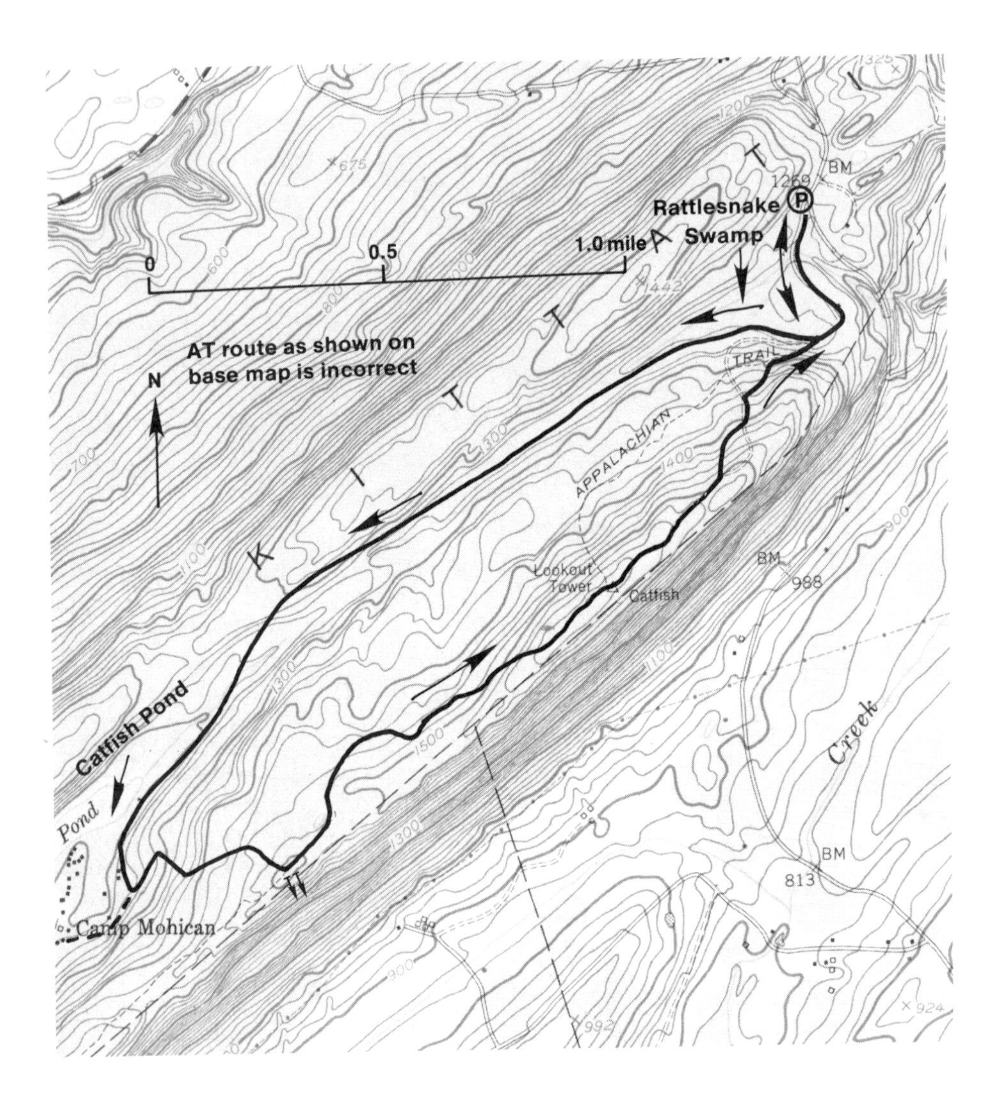

left off the gravel road, heading uphill through the rhododendrons. Continue straight ahead past Rattlesnake Springs on the left, and look for the orange markers of the Rattlesnake Swamp Trail. At a signed junction, the orange markers will lead you to the right, off the gravel road and onto a cut footpath. The footing, typical of trails on the Kittatinny Ridge, becomes extremely rocky almost immediately.

The Rattlesnake Swamp Trail continues to the left of and slightly above Rattlesnake Swamp. Some sections are deep and dark, dominated by hemlock and other shade plants, while other sections, with dead trees and high ferns, are open to the sun. As you leave the swamp, the trail, now traversing thick mountain laurel growth, enters a deep hemlock grove. Farther along the footing becomes mossy and in places quite wet. Cross over a small brook and begin to climb toward higher ground.

Don't be surprised if you startle a deer in this section, sending it crashing through the brush. After a stretch of much drier woods, the trail descends and crosses a small brook twice. Immediately after the second crossing, notice a large swamp (part of the drainage that feeds Catfish Pond) to your right. After about 45 minutes to an hour, Catfish Pond appears through the trees on your right.

Catfish Pond

As you walk past the northern end of the pond, enjoy the views of lily-covered water against the steep western banks, some of which are bare of foliage because of rock slides. The sounds of frogs fill the air in spring and summer. The trail follows an old road lined with both low- and highbush blueberries. The highbush blueberries, ripe in late July and early August, are delicious. Catfish Pond is the centerpiece of Camp Mohican, which has several buildings and is leased from the government by the Appalachian Mountain Club.

The Appalachian Mountain Club (AMC) is a Boston-based hiking club that has a strong presence in the White Mountains of New Hampshire and several other areas in New England. The club was founded in 1876 and was a model for the later Sierra Club. The AMC's Camp Mohican might be called a guide center: part nature center, part hotel, and part conference center. Workshops are held on weekends covering topics such as backpacking, canoeing, and birding. Hikers may stay overnight in one of their bunkrooms (with kitchen and showers) for $18 on Friday and Saturday nights, or $12 at other times. Since the AMC has been at Camp Mohican, the trails in the area have been very well maintained. On the second weekend of each summer month, volunteers do trailwork in exchange for lodging. Call 908-362-5670 (Wednesday and Thursday, 7 AM–9 PM) for more information about Camp Mohican.

The Rattlesnake Swamp Trail will gradually veer away from the pond and soon come to a junction where a sign indicates a turn to the left. After only a few hundred feet, the orange markers will direct you to turn left again onto a grassy road leading uphill. Just after the road swings to the right, the trail turns off the road onto a footpath and begins to climb the Kittatinny Ridge in earnest. The ascent is quite steep and takes you over large rocks and through clumps of laurel. After a few minutes of work, there is a temporary respite where the trail levels off before it resumes climbing, this time not so steeply. After meandering through another level section, the trail climbs once more, leading to the flat, level summit of the Kittatinny Ridge. Here, in dense blueberry bushes, a vast vista of forest and farmland is seen through the trees. Just a few steps ahead is a junction with the AT and a magnificent view over cliffs to the east and south.

After resting from the climb and enjoying the spectacular view, turn left and head north, following the white markers of the AT. The trail twists and winds along the broad summit through an open area of dead trees killed by gypsy moths. To the right are vistas out to the horizon. After about a half hour, arrive at the Catfish Pond fire tower, which is operational and manned during the fire season. The tower may be climbed for views in all directions. On a clear day even the distant Catskills are visible.

Continue straight ahead on the AT, which now follows the grassy utility road allowing access to the fire tower. Watch where the AT veers off to the left from this service road and begins to descend the ridge through an open area covered with blueberry bushes and ferns. The AT joins the service road again, now gravel, for a few hundred feet before turning right, back into the woods on a cut trail. After a descent through dark woods on a very rocky trail, come to a T-junction and bear right. After another 200 yards, the AT joins the gravel road once again, this time near Rattlesnake Springs, which you passed early in the hike. A right turn here will lead via the AT to the gate and your car.

BCS

5

Mount Tammany

Total distance: 4 miles

Hiking time: 3 hours

Vertical rise: 1200 feet

Rating: Moderately strenuous

Maps: USGS Portland, Bushkill; NYNJTC South Kittatinny Trails #15; WB #15; HRM #43; NPS Kittatinny Point Area Trails map

Overlooking the Delaware River on the New Jersey side of the Delaware Water Gap stands Mount Tammany. This mountain, a portion of the Kittatinny Ridge and located within Worthington State Forest and the Delaware Gap National Recreation Area, offers one of the steepest climbs in all of New Jersey as well as spectacular views from its summit. Because of its easy access from I-80, the trail to the summit is heavily used year-round, though particularly so in summer. Also in the area is Dunnfield Creek with its many falls and cascades, the Appalachian Trail (AT), and Sunfish Pond, making this location a major natural area in the state.

How to Get There

Take I-80 west to the Delaware Water Gap. As the highway enters the gap itself, turn off to the right, following signs to a rest area. If you miss this turnoff, take the next exit off the highway, the last exit in New Jersey, and follow signs to the Delaware Water Gap National Recreation Area Kittatinny Point Information Center (Bushkill, PA 18324; 908-496-4458). You will be able to find the rest area by passing the visitors center, crossing back under I-80, and bearing right. The trailhead is in the rest area, not at the parking area for the AT and Sunfish Pond.

The Trail

Begin the hike on the River Ridge (or Red-Dot) Trail, which leaves the rest area heading east. It is on the far side of the parking area just to the left of a small cascade that flows during wet periods. The trail, marked with red-on-white markers painted on trees, begins climbing almost immediately, a foreshadowing of things to come. After this brief elevation gain, the trail levels off, temporarily paralleling Dunnfield Creek well below on the left. Where the trail turns sharply right,

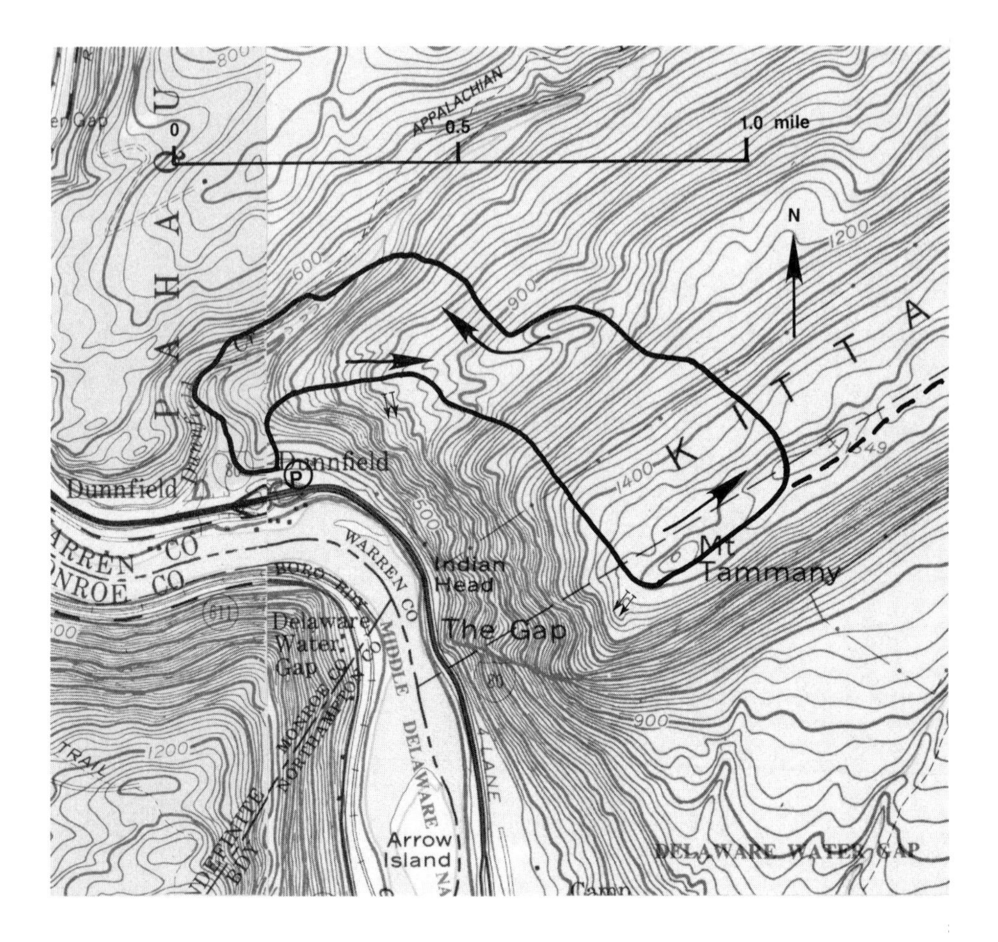

it begins a steady climb on a well-used, rocky path lined with evergreens, hemlocks, and rhododendrons. The sounds of the falls on Dunnfield Creek, even farther below now, are still in the distance. Watch for where the trail turns right, climbing over tilted but parallel beds of sedimentary rock.

After this last climb, you'll arrive at the first of several overlooks. Here, at the edge of a steep cliff and exposed to the elements, cedar trees struggle for survival. Below, looking south, the Delaware Water Gap opens in front of you. Mount Minsi on the Pennsylvania side is to the right and Mount Tammany to the left. Mount Minsi, which rises 1463 feet above sea level, is named after the Native Americans who lived in the area. Mount Tammany, at 1527 feet, is named after the Lenni-Lenape chief Tamenund.

The Delaware Water Gap, certainly one of the scenic wonders of New Jersey, is a 1200-foot-deep gorge carved by the waters of the Delaware River through the long, wall-like Kittatinny Ridge. Back in Cretaceous times, roughly 100 million years ago, the Water Gap did not exist. The entire area, which was once very mountainous, had been worn down by erosion to a flat plain that gently sloped toward the Atlantic Ocean some 40 miles away. Streams, which drained the land, meandered through this landscape on their way to the sea. In the late Cretaceous period the land began to rise, and the streams began cutting deeper channels.

As the land rose, the ancestral Delaware River found itself confronted with a major barrier—the relatively resistant rock that makes up the Kittatinny Ridge. This rock, made of the tough sandstone and conglomerate of the Shawangunk Formation, dips to the north at the entrance to the gap. These rocks and the red rocks that overlie them are warped into many folds. (The cross-section of the ridge exposed by the gap is a geology lesson in itself.) Right at the gap, the Kittatinny Ridge is fractured, its long continuity broken. Because of this structural weakness, the Delaware River has successfully maintained its course through this section of the Kittatinny Ridge. Today, the river continues to cut and remove rock as the land continues to rise slowly.

The Delaware Water Gap

After skirting a few more viewpoints, the trail crosses a brook and then passes a reliable spring on the left. After this brief respite, it once again begins seriously climbing the mountain ridge. Because of the rocky terrain, climbing this section is difficult in any season, but it can be particularly challenging and even dangerous in icy conditions. First you cross a boulder field; then, through a beautiful forest of hemlock and rhododendron, you must navigate a steep rock slab. Use both your feet and your hands when you need to, while still paying attention to the markers so as not to lose the trail. After leveling off temporarily through a more open forest, the trail begins climbing again on a rocky footpath high on the ridge. From here to the summit, the forest is sparse, offering little protection from the winds. Along the way, you will find a cedar-lined viewpoint on the right.

Just before you reach the summit, notice that the area to the left is open; a fire occurred here some years ago.

The former oak forest is being replaced by thick laurel growth. Finally you reach the summit. Here the oak forest stops at the edge of a 1200-foot cliff overlooking the Delaware River. Only scrub oak and pitch pine survive in this rocky, exposed environment. At the summit area, walk to the right and down over the exposed rocks, which offer you an expansive view west to Mount Minsi and the Blue Mountain Ridge behind it. The Pocono Plateau of Pennsylvania stretches out to the horizon in the north; in the south the plains of the Great Valley, and beyond it the Reading Prong section of the Highlands, extend to the horizon. If you walk down the exposed rocks of the summit you will see the Indian Head profile—located on a portion of the cliff below and to the north (upriver) of the viewpoint—staring out over the river.

From the summit follow the trail, now marked with blue, away from the overlook area. Heading northeasterly, the trail meanders along the summit ridge for about 0.25 mile, then bears sharply left near a viewpoint through the trees to the east. Do *not* continue straight ahead on the gray markers. A sign indicates that you are on the Blue-Dot Trail.

After a long, steady descent from the ridge over rocks, the trail swings to the left toward the river, following a nearly level walkway. Finally, after a long walk, the Blue-Dot Trail arrives at Dunnfield Creek near one of its many falls. The trail, now concurrent with the green-blazed Dunnfield Creek Trail, bears left and then right, crossing the creek on a wooden bridge. Here in this dark hemlock gorge are numerous cascades and plunge pools, the white water creating a sharp contrast to the dark rock it glides over. After following the right bank of the creek for a short distance, the Blue-Dot Trail reaches its terminus as shown by three markers on a tree. From here, follow the white markers of the AT downhill along the stream, and cross the creek again on a wooden bridge. Leave the AT here—it bears to the right—and follow the pathway out to the parking area. To reach the rest area and your car, walk along the parking area, keeping to the left. Look for and take a very small footpath that leaves the area heading south just past the last parking spot. This small path parallels the road below it on the right and leads to the rest area and its picnic tables.

BCS

6

Appalachian Trail Backpack

Total distance: 28.2 miles

Hiking time: 17 hours—allow 3 days, 2 nights

Rating: Strenuous

Maps: USGS Portland/Bushkill/Flatbrookville/Culvers Gap; NYNJTC North and South Kittatinny Trails, #15, #16, and #17; WB #15, #16, and #17; HRM #43 and #52B

Most hikers are aware that the Appalachian Trail (AT) is a marked footpath extending 2000 miles from Springer Mountain, Georgia, to Mount Katahdin, Maine. The summer of 1987 marked the 50th anniversary of its completion. The first section of trail was built in Bear Mountain/Harriman State Parks in New York State, and the last section completed was on a remote ridgeline in Maine between Spaulding and Sugarloaf Mountains cut by a crew from the Civilian Conservation Corps. Trail markers are white rectangles; side trails to water, viewpoints, and shelters are marked in blue.

The AT is often rerouted, and if there is a discrepancy between the markers and the guide or map, follow the markers. This backpacking trip begins at the Delaware Water Gap and follows the ridge of the Kittatinny Mountains generally north through Worthington State Forest and the Delaware Water Gap National Recreation Area. The terrain is rocky, and it is recommended that sturdy hiking boots be worn instead of sneakers. The hike is rated as strenuous because of the need for a backpack.

Squirrels and chipmunks are numerous and are always attracted to campsites where food scraps are available. Their sharp teeth can do a tremendous amount of damage to tents and packs. To avoid such damage, at night and whenever your campsite is unattended, put all food into one large plastic bag and string it on a line between two trees. Because these little animals are adept climbers, the bag should be a minimum of 6 feet away from the nearest tree or large branch.

Most natural water sources along the trail are liable to be contaminated and should be purified before use by boiling, filtering, chemical treatment, or a combination. Open ground fires are not permitted in the Delaware Water Gap National Recreation Area, so a portable camp stove is essential. Camping is permitted along the trail with certain restrictions, and you should check on regulations with the ranger at the Delaware Water Gap Visitor Center before setting out.

Because the term "rattlesnake" is used frequently in these parts, it is often assumed that timber rattlesnakes are numerous. In fact, this snake is on the New Jersey list of endangered and rare wildlife species. Do not meddle with any snakes you encounter, however; most retreat quickly unless interfered with.

This hike requires transportation at each end. The best arrangement is to leave the majority of cars at the end point, using as few cars as possible to transport all the hikers back to the other trailhead. If you are willing to do some investigation on where cars should be placed, you could walk the three following sections of the AT as day hikes.

How to Get There

Leave one car at Culvers Gap—the end point of this hike—at the parking lot on Sunrise Mountain Road. To reach this lot from US 206, turn east onto Upper North Shore Road just north of Culvers Lake, 3.4 miles northwest of Branchville; then immediately turn left onto Sunrise Mountain Road. The lot is at the first bend on the left (west) side of the road.

Drive to the Delaware Water Gap. You can park either at the Delaware Water Gap National Recreation Information Center (Bushkill, PA 18324; 717-828-7802 or for information out of season, 717-588-2451), south of I-80 at the gap; or at the Dunnfield Creek Natural Area. The latter lot, which is east of the information center, is often crowded. It can be reached by turning left at the underpass under I-80, then making another left onto a paved road. Go to the parking lot on the right with the sign DUNNFIELD CREEK NATURAL AREA.

The Trail

First Day: Delaware Water Gap to Catfish Fire Tower

Total distance first day: 12.6 miles

Hiking time: 7 hours

Vertical rise: 1000 feet

Hoist your backpack and enter the woods at the far end of the Dunnfield Creek Natural Area parking lot. Follow the stream's right bank until the trail crosses a substantial wooden bridge and parallels the stream on the opposite side. The trail leads steadily upward, away from the stream, through a mixture of deciduous and coniferous trees and ferns. Look to the right: You can see distinct layers of rock on the opposite bank. Look down as you climb high above the stream to see numerous pools and waterfalls and enjoy this delightfully cool section.

A campsite is marked by signs here, although it is probably too close to the start of this trip to be useful for overnight accommodation. Because the other of the area's two campsites was recently closed, this site tends to be overcrowded. No fires are permitted and a stay of only one night is allowed.

Back on the main trail, 0.5 mile from the start of the hike, the woods road forks. There is a metal sign with a painted map at this junction, and the blue trail to Mount Tammany leads away to the right. Follow the left trail through small sweet chestnut trees,

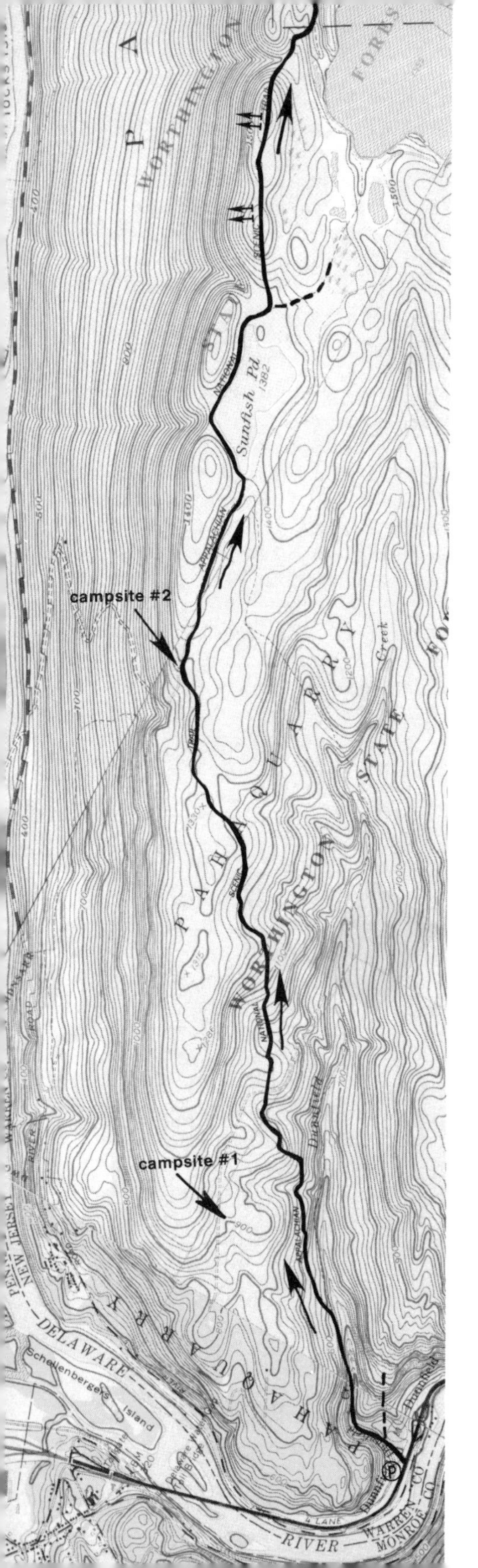
campsite #2
campsite #1
Sunfish Pd
WORTHINGTON
DELAWARE
RIVER
Schellenbergers Island
NEW JERSEY
PENNSYLVANIA
WARREN CO.
MONROE CO.

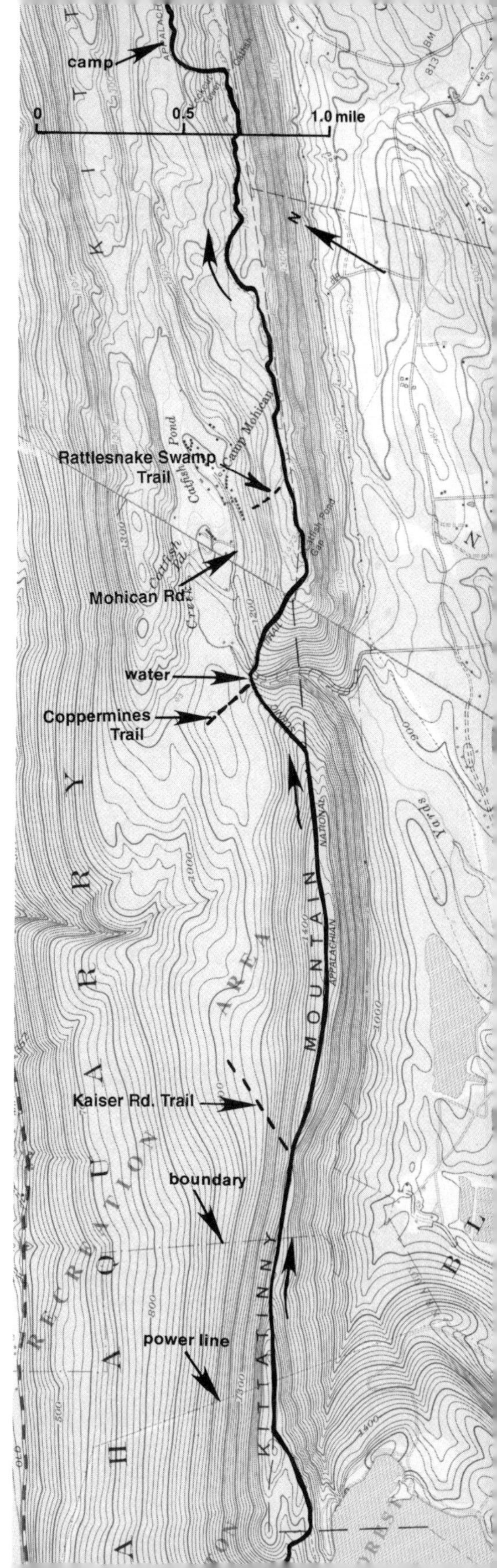
camp
0
0.5
1.0 mile
N
Rattlesnake Swamp Trail
Camp Mohican
Catfish Pond
Mohican Rd.
water
Coppermines Trail
Kaiser Rd. Trail
boundary
power line
KITTATINNY
MOUNTAIN

which will probably not reach maturity because of blight; the disease practically destroyed these trees in the 1930s. The blue trail and Dunnfield Creek are visible below.

Still climbing, the woods road changes dramatically into a rocky trail and at 1.5 miles reaches an intersection with the Beulahland Trail. Your route climbs still farther before leveling out, paralleling the ridge of the Kittatinny Mountains to the right. By now you have been on the trail for about an hour, and after another 30 minutes through an open area on a rocky trail with tall mountain laurel, you will reach the intersection for the Backpacker Campsite (#2 on this map). Another 40 minutes brings you to the southern tip of Sunfish Pond. The center of much environmental controversy, this glacial lake is 1380 feet above sea level and is considered a natural geological oddity. Just to the left of the trail here is a stone monument dated 1970. Walk straight ahead to the shore of Sunfish Pond, then turn left to follow the trail around the western shore. The no-camping regulation is strictly enforced at Sunfish Pond.

The trail is now rocky and narrow. It shortly crosses a small outlet from the pond, climbs, turns right, and descends again to the water's edge. Many rocky areas on the shore of the pond invite the traveler to rest. In one area, we came across a stony beach where industrious folk had built many Stonehenge-like edifices. This nondestructive graffiti must have kept someone busy for many hours.

At the end of Sunfish Pond, the trail moves back deeper into the woods, and a dependable spring can be found 600 feet to the left of the trail. In this section, a blue-marked trail enters from the right and a turquoise-marked trail from the left.

The trail levels out after a short climb, turns left, and descends again through magnificent mountain laurel. Two-and-a-half hours into the hike (about the 4.5-mile point), cross a small brook. After climbing a short way, it is possible to make a detour to the left of the trail to see the Delaware River and the Pennsylvania Mountains. Within 30 minutes, a power line crosses the trail; slightly farther ahead, where the trail reaches the crest of the ridge, there are views in both directions. Walking slightly to the left improves the view of the river and Pennsylvania. Directly ahead Catfish Fire Tower is visible, and to the right the Yards Creek pumped water-storage ponds can be seen.

The Yards Creek Pumped Storage Electric Generating Station began operation in 1965. The upper reservoir was created from two small swampy areas on the mountaintop, and the lower, about a mile east and approximately 700 feet below, is located on Yards Creek. An auxiliary reservoir, now part of a Boy Scout camping area, is just to the north of the lower Yards Creek reservoir.

The trail remains high on this slabby terrain for a short distance. The bow in the Delaware River, which is not visible from other places, can be seen from here. On a clear day the Catskills are also visible. Just as the trail begins to drop, there is a large AT sign on the boundary between Worthington State Forest and the Delaware Water Gap National Recreation Area.

The trail continues downhill on the ridge—called Mount Mohican—with glimpses of the views seen previously, until it reaches a sign for a spring 0.3 mile down the Kaiser Road Trail. Continue ahead until the Kaiser Road Trail turns to the left and the AT makes a right. About a mile from the right turn, the trail becomes rockier and, descending steeply through mountain laurel, eventually reaches a stream crossing at Mohican Road. This stream is a dependable water source. You have now walked about 9 miles and as it will soon be time to make camp, you should collect water here for overnight use.

Coppermines Trail soon enters from the left. New Jersey claims the first copper mine opened in America by Dutch settlers in the Kittatinny Mountains around 1640. The Coppermines Trail leads to a number of mines that can still be entered and explored by flashlight.

Cross Mohican Road and immediately enter the opposite woods. It will take about 10 or 15 minutes until the trail emerges onto a ridge with a view of an agricultural valley to the right. This section of the trail is spectacular—it travels along the side of the ridge through cedar and scrub pines. There is a sharp drop-off, and if you look back, Yards Creek Reservoir is visible in the distance. A short way along this ridge is a sign to the left for RATTLESNAKE SWAMP TRAIL and another for CATFISH POND, only 0.5 mile distant. The trail turns away from the ridge and climbs slightly left, then descends and passes through a more open area with many dead trees.

After the trail leaves the ledges, it passes areas that could be used for camping, but we recommend you proceed just beyond Catfish Fire Tower. This tower, built in 1922, is 60 feet high, and it is well worth climbing the stairs to the splendid 360-degree view if the opportunity is available. The elevation here is 1565 feet, and it is possible to see the Catskills in the distance and, closer in, Sand Pond.

From Catfish Fire Tower, the trail descends on an old jeep road toward Millbrook-Blairstown Road. There are some ideal campsites just past the fire tower, both left and right of the jeep road. It is your responsibility to comply with camping regulations.

Second Day: Catfish Fire Tower to Junction with Trail to Buttermilk Falls

Total distance second day: 7.8 miles

Hiking time: 5 hours

Vertical rise: 1000 feet

Still heading north, the trail leaves the jeep road, turns left, and descends slightly on a rocky path overlooking a different valley until it rejoins the jeep road. Then it once again leaves the jeep road, veering left and reentering the woods to the right through a lush section. At the foot of a steep descent on a narrow, rocky trail winding through tall mountain laurel, turn right at the power line and proceed through an extensive rhododendron thicket onto a gravel road. Turn left on the gravel road and look for Rattlesnake Spring in the left bank at the side of the road. This spring is delightful and can be depended upon for water for today's hike. The next water is approximately 5 miles ahead.

Walk back to where the AT joins the wide gravel road and continue on the AT until it shortly makes a sharp turn to the left. You will reach paved Millbrook-Blairstown Road within approximately 35 minutes of leaving your campsite.

Turn left on the paved road and, after a very short walk, enter the woods again on the right where there is a register. After signing in, take the left fork. At the beginning of this section, the trail is wide and passes a swamp on the left. The path is high on a ridge above this wet area, with glimpses of an even higher ridge on the right. After about 10 minutes of walking,

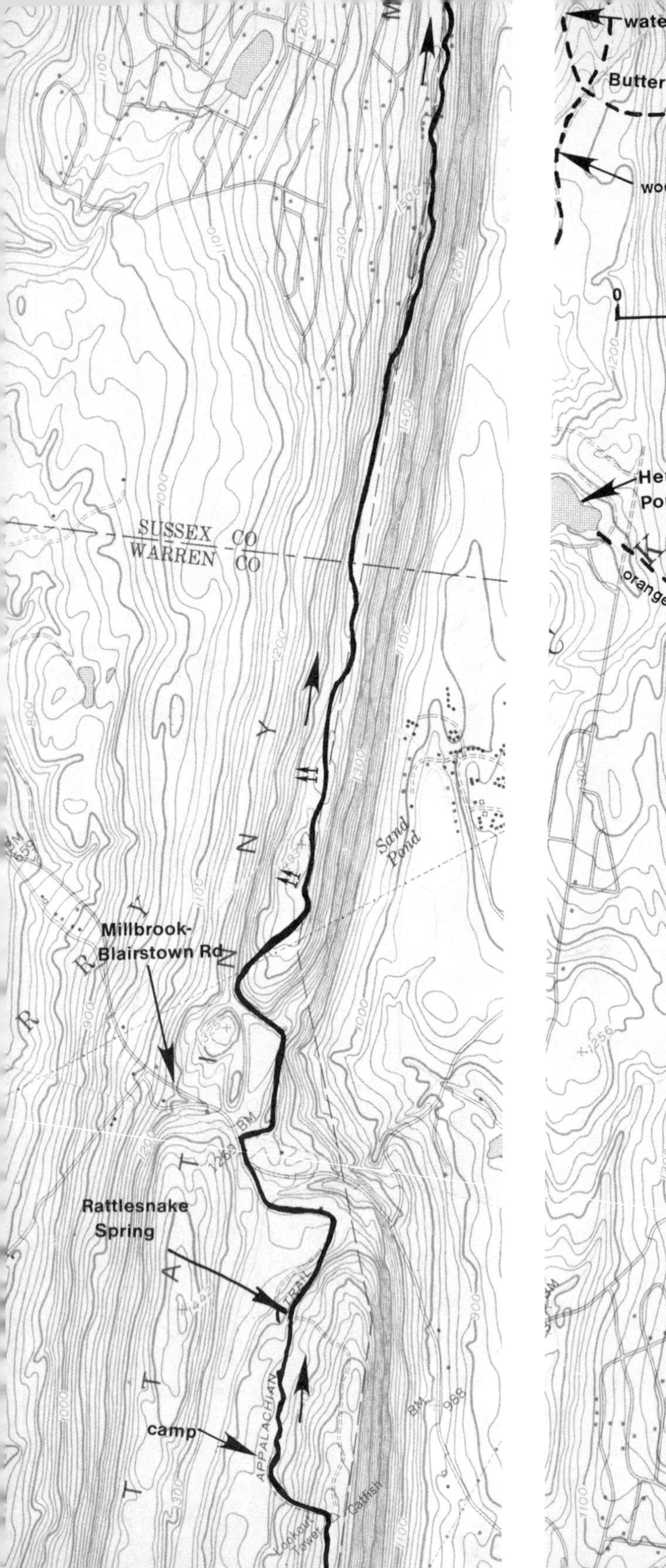
SUSSEX CO
WARREN CO
Sand Pond
Millbrook-Blairstown Rd
Rattlesnake Spring
APPALACHIAN TRAIL
camp
Lookout Tower
Catfish

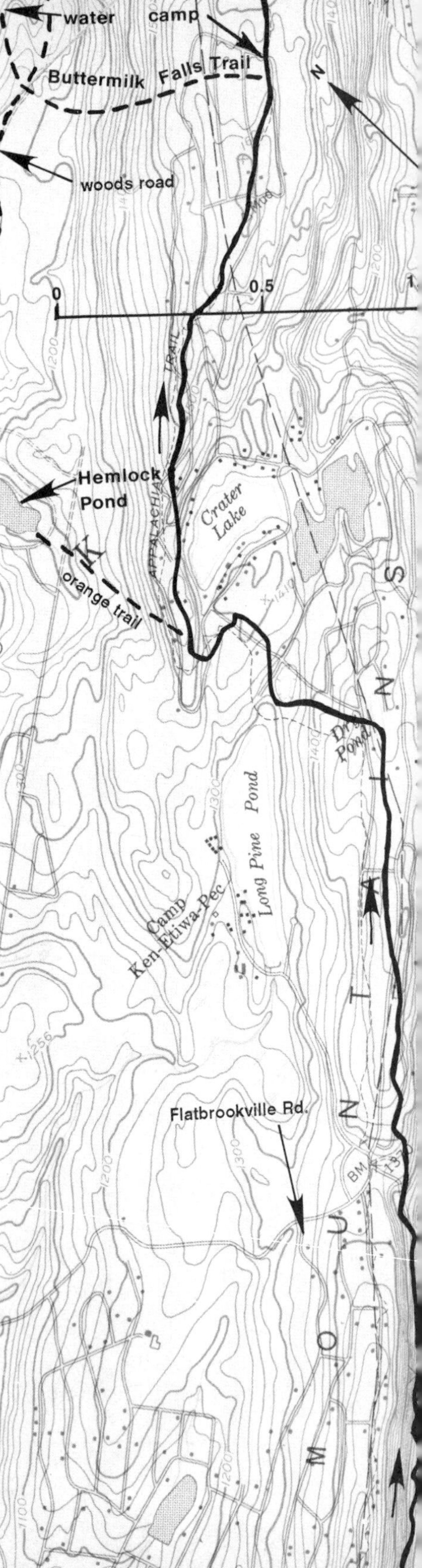
water
camp
Buttermilk Falls Trail
woods road
0
0.5
Hemlock Pond
Crater Lake
orange trail
APPALACHIAN TRAIL
Dry Pond
Long Pine Pond
Camp Ken-Etiwa-Pec
Flatbrookville Rd.

watch for a sharp turn to the left that detours around the northern end of the swamp away from the road. The trail becomes narrower, then opens out at the top of a short climb. There is a rocky bank on the left, and a careful watch is necessary for a sharp right turn leading steeply uphill. This turn was obscured by a blowdown at the time of this writing, and if you miss it, power lines soon come into view. You do not need to backtrack, however. By bushwhacking underneath the power lines to the top of the hill, you can easily find the trail again on the right. The Wallkill Valley and Pocono Plateaus are visible from the clearing at the top of the hill. Several small cedars are scattered around this viewpoint, and the power lines march down the hill with Sand Pond.

The view to the east continues as you follow the ridge. Markers are not clear in this section. The main trail is shortly joined from the right by one marked with a mix of diamond-shaped red and white metal emblems. Fairview Lake is visible through the trees to the right. The wide, rocky road is high on a ridge, and it very shortly passes a large boulder on the left from which views of the valley to the west are available. There is another register at this point.

After about 5 miles and just before reaching paved Flatbrookville Road, look for a water pump on the left. If you miss it, there is also a spring contained in a metal pipe about 0.1 mile down the hill on Flatbrookville Road on the right (east) side of the road. After emerging onto the road, turn right, walk a few steps down the road, and turn left into an area of small white pines. Two or 3 minutes later, cross a woods road. Walk straight ahead and register on the left.

The trail is in a pretty area here—narrower and cut through mountain laurel. It is clearly marked and descends steeply through rock slabs until it reaches a rock-strewn bog on the right. If you look back and to the left through the trees, you can see Long Pine Pond. Various lakes and ponds in the vicinity are all potential sources of water, though all water should be treated before drinking. Cross a gravel road by bearing slightly to the right, and reenter the woods on the left. Observe the outcrop of rock to the left—the trail is routed over this. At the top of this escarpment, you cross another gravel road and are rewarded by a good view to the west. Within a few minutes, you can get a view of Crater Lake (or Lake Success) by taking a blue-blazed trail to the right. A metal post is embedded in the rock at this viewpoint.

The walking is very easy on a wide, grassy trail that soon makes a sharp left turn. Notice the pipe to the left of this turn; there may have been a spring here at one time. Views of Hemlock Pond are available at this point, and the orange trail to Hemlock Pond is marked practically at the crest of the rise.

This attractive section is still on a slightly uphill gradient, with more views of Crater Lake to the right. The trail is on a ledge, with the ground dropping down to the left and rising to the right—a rock-slab slope dotted with white pines. Two other trails join the main path here from the right and the left, and soon there is a marked left turn onto a gravel road, followed within 100 yards by the blue-blazed trail to Buttermilk Falls on the left. This trail is marked by a wooden sign.

One of the many secluded and attractive campsites in this location should be chosen for the night. A prime site is found by proceeding down the AT approximately 100 yards from the BUTTERMILK FALLS sign and turning left onto a wide, grassy woods road. Within a minute you will find a delightful, flat, grassy opening with a beautiful white pine at each end. After setting up camp, water and a refreshing wash are available by taking a side trip (1.75 miles) to Buttermilk Falls. The trail to the falls is very steep, but (except in dry weather) it is not necessary to go all the way to the falls for water. Ten minutes down the trail, you cross a woods road; in another 5, you hear the sound of water. Where the trail goes downhill and makes a sharp left turn, go straight ahead a few more yards to a group of two or three pools of water. If these pools should be dry, follow the streambed down to find a suitable water-gathering spot. On the way down, the trail passes through several open blueberry patches, which in season might provide a snack.

If you prefer not to add this side trip for water to the day's walk and want to camp closer to a water supply, continue for approximately another mile until the trail descends to a stream crossing. Water is available farther still, about 200 feet down a blue-blazed trail to a dependable spring. The beautiful campsite at the head of the Buttermilk Falls Trail (described above), however, might make the extra effort to get water very worthwhile.

Third Day: Buttermilk Falls Trail to NJ 206 at Culvers Gap

Total distance third day: 7.8 miles

Hiking time: 5 hours

Vertical rise: 800 feet

After you leave camp, the gravel road bends to the right departing from the AT, which turns left on a narrow footpath into the woods. Follow the AT. Two good views west to the Poconos are available here (one of them via a blue-blazed trail on the left) before the trail descends steeply through a rocky section. At the next fork, turn right and cross a stream (the alternate camping spot past the Buttermilk Falls area).

The trail now goes through a mature hemlock and sheep laurel grove. A few minues after the stream crossing, it makes a sharp left turn to begin the climb up Rattlesnake Mountain. This section has been burned out and consequently is quite open. Rattlesnake Mountain (1492 feet) was once called Columbus Mountain. As you approach it, the route up through the boulders and white pines becomes clearer, and during the ascent, good views become more and more apparent to the left until the entire panorama is visible from the summit. This vista includes Normanook Fire Tower and High Point. Walk slightly to the right to reach the highest point.

Continue northward, gently descending on a narrow, rocky trail through many small pine trees toward a short swampy section, which is easily crossed by rock-hopping. This swamp is approximately 2 miles from the Buttermilk Falls area. Within 0.5 mile, the trail has climbed to a rocky area where it turns right onto an old dirt road and begins to descend again. Quick Pond and Mecca Lake can be seen. This road is wide and obviously used by four-wheeled vehicles.

Just to the left of the road are cages and blinds in disrepair. This banding facility was once operated by members of the New Jersey Raptor Association and the Raptor Trust in cooperation with state and federal agencies. Raptors migrate during the fall in great numbers along the Kittatinny Ridge and were banded at this site.

When the road bears left, the trail

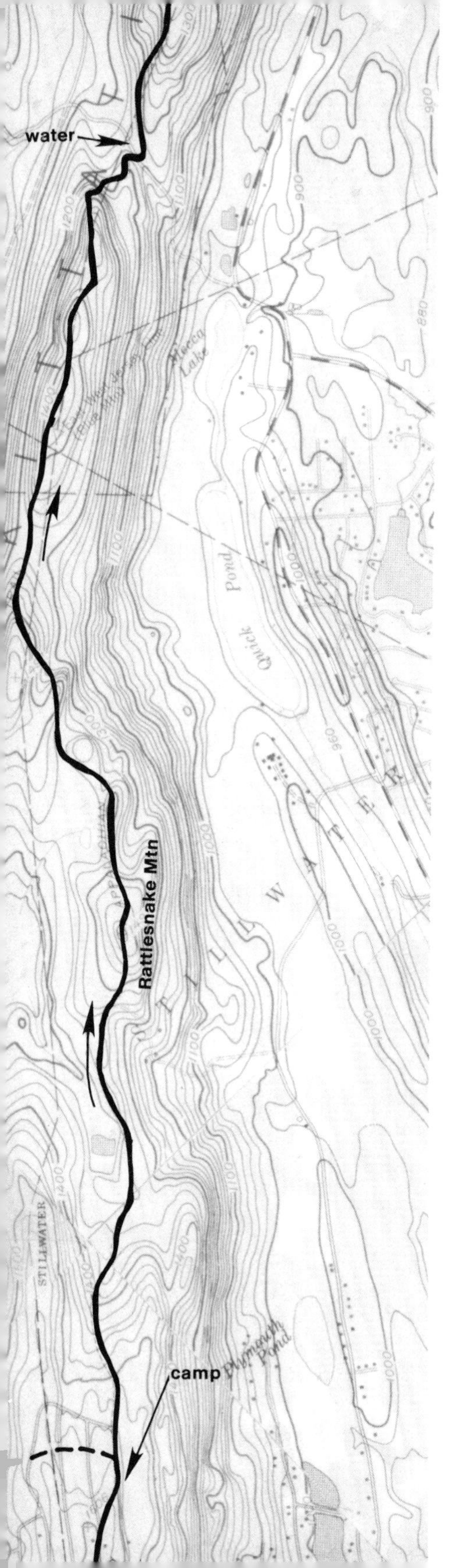
water
Quick Pond
Rattlesnake Mtn
camp
Plymouth Pond
STILLWATER

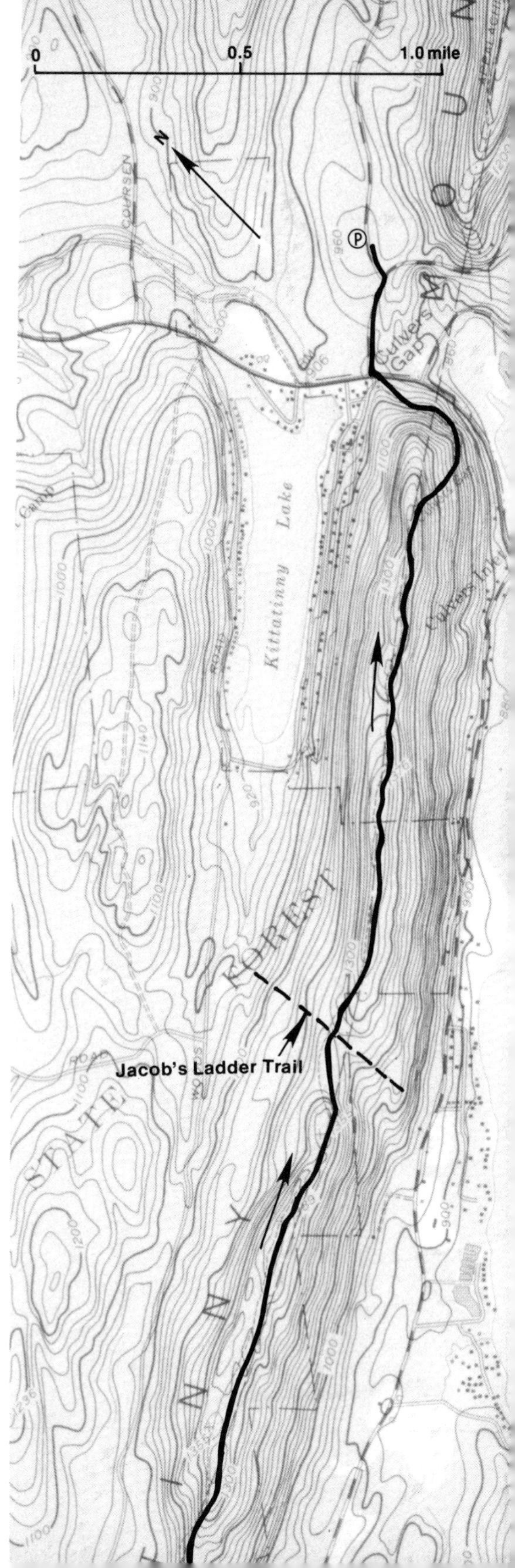
0
0.5
1.0 mile
N
Culvers Gap
Kittatinny Lake
Jacob's Ladder Trail
STATE
FOREST

turns right and begins to climb through white pines. There are views to the left from the rock ledges and, at the top of the ridge, extensive views of the Wallpack Valley and the Poconos, before the trail moves back into the woods on rocky terrain. This high area is commonly known as Blue Mountain, and the larger area of water you glimpse through the trees is Lake Owassa. You will see this lake more clearly later. The general trend is now downhill, becoming more steep as you approach Brink Road. As the trail leaves the wooded section, you can see the next ascent ahead.

Brink Road is 4 miles from the Buttermilk Falls camping area. There is a shelter here with a spring, which is reached by a blue-blazed trail to the left. Uphill from Brink Road is a pretty area with tall mountain laurel, white pines, massive rhododendrons, and hemlock. The climb is short, lasting only about 10 minutes, and the trail remains on the crest of the ridge for a similar amount of time. Just before a rocky, wet area on the right of the main trail, watch for the first unmarked side trail leading to an overlook and, after about another 0.5 mile, for a second unmarked trail leading to an observation point of Lake Owassa. The trail now alternately rises and falls until the final drop to US 206.

Jacob's Ladder Trail, with blue-silver markings, is reached another 0.5 mile from the viewpoint of Lake Owassa. The first view of Culvers Lake, seen here through the trees to the right, is probably not available in summer when the trees are in full leaf. Near the end of the trip is a large cleared area. From this vantage point, Culvers Fire Tower, Culvers Lake, and US 206 are apparent straight ahead and Lake Owassa, behind. The trail turns back into the woods, reaches another clearing with US 206 visible on the right, and emerges onto a gravel road. Traverse the side of a hill, and be careful not to miss the turn to the right. Continuing on the gravel road will lead to US 206 but involves crossing private property.

Use the AT on the north side of Route 206 to reach the parking lot on Sunrise Mountain Road. Walking a little farther on US 206 brings you to Worthington's Bakery (201-948-4490). Its delicious products are highly recommended as a reward for your efforts.

SJG

HIGHLANDS PROVINCE

7

Hoeferlin Memorial Trail

Total distance: 12 miles

Hiking time: 6½ hours

Vertical rise: 700 feet

Rating: Moderately strenuous

Maps: USGS Ramsey/Wanaque; NYNJTC North Jersey Trails #22; WB #23; HRM #15

This hike is almost entirely on the Hoeferlin Memorial Trail. The trail was originally called the Suffern-Midvale Trail; its name was changed to honor well-known trailblazer and mapmaker William Hoeferlin. Bill was the originator of the Hikers Region Maps, which he prepared and published, some of which are still available. He also founded the Wanderbird Hiking Club and served the New York–New Jersey Conference in many capacities for more than three decades. He conceived and published *Walking News*. This periodical, designed to keep the hiking public informed of trail modifications, included hike schedules and was the forerunner of today's *Trail Walker* (New York–New Jersey Trail Conference). He died in 1970 at age 72 while leading a small group of hikers on the trail.

Other trails used in this hike are the Silver and Red/Silver Trails within the Ramapo Valley County Reservation trail system (PO Box 225, Oakland, NJ 07436; 201-646-2680), the Cannonball Trail, and, at the end of the hike, the blue-marked MacEvoy Trail.

During the hike, the trail leaves the Ramapo Valley County Reservation, proceeds through Ringwood State Park (crossing land belonging to the Boy Scouts of America), and traverses the eastern section of the Ramapo Mountain State Forest. The Ramapo Mountains are not especially high—they rise no more than 800 feet above the bordering valleys of the Wanaque River on the northwest and the Ramapo River on the southeast. The Ramapo River valley was the site of a trading post, established perhaps as early as 1710, which attracted squatters to this location. Since colonial days, the ancestry of the Ramapo Mountain people has been a mixture of Native American, African American, and European, resulting in their social isolation as a separate racial group and in their feeling that they are "different" from their neighbors. Today they are a relatively small group—about 1500—living in Mahwah and Ringwood, New Jersey, and Hillburn, New York.

How to Get There

This hike requires transportation at both ends of the trail. Leave one car at the Ramapo Valley County Reservation on the north side of US 202, approximately 2 miles from NJ 17 at Mahwah, and the other at the Ramapo Mountain State Forest parking lot. From the east take NJ 208 (which becomes West Oakland Avenue), then turn north onto Skyline Drive at its junction with West Oakland Avenue. The parking lot is on the west side of Skyline Drive, 0.3 mile from that junction.

The Trail

With your back to the road at the reservation parking lot, cross the blacktop and enter the woods at the lower left-hand corner of the lot. Look for three metal markers on a tree to the right of the footway leading through a gap in the fence. After a short distance through the woods, there is a building and a fountain to the right. Go straight across the road, past a small pond on the left. Camping is permitted here (information is available from the Bergen County Park Commission at 201-646-2680). The route is on a wide dirt road, which first crosses a wooden bridge over the Ramapo River and then immediately passes Scarlet Oak Pond on the right.

At the end of the pond, the road becomes paved and climbs to the left. There are dirt roads on both the right and left that you should ignore—the best route is the one that is alternately dirt and blacktop. It has metal markers indicating the silver trail and is the reservation service road to MacMillan Reservoir.

Within about 20 minutes, you will hear cascades to the left. Although there are paths leading down to the water, they are dangerous. It is possible to see the cascades when the leaves are off the trees. As the metal-marked silver trail bears left, a sign indicates the Ridge Trail (white), and a dirt path join from the right. Stay on the silver trail, which continues to climb, crosses several stone bridges over streams through prolific jewelweed, and bends sharply left as it approaches MacMillan Reservoir. Spend a few minutes at the reservoir by turning right and walking to the water's edge.

Back on the silver trail, climb steadily uphill on a rocky path paralleling the reservoir. Pass the yellow/silver trail and the Marsh Loop Trail on the left. The Marsh Loop is marked with red, although on some maps it is shown as unmarked. Within 25 minutes you will reach the junction of the blue-marked Ridge Trail. Stay on the red/silver trail straight ahead, winding through the woods on a narrower path. Just over the crest of the hill, red/silver markers are evident, and farther on at the lowest point in the trail, the silver trail exits to the left. Continue straight, noting the three red/silver markers on a tree to the right of a small stream crossing. Ten minutes sees you through this section, which is sometimes narrow and muddy.

The trail widens and descends to meet a wider, grassier woods road. Bear left until you reach a pipeline within a few minutes, then walk straight ahead on a wide gravel road, avoiding the poison ivy to the right of the trail. Red/silver markers are still visible and lead to a T-junction at the edge of

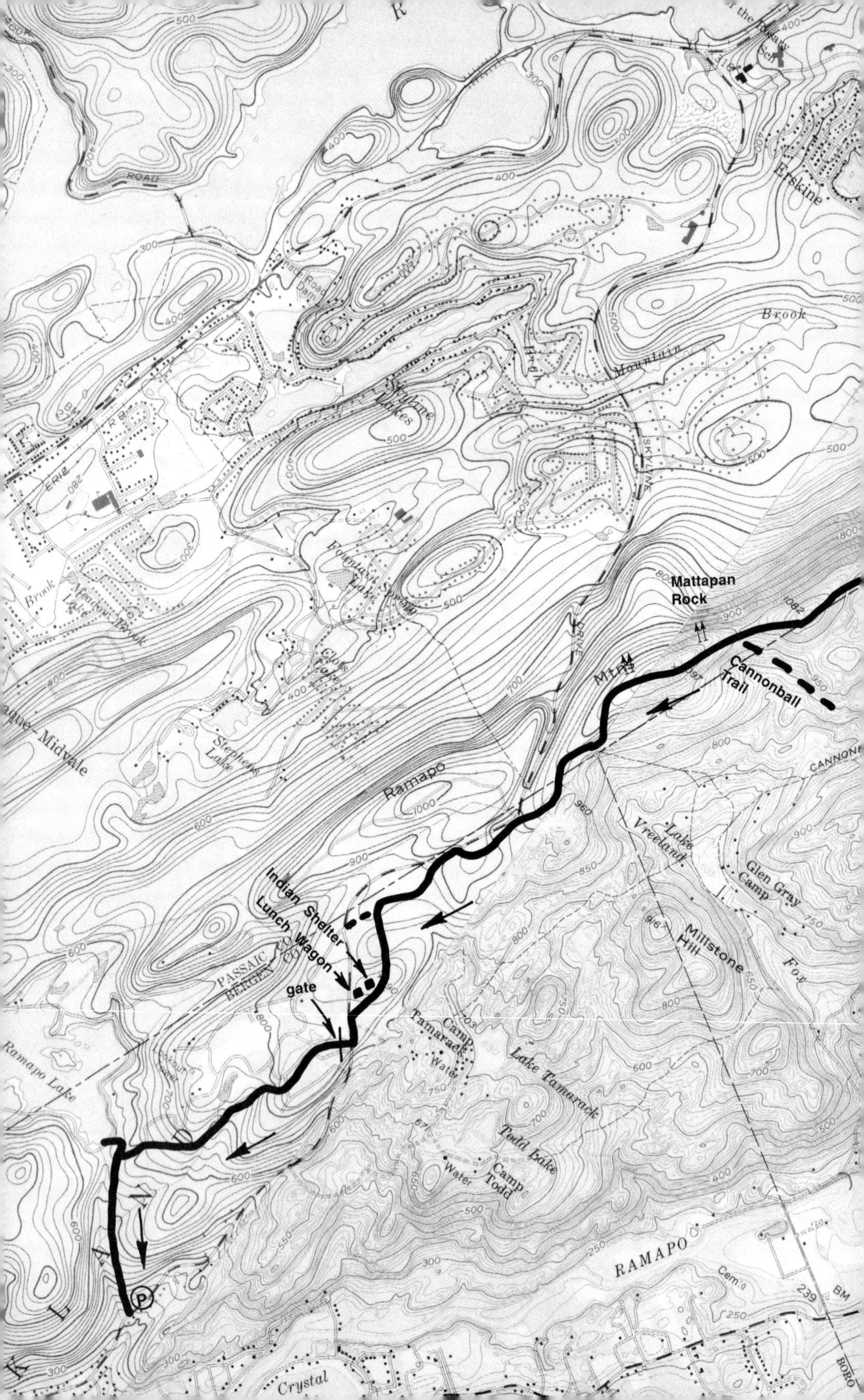

Mattapan
Rock
Cannonball
Trail
Indian Shelter
Lunch Wagon
gate
Ramapo
Mtn
Erskine
Brook
Mountain
Skyline
Lakes
SKYLINE
DRIVE
Fountain Spring
Lake
Clove
Lake
Stephens
Lake
Meadow Brook
Lake
ERIE
RD
ROAD
Lake
Vreeland
Glen Gray
Camp
Millstone
Hill
Camp
Tamarack
Water
Lake Tamarack
Todd Lake
Camp
Todd
PASSAIC CO
BERGEN CO
Ramapo Lake
Lookout
RAMAPO
Cem
BM
Crystal
CANNON

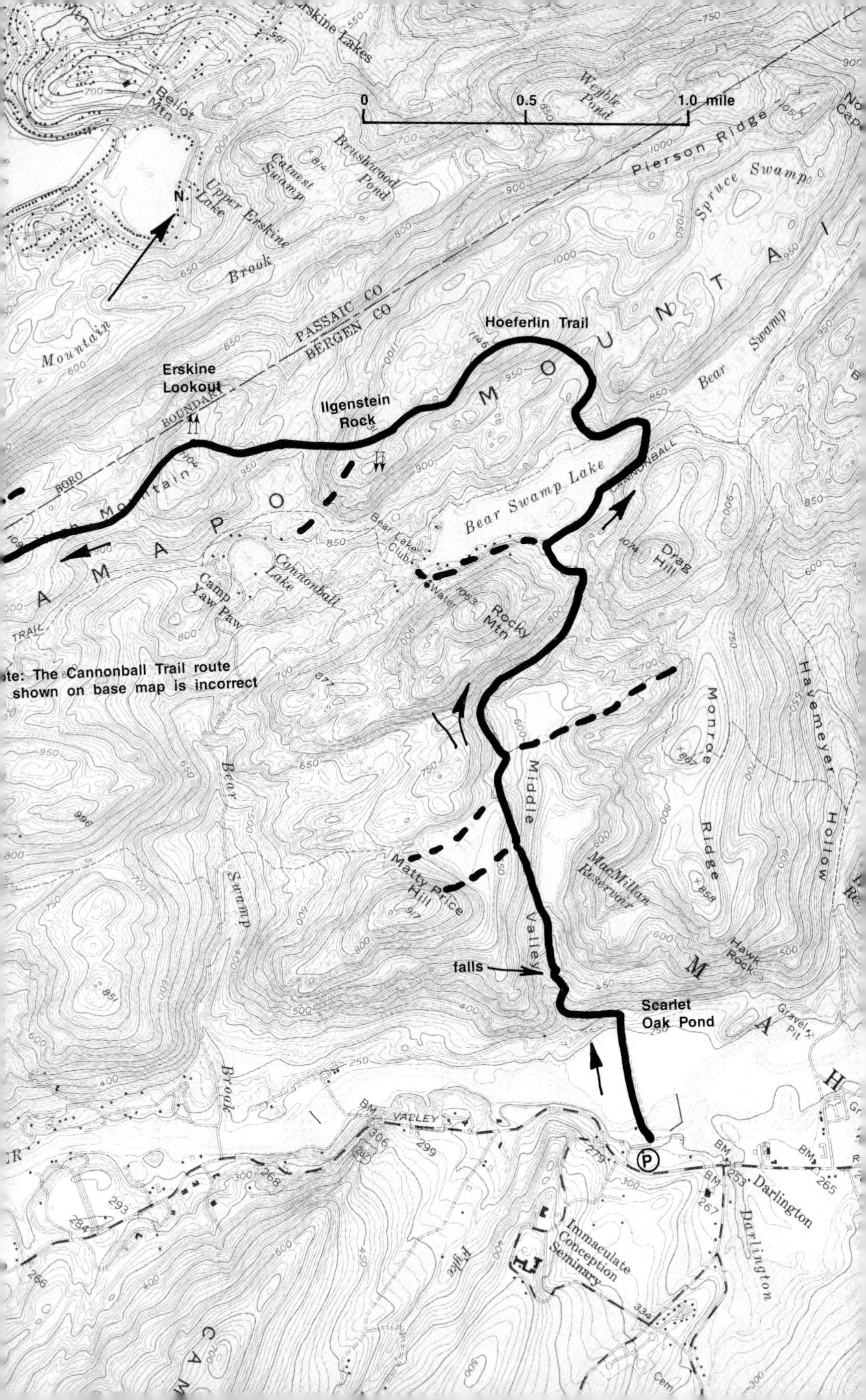
0
0.5
1.0 mile
N.
Hoeferlin Trail
Erskine Lookout
Ilgenstein Rock
ote: The Cannonball Trail route
shown on base map is incorrect
falls
Scarlet
Oak Pond
Upper Erskine Lake
Erskine Lakes
Bellot Mtn
Catnest Swamp
Brushwood Pond
Pierson Ridge
Spruce Swamp
Bear Swamp
Brook
Mountain
PASSAIC CO
BERGEN CO
BOUNDARY
BORO
R A M A P O   M O U N T A I N
Bear Swamp Lake
Bear Lake Club
Cannonball Lake
Camp Yaw Paw
Water
Rocky Mtn
Drag Hill
CANNONBALL
TRAIL
Monroe Ridge
Havemeyer Hollow
Middle Valley
MacMillan Reservoir
Matty Price Hill
Bear Swamp Brook
Hawk Rock
Gravel Pit
VALLEY
BM
Darlington
Immaculate Conception Seminary
Cem

Bear Swamp Lake.

Turn left at the intersection with the blue-marked Shore Trail onto a leisurely, wide gravel road parallel with the water. Blue paint markers are visible on the first tree. To the right, about 10 minutes along the gravel road, a ruined building is visible. The gravel road becomes paved and bears right, descending toward the outlet of Bear Swamp Lake. The paved road then continues to the left. Turn left immediately after crossing the bridge onto the red-marked Cannonball Trail, indicated by three red markers on a tree at the right. Do not take the Shore Trail to the right; it continues on around the lake. Markers on the Cannonball Trail are mixed; some have a white "C" on a faded red paint background, which means the trail should be regarded as white-marked in accordance with trail custom, although the New York–New Jersey Trail Conference map #22 designates the Cannonball Trail as red. The road in the valley (now US 202) was not held securely by the Continental Army during the Revolution, and the Cannonball Trail was originally a secret military highway used by Revolutionary soldiers to transport weapons and munitions.

The Cannonball Trail climbs slightly and continues along the base of a rocky ridge on your right for approximately 10 minutes. Notice how well the woods road has been constructed and built up on the left. After crossing an old foundation and approaching a stone wall that the trail parallels at a distance, you will see the three white blazes of the Crossover Trail on a tree to the right. Watch carefully for these blazes and turn onto the trail. If you walk for more than 15 minutes on the Cannonball Trail, you have probably missed your turn.

The Crossover Trail almost immediately makes a sharp right turn steeply uphill. The route is a little obscure, and at the top of the first pitch it makes a right along the top of the rocky outcrop. Look back at this point to confirm the white marker. Still climbing, although not so steeply, the trail bears left by the side of a huge rock, goes through a rock gully, swings left through a break in the rocks, and emerges onto higher ground. Markers are infrequent but lead you to the right along the ridge again. From the parking lot you have now climbed 900 feet. You will see the co-mingled yellow blazes of the Hoeferlin Memorial Trail. Just to the right is the viewpoint called Ilgenstein Rock—an admirable spot to take a break. On a clear day the view includes the New York City skyline to the extreme right, Bear Swamp Lake immediately below you, the cut of the pipeline, Drag Hill to the left, and a tremendous panorama ahead of you.

When you leave this viewpoint, take great care to follow the yellow markers where they are not co-mingled with the white. The route is generally back in the direction from which you came, but the Hoeferlin Memorial Trail, which you should now be following, runs slightly to the right of your route to the viewpoint and through Ringwood State Forest. At this point the trail drops close to 200 feet, sometimes on slabs that can be slippery when wet. Bear right on the yellow-marked Hoeferlin Memorial Trail, which continues on undulating rocky ledges until it reaches an outlook to the northwest at High Mountain called the Erskine Lookout. The view toward the Wyanokies includes Lake Erskine, Upper Erskine Lake, and the Wanaque Reservoir. Here the trail leaves state forest property to cross Scout property. This is an excellent place to pause.

After Erskine Lookout, many private Boy Scout trails join and leave the main trail. They are not generally open to the public. Stay on the Hoeferlin Memorial Trail along the ridge, noting intersections with the red Ringwood-Ramapo Trail, which joins from the right, and the Cannonball Trail from the left. The Hoeferlin Memorial Trail enters the Ramapo Mountain State Forest soon after the merging of these two trails.

On this hike you will see many signs of development, and this area is no exception. Both the Cannonball and the Hoeferlin Trails turn left onto a wide gravel road that leads up to a communications tower complex, and then turn right almost immediately back into the woods.

A wide, grassy crossroads is reached about an hour from the Erskine Lookout. The path to the left is a red-marked Boy Scout trail not open to the public; the one to the right, marked with white, leads to a viewpoint. This lookout, at Mattapan Rock, is only 2 or 3 minutes down this wide path; the view is much like that from Erskine Lookout. Traffic on Skyline Drive can be heard clearly and sometimes also seen from the ledge.

At the crossroads, the Hoeferlin Memorial Trail on the right is marked both with yellow and with the CANNONBALL sign. The first mountain laurel to be seen on the hike grows in this section, and the trees are less dense. The trail parallels Skyline Drive then, 15 minutes from the crossroads, descends toward it. Climb over the guardrail and turn left onto the road. At the end of the Oakland Disposal Area parking lot (which you immediately encounter on the left), there is a trail marker on a gate.

Cross this gravel area and walk back into the woods through a low-lying section, again paralleling Skyline Drive. The trail next makes a turn to the left and crosses a small stream. Watch carefully: The Cannonball Trail continues ahead across several blowdowns, while the Hoeferlin Memorial Trail—which you take—turns left away from Skyline Drive. There is a double yellow blaze on the left side of the trail to alert you to this turn; you have missed it if you find you are approaching Skyline Drive for the second time.

The trail climbs steeply to a level, rocky outcrop where the terrain is more open, then it almost immediately loses elevation as it passes the Indian cave and travels back down to Skyline Drive. On the descent, watch the rocks to the right closely to find the yellow arrow pointing to the site of the Indian shelter.

This rock shelter was rediscovered in 1980, and fieldwork took place at the site during the following 4 years. Nearly 3000 stone artifacts were found, including an unusual effigy, which is thought to have been used as a "dream stone" or a "wish stone" either to arouse the bear spirit or to conjure up a magic vision to guide the hunter's destiny. It is believed that the cave was used as a seasonal hunting shelter during the fall, probably from 5000 B.C. to perhaps 1600 A.D. A rock and soil wall had formed naturally in front of the cave, giving protection from the weather and also hiding the inhabitants. The shelter is approximately 6 feet by 12; this, together with the location of the hearths, leads archaeologists to believe that only two hunters were in residence at a time. Pause a while in this sheltered spot and imagine how life was for these ancient people before modern man disturbed the tranquility of this cave.

You will reach Skyline Drive almost

immediately after leaving the shelter. Walk toward the Boy Scout sign for Camp Tamarack and cross the road, reentering the woods at the lower end of the parking lot through a gate. Two yellow markers confirm your location. Just as the road bends right (there is a utilities shelter on the right), the trail turns back into the woods to the left with two or three large boulders at each side. It is wide and flat and looks like it might once have been a gravel road.

Soon after a large pile of boulders (with trees growing on the tops), there is a right bend in the trail and a jog across the same woods road. The trail now wanders through the woods, marked at times with yellow-painted can tops, and parallels the road, crossing streams from time to time. About 45 minutes from Skyline Drive, the trail finally emerges onto the road. Turn left and walk toward Ramapo Lake, noticing the blue trail on the left just before you reach the water. This trail is the route out to your car; however, allow some time to sit by the lake. On our last visit there was a large black snake swimming close to the shore. Fishing is permitted in Ramapo Lake, but not swimming. There is a ranger station on the western shore, and the northern shore is wild and open to hunters as well as to hikers. Ramapo Lake was formerly called Rotten Pond; the name probably originated with Dutch settlers, who called it Rote Pond because of the muskrats they trapped there. It has also been known as Lake LeGrande.

Turn back and take the blue-marked MacEvoy Trail on the right side of the road up over a short bank, after which the trail levels out. Although after the first blue marker it is 10 minutes until you see another one, the road is wide and there little confusion over which way to go. Cross a small stream and walk down some short, rocky descents. You will reach the parking lot about 20 minutes from Ramapo Lake.

SJG

8

Ringwood Manor Circular

Total distance: 1.5 miles

Hiking time: 1¼ hours

Vertical rise: 250 feet

Rating: Easy

Maps: USGS Greenwood Lake (NY/NJ); NYNJTC North Jersey Trails #22; WB #23; HRM #15; DEP Ringwood State Park

Ringwood Manor, part of the larger Ringwood State Park (PO Box 1304, Ringwood, NJ 07456; 201-962-7031), is located in northeast Passaic County. The history of the area is closely tied to the local iron industry, which started at Ringwood in 1740. The products of the forges and furnaces were of much importance to the colonies during the Revolutionary War. Troops were stationed here, and George Washington made Ringwood his headquarters on several occasions. Robert Erskine, manager of the mines, served General Washington as surveyor general and prepared many of the maps for the campaign against the British.

The property was purchased by Peter Cooper in 1853. Cooper, a New York philanthropist, is best known as the founder of Cooper Union Institute. The property last passed to Abram Hewitt, a famous ironmaster. He had become a family friend of the Coopers and later of their daughter Amelia. The greater part of the present mansion was built from about 1810 to 1930. It was always used as a summer house; winters were spent in New York City.

In 1936, Erskine Hewitt donated the Manor House and 95 acres to the state of New Jersey. His nephew, Norvin Green (namesake of nearby Norvin Green State Forest), made an additional gift to bring the total to 579 acres. Later purchases, using Green Acres funds, continued up to as recently as 1978. The park now extends east into Bergen County, connecting with Ramapo Mountain State Forest and a Bergen County reservation to form a large network of public lands. An extensive network of trails in the area was developed in the 1970s by volunteers coordinated by the New York–New Jersey Trail Conference.

In recent years, Ringwood State Park, especially on the eastern side of

Sloatsburg Road, has become a very popular mountain biking area. The bikers are supposed to stay off the marked hiking trails, but many are either unaware of or ignore the rule. Clearer use signage is needed and may be forthcoming.

How to Get There

Ringwood Manor is on Sloatsburg Road, just south of the New York–New Jersey border. Access to this road is from County Road 511 (1.8 miles north from Skyline Drive) or from NY 17, just south of the village of Sloatsburg, New York (3.6 miles north of the New York–New Jersey border). The area has many roadside directional signs for this park and the adjacent Skylands Botanical Gardens (see Hike 9). As in many state parks, there is a fee for parking from Memorial Day to Labor Day. New Jersey residents older than 61 can get a pass that allows free parking at all state parks and forests (see Introduction).

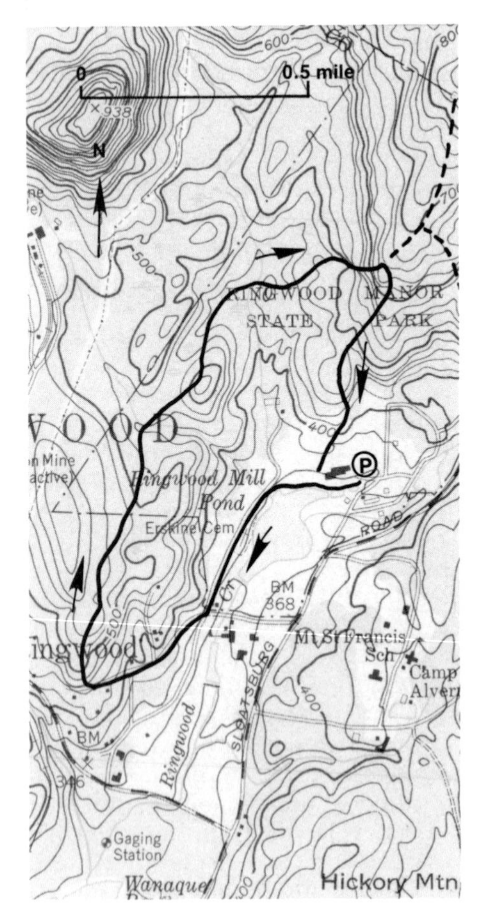

The Trail

History is everywhere at Ringwood Manor, and it is a fine idea to combine your hike with a tour of the Manor House. Call ahead to determine their house tour schedule. The hike commences at the park office, where maps and brochures are usually available. Heading out toward the clearly visible Sally's Pond (a local name; the USGS and NYNJTC maps show this pond as Ringwood Mill Pond), turn right, passing the Manor House porch. Walk through the wrought-iron gates (standing by themselves on the lawn) and continue to the far side of the pond. Pass a row of large oak trees and come to a dirt road. Bear left and watch for the first sign of a blue-marked trail on a telephone pole. The trail is nameless, but you will follow its blue markers throughout the hike. The pond is stocked with bass and pickerel, but fishing is, of course, subject to the various New Jersey laws. Inquire at the park office.

Continue along the shore with the pond on your left. The road is well marked with both the blue blaze and another—a red dot on a white background. The latter denotes the abandoned Bus Stop Trail and follows the blue trail before branching off to a public bus stop.

Start down the road and cross a small stream on a bridge. Note the rust-colored rocks, indicative of the iron ore present throughout the area.

Gravestones overlooking Sally's Pond in Ringwood Manor

Along the shore, the route passes several small graveyards. Pause and browse. Names such as Morris, Paterson, Erskine, and Hewitt are central to regional history. Many of the graves are small—children died often in the 18th and 19th centuries. Cedar trees add to the tranquility of the area (unless you made the mistake of coming late on a summer weekend!). The large building visible across the pond is the sanctuary of the Order of Saint Francis.

Pass the end of Sally's Pond and take the right fork of the road uphill, as always following the blue paint markers. The deteriorating houses here were acquired when the area became parkland. They are now used by various state agencies.

Ignore the dirt road on the left and continue uphill, following the main gravel road. As the route crests and then begins a gentle drop, watch the blazes carefully. Two blazes together indicate a sharp right turn onto a woods road, which you take. (If you go too far, you'll soon see a paved highway—Margaret King Avenue.) The woods road continues uphill and is generally level, with short pitches up and down. This place is good for observing the surrounding woodlands. In spring, flowers abound: jack-in-the-pulpit, rue anemone, spring beauty, and trout lily, to name just a few. Watch for a large rock to the left of the trail with a green metal marker on top. Called benchmarks, these have been placed (many on the summits of mountains) by the United States Geological Survey throughout the country. They generally identify key spots in the government's mapping work. This one, however, is a remnant of the Cooper Union Camp.

About 45 minutes into the hike, the trail crosses a pipeline. This area provides a nice view, marred by some illegal dumping. Continue across the path of the buried pipeline, as the marked trail takes a short jog to the right. The trail is narrower now, and the woods are deeper. Soon you reach a lovely stream. Note the rusty red rocks—iron ore. This spot is a good place for a break. Pull up a rock and have a snack.

The trail follows the stream for a short distance then crosses it on some stones. Watch your footing here! The path again heads into the woods. Note the large stumps, evidence of past logging activities. Beech, oak, maple, and dogwood abound in this area. Soon, off to the left, is a large water-filled rectangle. This depression is an old mine pit. Note again the rust-colored rocks. The trail continues across a small stream. Watch out for some poison ivy here. If you are not yet sure what to watch for, avoid all three-leafed plants and vines.

The trail turns right, following an old woods road downstream. There may be some wet, muddy stretches here—just walk to either side into the woods to avoid them. The trail passes under a canopy of 10-foot trees, forming a lovely arch. More flowers are here, as well as some false helibore and skunk cabbage.

Upon reaching an intersection with a wide road, follow the blue markings that indicate a right turn (downhill). The white-blazed trail, which follows the road to the left, makes an interesting, if somewhat longer, alternate return route. Should you decide to take the longer route, just follow the white markings carefully. There is one sudden turn right off the road that you could miss. Although the white trail is well marked, it is easy to lose concentration when walking along such a wide and obvious footway. The white trail, which adds about 0.5 mile to this hike, will return you to Ringwood Creek just upstream from the Manor House section of the park. To be back in sight of the Manor House within a few minutes, though, follow the blue blazes right. Perhaps you have time now for a tour?

HNZ

9

Skylands Manor

Total distance: 7 miles

Hiking time: 3½ hours

Vertical rise: 700 feet

Rating: Easy to moderate

Maps: USGS Ramsey; NYNJTC North Jersey Trails #22; WB #23; HRM #15; New Jersey Department of Environmental Conservation, Division of Parks and Forestry: Ringwood State Park; Skylands Association Self-Guiding Tour map of the gardens available from the register at Parking Lot A

Like Hike 8, this hike is located in Ringwood State Park (PO Box 1304, Ringwood, NJ 07456; 201-962-7031) in the northernmost part of New Jersey. Trails used are the Ringwood-Ramapo (red), Halifax (green), Crossover (white), Cooper Union (yellow), and Cupsaw Brook (blue). The itinerary affords an opportunity to linger in Skylands Botanical Gardens and to walk past Skylands Manor House. The peacefulness of the hike is somewhat spoiled by the noise of shooting—Thunder Mountain is a shooting range—but the sound is less obtrusive along certain sections of the hike and at certain times of day.

How to Get There

From Sloatsburg Road, turn onto Morris Drive just south of the New York–New Jersey border from Sloatsburg Road. Access to Sloatsburg Road is from County Road 511 (1.8 miles north of Skyline Drive) or from NY 17, just south of the village of Sloatsburg, New York (3.6 miles north of the New York–New Jersey border). Approaching on Sloatsburg Road from the northeast, pass Ringwood Manor and Sally's Pond on the right, and turn left into Morris Road about 0.75 mile farther at the sign for Thunder Mountain and the Holy Name Friary. From the southwest, Morris Road can be found approximately 0.5 mile past Margaret King Avenue.

Park at Shepherd Lake. (There appear to be alternative spellings to the lake's name; USGS maps and the *New York Walk Book* spell it "Sheppard.") To reach the lake, turn left as you approach the two stone eagles, pass through a pair of iron gates, and drive past the gatehouse. There is no charge

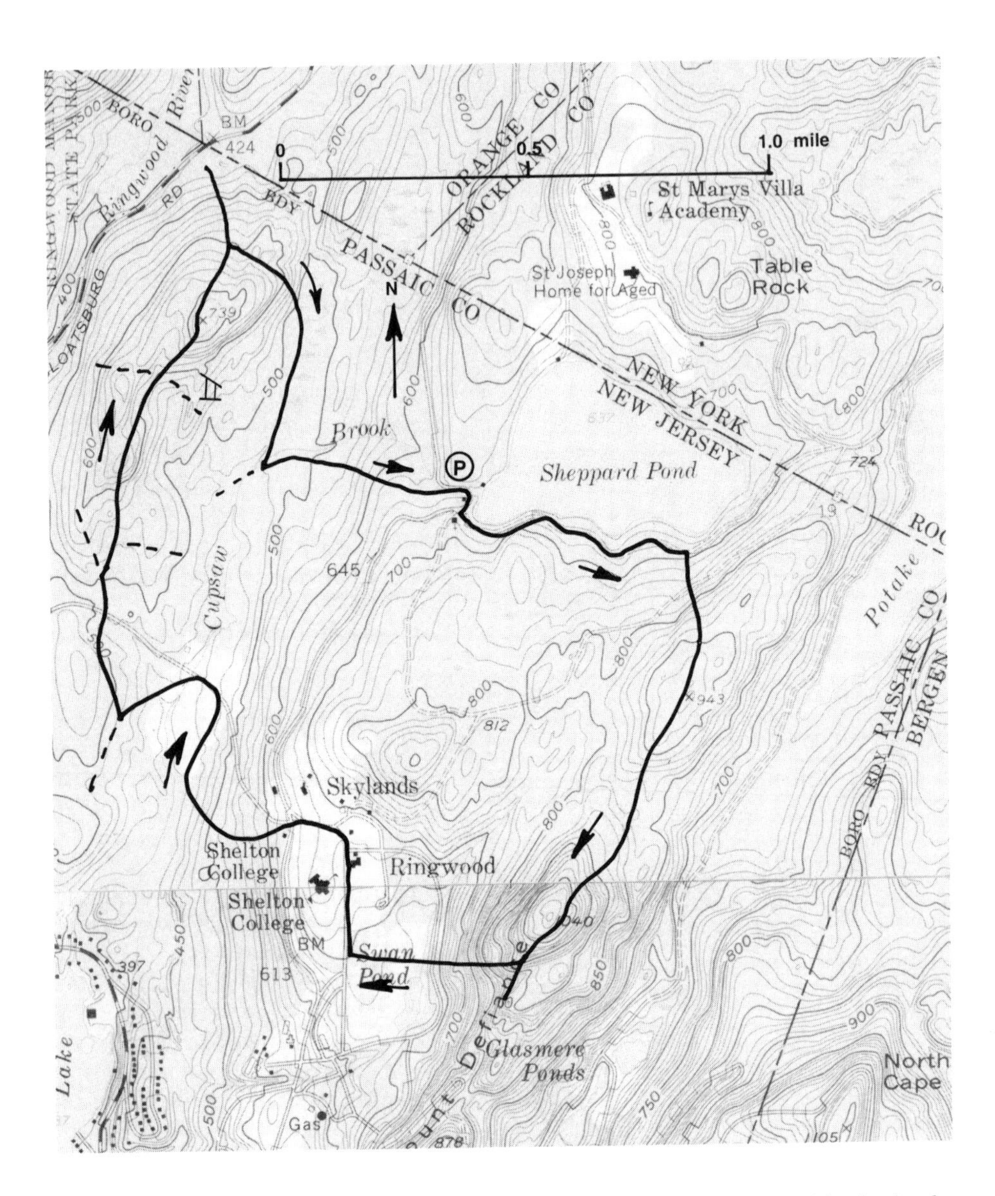

for parking out of season. In the swimming season, fees vary between $5 and $7 according to the day of the week.

The Trail

Shepherd Lake is approximately 1000 feet above sea level, and the water remains cool because it is spring-fed. St. Luke's Chapel stands on a knoll behind the parking area, and the lake is immediately in front with the bathhouse on the left and the boathouse on the right. With the lake in front of you, walk to the right—toward the boathouse and past the DO NOT ENTER sign and the first red marker. Proceed, at first on gravel, then on a substantial woods road that hugs the lakeshore. The first footpath used in the hike, the Ringwood-Ramapo Trail, is marked in red and soon passes through two stone pillars and the remnants of a gate. Only a portion of this trail, which extends from Ringwood Manor to the Ramapo Mountain State Forest, is used on this hike.

After about 7 minutes along the woods road, and just after passing a leaning tree and a bend in the road, watch the right side closely for a wooden post and the red turn signal that indicates the trail leaving the road and entering the woods. This narrow foot trail parallels an old, eroded woods road and emerges onto it after 5 minutes of steady climbing. Follow the red markers across another woods road, climbing a little more steeply until the trail flattens out. In winter, you can see the long ridge and the high point of Mount Defiance through the trees. In spring you may hear spring peepers at this point.

The trail now moves slightly downhill and, about 20 minutes after entering the woods, crosses a pipeline. It then continues straight to reenter the woods, almost immediately climbing through boulders. Bear to the right if you find the next marker difficult to spot. Farther along, a large isolated boulder stands to the right of the trail. After a short flat section, the trail begins to climb again to an excellent viewpoint to the north. To the left you can see Cupsaw Lake.

Leaving the viewpoint, walk uphill again for another couple of minutes, then begin to descend, at first gently and then more steeply through boulders. The trail bears right along the base of some interesting cliffs and provides a view through the trees of Pierson Ridge to the left.

Within 10 minutes, turn right at the cairn that marks the intersection of the Halifax and the Ringwood-Ramapo Trails. The Halifax Trail is marked by a green square on a white background. Here the footway is smooth and slopes gently upward, with the cliffs still on the right. Within a couple of minutes, the cliffs come to an end and the trail begins to descend.

Within a few minutes you reach a fork. This hike follows the green trail to the left, but it is well worth taking the short side trip on the path to the right that leads to an excellent view of Skylands Manor and Cupsaw Lake. This viewpoint is also home to a well-shaped cedar tree that will be visible when you walk past the Manor House later.

Return to the green trail, which now descends quite steeply. The trail switchbacks, and it was probably constructed as a bridle path many years ago. Look for and admire the stone construction supporting the downhill side of the path. Within about 20 minutes the combination of three green markers indicates the end of the Halifax Trail and a junction with the (white) Crossover Trail.

There is a decision to be made at this point. One option is to turn right and follow the white markers of the Crossover Trail until you reach Parking Lot A. However, we suggest that you make the right turn on the white trail, but almost immediately turn left onto a woods road between two large stones. Walk past a large stand of evergreens and through the gate ahead into the cultivated, peaceful Skylands Botanical Garden.

The New Jersey State Botanical Garden was originally a working farm assembled from pioneer farmsteads by Francis Lynde-Stetson. In addition to outbuildings and gardens, it included a vast lawn used as a nine-hole golf course. Many famous people were guests of this prominent New York lawyer at Skylands Farms. The estate was sold in 1922 to Clarence McKenzie Lewis, an investment banker and a trustee of the New York Botanical Garden, who pulled down the Stetson farmhouse and replaced it with the Tudor mansion now on the site.

Once through the gate and past the small stream, bear right on the grass toward a wooden seat dated 1991 and dedicated to Humbert "Al" Cincotti, a Skylands volunteer. Turn right; when you reach another gate, turn left and admire the stone birdbath; continue toward a curved wooden bench on the grass to the right. Go through another gate into an open field. The Manor House is visible to the right. The fences and gates are probably needed to keep the deer from eating the ornamental shrubbery. Explore these gardens now or after your hike.

Walk straight ahead toward Maple Avenue (the paved auto road). Cross Crab Apple Vista, pass underneath an arbor, and turn right when you reach the road, about 45 minutes from the Halifax Trail. Look up to the right as you walk to see the cedar tree and rocky outcrop of the viewpoint you just left.

Maple Avenue takes you past Skylands Manor House on the left. This house was designed by John Russell Pope and built from stone quarried from Pierson Ridge. The building's weathered facade and the sags and ripples in its slate were deliberately introduced to make it appear older. Clarence Lewis collected plants from all over the world (including the New Jersey roadsides), resulting in the fine collection now to be seen in the Botanical Gardens. He also planted most of the trees framing the house. The state of New Jersey bought Skylands Gardens in 1966 as the first property purchased under the Green Acres program. Skylands was later designated the state's official botanical garden.

Although the Manor House is mostly closed to the public, it is opened (and often decorated) on certain dates during the year, such as Mother's Day and the Christmas season. Sixty gardeners were employed during Mr. Lewis's ownership, but volunteers now help out. For information on volunteering and for minimal-cost membership in the Skylands Association, call 201-962-7527. The Skylands Association is a nonprofit organization founded in 1976 to assist with the preservation and restoration of the gardens and manor house.

Continue down Maple Avenue, past the rest rooms and visitors center on the right, until you reach Parking Lot A. This lot is the one at which you would have arrived if you had followed the Crossover Trail instead of walking through the ornamental gardens. White markers on a boulder direct you to bear left when the road forks. The two stone statues that you passed in the car on the way in are on either side of this road. If you need to curtail the hike at this point, turn right and walk down the road to the Shepherd Lake parking lot and your car.

Continue the hike by returning to the woods at the wooden TRAIL sign on the left. The large entry signboard is on the right. Follow the white markers of the Crossover Trail downhill, ignoring two unmarked trails coming in from the left. This section tends to be muddy, especially in spring. Confirm that you are still on the white trail by observing the wooden post to the left of the trail, with two white markers indicating a right turn. At this point the route nears a fenced-in water treatment facility. Almost immediately you reach a pipeline. The trail turns right (confirmed by a white marker on a wooden post to the right at the top of a short rise) and follows the pipeline to Morris Road. Approximately 45 minutes will have elapsed since you entered the gardens.

Turn left down the road, cross the stone bridge labeled 235 PASSAIC COUNTY above Cupsaw Brook, and within 20 yards turn right through two large evergreens, back into the woods, climbing slightly. Some of the markers are now paint blazes, but some are white metal rectangles affixed with nails.

The trail continues to climb gradually, crosses over the ruins of a stone wall, and quite soon reaches the junction of the Cooper Union Trail, marked in yellow. Turn right, uphill, on the Cooper Union Trail. A junction with the Cupsaw Brook Trail, marked with three blue blazes, is at the top of the rise a little way ahead. You may shorten the hike here by taking the Cupsaw Brook Trail to the Ringwood-Ramapo Trail, and thence to your car. This route, however, continues easily uphill on the Cooper Union Trail, and in about 10 minutes reaches an excellent viewpoint, elevation 680 feet, facing Mount Defiance.

Beyond the viewpoint the trail descends slightly along a ridge with a shallow drop-off to the left and a steeper one to the right. After another 10 minutes of walking, you can see the Cooper Union Shelter downhill to the right. At this point the Ringwood-Ramapo Trail (red) comes in from the left and joins the yellow Cooper Union Trail for a short distance. Just a few yards ahead, the Ringwood-Ramapo Trail leaves to the right. Follow the red markers down to the shelter for a short break, if you wish, then backtrack to resume easy walking downhill on the now much wider Cooper Union Trail.

Within 10 minutes after leaving the shelter, the trail moves more steeply downhill. Watch carefully on the left for the three blue markers indicating a right turn into the woods on the Cupsaw Brook Trail. (If you miss these markers you will find yourself at the bottom of the hill on a pipeline and will need to retrace your steps.) The trail begins to climb, but because the footway is not as well established here as on the other trails, be sure to follow the blue markers. Walk down through boulders scattered with evergreens and, after another 5 minutes, emerge onto another woods road with a pipeline going uphill immediately in front. Turn right, still following the blue blazes, bearing first left and then right to follow a tributary of the Cupsaw Brook for a short distance before the trail moves away from the stream. If the leaves are off the trees, Cupsaw Mountain can be seen to the right.

Within approximately 15 minutes, the trail moves closer again to the stream, which is now considerably bigger. After another 10 minutes, turn left at the junction with the Ringwood-Ramapo Trail. Quite soon Cupsaw Brook comes into view, but the trail bears left and crosses a watercourse, then the main flow, on large boulders. Exercise caution, as the boulders might be slippery. (The trail markers are a mixture of red paint [blazes] and round metal disks.) Cupsaw Brook is now to the left of the trail. About 15 minutes after the stream crossing, the trail climbs up through large boulders and—if the water is high enough—through cascades. After about 15 more minutes, it flattens out again and walking becomes easier. Turn left when it emerges onto a wide woods road. If you glance to the right you may see an abandoned bulldozer. Almost immediately you reach the parking lot and your car.

SJG

10

Governor Mountain

Total distance: 3.5 miles

Hiking time: 2½ hours

Vertical rise: 400 feet

Rating: Easy

Maps: USGS Wanaque, Greenwood Lake (NJ-NY), Sloatsburg (NJ-NY); NYNJTC North Jersey Trails #22; WB #23; HRM #15; DEP Ringwood State Park

This hike leads to a peninsula of state-owned land in the southwest section of Ringwood Manor State Park (PO Box 1304, Ringwood, NJ 07456; 201-962-7031). In 1936, Erskine Hewitt deeded the Manor House and 95 acres to the state for preservation. His nephew, Norvin Green, gave New Jersey considerable lands. Additional purchases in the 1960s and as late as 1978 brought the park to its present size. Because the boundaries of Ringwood couple with those of Ramapo Valley State Forest and Ramapo Valley (Bergen) County Reservation, an extensive and varied trail network now exists. Most hiking trails in this region are maintained by volunteers coordinated by the New York–New Jersey Trail Conference. In recent years, this has become a very popular mountain biking area. The bikers are supposed to stay off the marked hiking trails, but many are either unaware of or ignore the rule. Clearer use signage is needed and may be forthcoming.

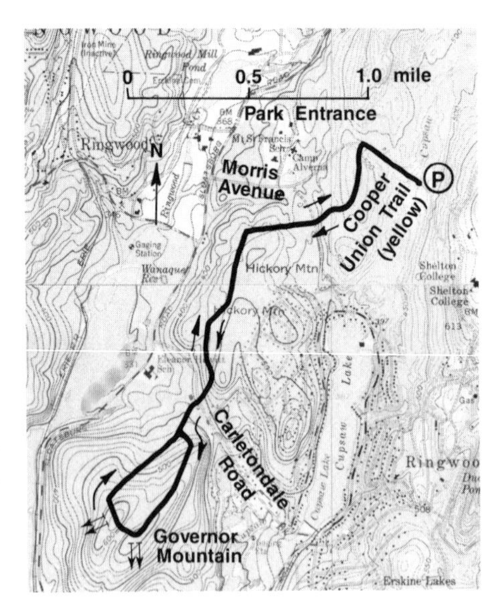

How to Get There

Drive along Sloatsburg Road to Morris Avenue, the entrance road to the Skylands Section of Ringwood State Park. Sloatsburg Road can be accessed from NY 17 just south of the town of Sloatsburg, New York (3.6 miles from the New York–New Jersey border), or by driving north 1.8 miles on County Route 511 from its junction with Skyline Drive. The area has many roadside directional signs for Ringwood and Skylands.

Proceed east on Morris Avenue for 1 mile, past the wooden entrance posts (0.4 mile) and across a small bridge at the end of a downhill section. The bridge has rock-faced sidewalls. Just past this bridge on the left is a wide dirt-and-gravel-surfaced parking area (unsigned).

The Trail

The Cooper Union Trail, which starts near the New York–New Jersey border, crosses Morris Avenue back at the top of the hill you just drove down. Cross the bridge and walk up the road for 5 or 10 minutes till just short of the crest. Avoid the white-blazed trail you may notice going off to the right. Keep to the roadway: The sides are resplendent with poison ivy! Take a well-marked yellow-blazed trail south (left). It enters the woods on a wide path through a deep cut in the embankment. The trail wanders through open hardwoods for less than 10 minutes before coming to a pipeline. Follow the blazes right along the pipeline down through a wet muddy area. As the pipeline right-of-way again begins to rise, the trail will leave the pipeline, heading left. For the next half hour or so, the trail continues south until it reaches Carltondale Road. There are several well-defined but unmarked trails branching off, but only one turn. Stay with the blazes.

The trail crosses Carletondale Road (room for one small car to park) and almost immediately levels out and heads into deep woods. There is some evidence of illegal mountain biking but the trail is, for the most part, in good shape. The wide path passes through tall woods with a lush undergrowth. Indian pipe, as well as some poison ivy, is evident. In spring, wildflowers are abundant. Pass by a faint, dirt path going left to a school building yard and continue straight ahead.

In little more than 5 minutes, the trail splits, and a loop begins. Both forks are yellow marked. Take the left one—a 90-degree turn. Note the large hemlock tree in this particularly dense sector. The trail begins an uphill course here, gently at first and then more steeply. The steep parts of this hike are, however, always short-lived. At the top of the rise, the woodland thins out and gives way to more grasslands and open areas. The cedar trees here are especially lovely, large specimens with their typical symmetrical shapes. This stretch also has patches of poison ivy, so stay on the trail and be attentive, especially if you have children or the dog along.

The footpath narrows with gentle ups and downs as a plateau of the mountain, interspersed with some dense underbrush, is traversed. There are small outcrops of rocks, blackberry bushes, more cedar groves, and moss patches. Though there is some evidence of illegal camping in this area, the moss on the trail is indicative of the generally light use. The walking is pleasant, and the underfooting is soft. Most people go in and out to the upcoming vista using only the exit route of this hike. They see the fine view at the summit but miss this peaceful section.

After crossing a wet area on some stepping-stones, the trail swings steeply up toward a panoramic viewpoint known locally as Suicide Ledge, just below the true summit of Governor Mountain. At a 600-foot elevation and some 300 feet above the water, the view is extensive. Below and ahead is the Wanaque Reservoir. Across the water, Board and Windbeam Mountains are prominent, the territory of the popular Stonetown Circular hike. Farther south are the hills of Norvin Green State Forest (see Hike 11).

Unfortunately, this area also attracts people who leave considerable litter. Each spring, volunteers organized by the New York–New Jersey Trail Conference sponsor a Litter Day. Hikers cover many of the trails in the bistate area. Governor Mountain has received special attention over the last several years and is much cleaner, at times, than it used to be. Each time we take this pleasant walk, we bring along a litter bag and spend 10 minutes cleaning up. It seems that "litter attracts more litter," so if we leave it clean, we hope it stays that way longer . . . at least, that's the theory.

According to Ringwood Borough historian Bert Prol, the name Governor Mountain is presumably a corruption of Gouvernour, the family name of early owners (until 1764) of the Ringwood Ironworks. There was a beacon here during the Revolutionary War, part of a system linking Ramapo Torne Mountain near Suffern, New York, and Federal Hill in Pompton Lakes. For more on the history of this area, see Hike 8.

Leaving the viewpoint, turn right, uphill, to the actual summit of the mountain and follow the yellow blazes straight ahead. Ignore the local white paint here. You will soon pass a large glacial erratic on the left side of the trail. These boulders, quite common in New Jersey, were left behind as the glaciers of the ice ages retreated and melted. The large ones attest to the awesome power of nature's force.

Passing through a conifer grove and descending a little more steeply, the trail bends right, crosses another wet area on rock steps, and swings back to its original northward course. In a few minutes, you'll be back at the trail fork, having completed the loop. Continue over the same route upon which you entered, following the yellow markers. Be careful to take the one well-marked turn shortly before the pipeline.

The entire hike, including some time to linger at the summit, can be walked in 2 hours or less. The best time to journey forth is early on a weekend morning when you may be alone on the mountain and have the trail and viewpoint to yourself—your own personal "wilderness."

HNZ

11

Norvin Green State Forest

Total distance: 6.5 miles

Hiking time: 5 hours

Vertical rise: 1000 feet

Rating: Moderately strenuous

Maps: USGS Wanaque; NYNJTC North Jersey Trails #21; WB #20; HRM #37

The Wyanokie ridge, which forms part of the New Jersey highlands, dates back to the Precambrian period, and many of the rocks in the area are more than 600 million years old. These hills were here long before there was a Wanaque Reservoir or a New York skyline to be seen from the viewpoints on this hike. Blue iron ore was abundant, and villages grew up around the iron mining operations and charcoal furnaces scattered throughout the area. Construction of the Wanaque Reservoir, which is visible from several high points in the area, was started in 1920, and the reservoir was filled by 1949. Many Native American names remain in these parts. Wanaque and Wyanokie mean "sassafras"; other Native American words will be noted in the text of this hike.

This hike offers spectacular views, pleasant walking in the woods, and the possibility of swimming en route. Partially on private land and partially in the Norvin Green State Forest (c/o Ringwood Park, RD Box 1304, Ringwood, NJ 07456; 201-962-7031), the hike uses one of the largest concentrations of trails in New Jersey, including the Mine Trail (yellow) and the red-marked Wyanokie Circular Trail, although from time to time the route is marked with additional colors. The Wyanokie area borders the reservoir. It is important not to trespass on the Northern Jersey District Water Supply Commission property.

How to Get There

Norvin Green State Forest is accessible from County Route 511, reached from the north by way of Skyline Drive or from the south by NJ 23. Turn west on West Brook Road about halfway along the Wanaque Reservoir. The road soon crosses the reservoir on a causeway, then parallels the water on the left. Shortly beyond the end of this reservoir inlet is a junction with Stonetown Road to the north. Bear

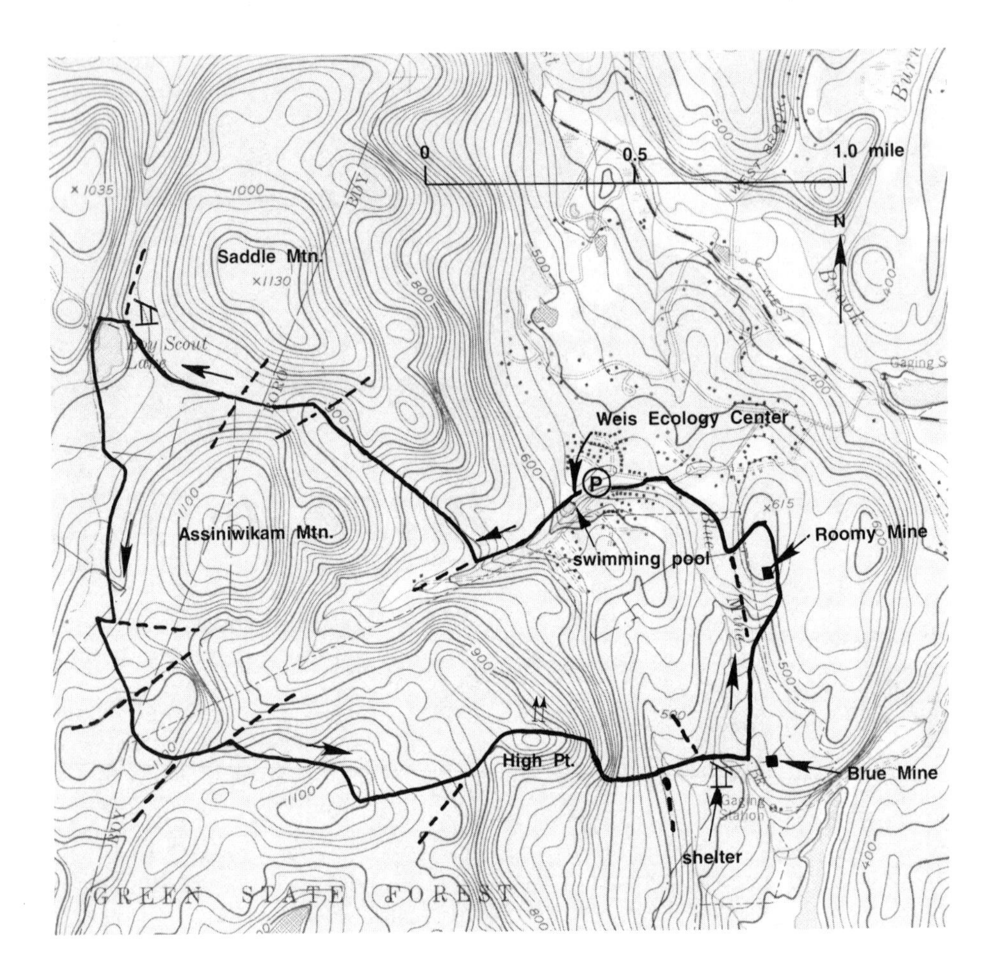

left on West Brook Road, and after about 0.5 mile look for Snake Den Road on the left. Drive uphill, bearing left, past private homes to the main gate into the Weis Ecology Center.

The hike starts at the Weis Ecology Center (201-835-2160), now operated by the New Jersey Audubon Society. Park either outside the gate or in the center's parking lot, on the left just inside the gate. This gate is locked during the winter months, when the office is closed. Overnight accommodations are available at moderate charges. The visitors center is small but worth a visit to pick up their trail map and information on their programs and workshops.

The Trail

Walk across the ball field and picnic area, keeping the stream on the left. Soon the spillover from a swimming pool will be in sight. Carved out of the hillside by hand more than 60 years ago, this Olympic-sized pool has been donated to the community. For information or a membership application, call 201-835-0546 or 212-545-1000.

Veer right to a bulletin board and a wooden post bearing three Ws painted in green. On the right is an old basketball court with additional picnic tables in the rear. Ahead is a short steep climb on a wide woods road but, just at the base, the trail turns left uphill into the woods toward the stream on a narrow hiking trail. After you pass the cement holding tank on the left, watch the trees for red, blue, and green markers. Bear right, staying with the green Ws—do not cross the stream, as that trail leads to Snake Den Road. You will soon reach the junction with the Hewitt Butler (blue) and the Otter Hole (green) Trails. Follow the green-painted W Trail across a wooden plank bridge to the left. The trail climbs slightly, following the stream on the right and crossing two more smaller wooden plank bridges; after this the trail bears left, still climbing slightly. Within about 10 minutes from the start of the hike, you will see an old bridge abutment on the left and the first yellow markers of the Mine Trail, looking rather like fried eggs.

Begin to follow the Mine Trail. Do not cross the stream on the left, but follow the yellow markers up a wide rocky path. Soon you will see markers indicating that the W Trail goes both left and right (though we suspect that the markers on the right are incorrect). Continuing to gain elevation on a trail that is narrower and less rocky underfoot, you will see both Mine and W Trail markers, and—at one point on the right—three music notes in faded green paint. The Mine Trail makes a sharp right at the junction with the Otter Hole Trail, marked with a green rectangle. Within 30 minutes from the beginning of the hike you will see a post indicating an intersection with the Wyanokie Crest Trail (yellow squares without the white surround).

Stay on the Mine Trail, confirming your route by looking for the letter M above the first paint blaze. This trail is very pretty in the spring when the mountain laurel is in bloom. Cross a shallow stream (with a small waterhole in season); within 10 minutes, pass to the left of the lean-to and arrive at Boy Scout Lake.

Follow the broad, grassy road to the wide wooden bridge and cement overflow across the lake's outlet. Permission to swim in the 5-acre lake may be obtained from groups using the camp. This 150 acres is called Camp Wyanokie. There is a dining hall, six lean-tos, two pit toilets, a large, flat area for tents, and tested drinking water. Overnight camping is permitted for a small charge. Make your application to the Borough Administrators Office, Gould Avenue, North Caldwell, NJ 07006; 201-228-6410.

Markers are sparse in the vicinity of the lake, but walk past the dining hall—called the Lion's Den—keeping to the left of the building and up a slight hill to the gravel road where there is a distinct red marker to the left. Walk toward this marker and, when you see two roads facing you, take the upper (right-hand) road past the water pump.

The wide gravel road, which is sometimes very wet, parallels the lake for a little while, then climbs slightly, passing several private homes. This part of the trail has been rerouted recently. Within a few minutes the trail turns left into the woods and soon crosses a small stream. The red markers lead uphill through hardwood and laurel.

The next section of the Wyanokie Circular Trail skirts Assiniwikam Mountain and is bisected by several other trails. It is important to follow the red markers. After another brief climb, the trail arrives at a T-junction with the yellow-marked Wyanokie Crest Trail. Turn right. Follow the red blazes of the Wyanokie Circular Trail while they co-mingle with yellow markers down to a woods road where the white-blazed Macopin ("wild potato") Trail begins. Cross the woods road. After about 10 minutes of walking through some high laurel, the yellow trail continues straight while the red trail turns left. Follow the red markers. If you find yourself walking a route only marked in yellow, you have missed your turn.

At the bottom of a rocky section, at a junction with the Otter Hole Trail, turn left. The green-marked Otter Hole Trail and the red-marked Wyanokie Circular Trail travel together for approximately 10 minutes on a wider path.

The next turn is to the right and is indicated by two signs on the trees. Ignore the green trail, labeled the GLEN WILD FIRE ROAD, which continues straight ahead. Turn right by the tree carrying a metal plate that says WYANOKIE CIRCULAR. Watch the right side of the trail for a large boulder split cleanly in two. An orange-blazed trail leaves to the right just past the split boulder. Follow the red trail around to the left.

Ten minutes past the Glen Wild Fire Road junction, the route crosses a distinct path at right angles. This may be an inspection path for an old water pipeline that crossed here; almost immediately rusty sections of this pipeline are visible to the right. A few minutes later, the trail emerges onto a large rock outcrop. This area has been hard hit by gypsy moth caterpillars in recent years. Wild grapes can be gathered in season, and black snakes and grouse have been seen in this section.

Leaving this outcrop, bear left until you reach a stony junction with the blue-marked Hewitt-Butler Trail. There is a delightful specimen of a young sassafras tree here. The Wyanokie Circular Trail is apparently not much used in this section, for it is a little indistinct and overgrown. It is well marked, however. Turn left toward High Point, noting that the trail is marked in blue as well as in the red of the Wyanokie Circular Trail.

The new Highlands Trail uses trails in the vicinity and its turquoise markers now appear. However, these markers end as the ascent to High Point begins because the route of this new trail was not fully determined as of this writing.

After a wet area, the trail turns and leads to the right over a small stream. At a large, flat boulder, the Hewitt-Butler Trail leaves to the left. Follow the red markers past an enormous boulder (with HIGH POINT written on it in white paint) until you reach the large slabs of rock that form High Point. Views appear during the climb, first on the right, then on the left, until at the top is a 360-degree view. You will see the Manhattan skyline and the Wanaque Reservoir, but be sure to turn your back to the reservoir and look for two power lines on the horizon. If you follow the left one with your eyes to the second ridge, you can see the pine paddies encountered earlier in the hike.

When the time comes to leave this superb viewpoint, seek the trail in the direction of the reservoir; the trail switchbacks steeply down the rock slabs. The original descent, totaling more than 500 feet, is steep and rocky, but a new trail has been constructed just a short distance down from the summit (watch for the sign for the WYANOKIE CIRCULAR TRAIL) to provide a less rocky, more gradual descent. The original route is still clearly visible but not recommended. The new route joins the old just prior to the connection with the Lower Trail (white) on the right, which is marked with three white paint rectangles. Proceed straight ahead to cross a stream on large boulders; the Mine Trail (yellow) comes in almost immediately on the left.

The trail continues to drop approximately 400 feet through rocky outcrops on a boulder-strewn pathway. At a junction with a woods road, keep left, and soon you will traverse a low-lying area and a grassy clearing. On the left side of the clearing is the Green Mountain Club shelter. This lean-to is situated in an attractive open area but is in exceptionally poor repair. For some time now, it has been reduced to rocky walls with a corrugated iron roof resting only a few feet above the floor.

Bear right past the shelter and look for the trail, which leaves the open area to the left. After a few minutes, the trail turns left, leading to a bridge over Blue Mine Brook. Turning right will bring you to one of the entrances to the Blue Mine—also called the Iron Hill, London, or Whynockie Mine. It is currently filled with water. The name came from the dark blue color of the mine's ore.

Until 1855, the ore was mostly used at a hot-blast charcoal furnace called the Freedom Furnace. For a short period after the Blue Mine's reopening in 1886, the mine produced about 300 tons of ore per month. Water in the mine was obviously a problem, and the mine was "de-watered" several times. This operation was quite difficult. Mine workers stood on a raft that sank lower as the water was pumped out. Their job was to remove the debris left clinging to the walls of the mine and to shore up the timbers in the sides of the shaft while keeping their balance on the raft. After another de-watering operation in 1905, the mine was not worked again.

Old stonework and concrete foundations can be seen near the mouth of this mine opening, and by exploring the surroundings you can detect other evidence of mining.

After crossing the bridge, turn left along the rocky, eroded path and walk for 5 minutes to where the yellow Mine Trail leaves the Wyanokie Circular. Follow the Mine Trail right to visit Roomy Mine. Five minutes of climbing will bring you to the entrance. Roomy Mine is also called Laurel or Red Mine; it was probably opened shortly after 1840. This mine is said to have been named for Benjamin Roome, a local 19th-century land surveyor. Extensive mining was carried on here through an entrance in the side of the hill above water level as well as from the surface. The ore was compact and mostly free from rock. The vein was about 4 feet thick with a pitch of 58 degrees, dipping sharply to the southeast.

Roomy Mine's passage can still be entered. With a flashlight, crawl through the mine entrance into an open-air section; the passageway itself lies straight ahead. Even in dry seasons there is water underfoot, but the passage can be walked for a distance of about 50 feet until it forks and dead-ends. Round dynamite holes are visible in the roof of the passageway. Exploring Roomy Mine takes about 30 minutes. Then proceed past the entrance on an elevated rocky path until, within 5 minutes, you reach the Wyanokie Circular Trail again. You can omit the trip to Roomy Mine by continuing straight on the Wyanokie Circular Trail from Blue Mine.

The route now climbs moderately, past a massive boulder on the left (unfortunately covered with graffiti). Walk through an area of spruce trees and the backyard of a private home, keeping to the right along a fence to Snake Den Road. Take a moment to appreciate the graciousness of the homeowner, who permits hikers to walk across his property. Turn left at the road and walk a minute or so back to the parking lot of the Weis Ecology Center.

SJG

12

Carris Hill

Total distance: 5 miles

Hiking time: 4 hours

Vertical rise: 580 feet

Rating: Moderately strenuous

Maps: USGS Wanaque; NYNJTC North Jersey Trails #21; HRM #37

Although this hike is only 5 miles long, the rugged terrain and possibly difficult water crossings make for an exciting and challenging day hike. Carris Hill is not the highest point in Norvin Green State Forest (c/o Ringwood Park, RD Box 1304, Ringwood, NJ 07456; 201-962-7031), but it includes a strenuous climb and an arduous descent. Good footwear is necessary, and take special care if you attempt this hike in winter—certain sections are on steep slopes of bare rock that could be difficult to navigate when covered with snow and ice. Post Brook, which you will cross four times, is normally on the dry side and easily crossed on rocks; after a snowmelt or heavy rain, however, it becomes a raging torrent and can present serious problems.

How to Get There

From NJ 23, follow County Route 511 north to Butler. After a series of turns, bear right at the railroad tracks on Main Street, then make a left turn at the T-intersection with Riverdale Avenue. From NJ 23 to here is 1.3 miles. Just 0.1 mile after this left turn, bear right onto Glenwild Avenue (sometimes called Glenwild—or Glen Wild—Road).

From I-287, exit 53, take the Hamburg Turnpike east to Bloomingdale. In just less than 2 miles, bear right onto Riverdale Avenue, then right onto Glenwild.

Proceed another 3.3 miles on Glenwild and park at the Otter Hole parking area on the right-hand side of the road. There is space here for about 10 cars.

The Trail

For the first part of this hike, you will be following the blue-marked Butler-Hewitt Trail, an 18-mile hiking trail that traverses the entire Wyanokie range. You will find blue markers just before the parking area heading north into the woods. Soon you will arrive at Otter Hole, a small cascade and falls on Post Brook, popular with the local

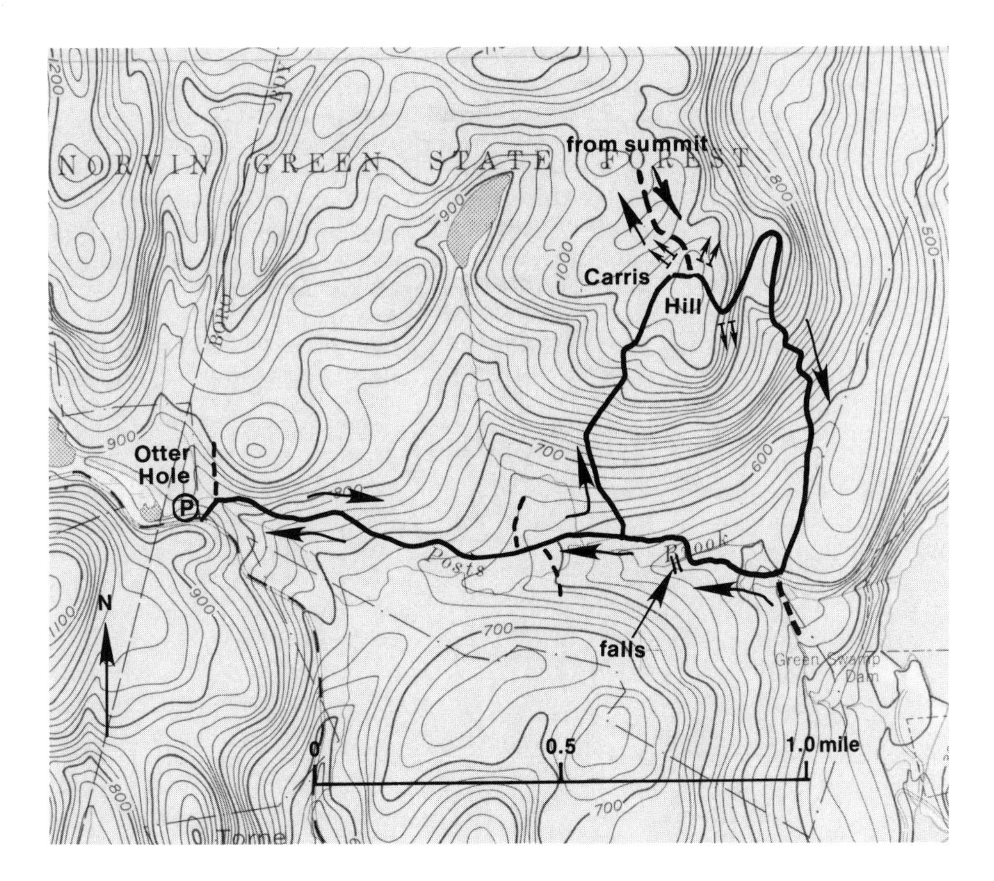

youth. It is normally possible to cross the brook on rocks, but if this is impractical or dangerous, you should abort this hike and try another one. (Just across the road the Butler-Hewitt Trail ascends the Torne, a summit with several fine views.)

After you leave Otter Hole, follow the blue markers to an intersection with the green-marked Otter Hole Trail. Stay right on the blue-marked Hewitt-Butler Trail, heading uphill and roughly parallel to Post Brook. From here to the summit of Carris Hill, your route will be concurrent with that of the new 150-mile Highlands Trail (see the introduction) marked with green- and blue-diamond blazes. After a short distance, the trail begins a long, steady decline. Be alert for a left turn—the markers direct you away from the woods road and onto a narrower footpath. The trail is now a little more rugged in places. About 15 to 20 minutes from the start of the hike, you will reach a junction with the yellow-marked Wyanokie Crest Trail. Bear left. For a short distance the two trails share the same path; in only 75 feet, though, the Crest Trail swings away to the left. Continue straight ahead, following blue markers along an old road that can be wet in places. Logs laid crosswise like railroad ties help keep your feet dry. To the right, catch glimpses and hear the sounds of falls and cascades as Post Brook now temporarily splits into two streams. Just ahead the trail goes to the edge of the brook and crosses another, smaller stream coming in from the left. You are at a junction of running waters, a place where streams merge. Immediately after this (potentially difficult) stream crossing, the Hewitt-Butler Trail turns left. Straight ahead is the Lower Trail. You will reach this point again on the return trip. The steady uphill climb to the summit of Carris Hill begins here.

At first the trail gains elevation very slowly as it snakes its way through the woods. Soon it gets rockier, although there is a temporary reprieve along the bed of an abandoned woods road. The trail then bears to the right, and the climb begins in earnest. The Hewitt-Butler Trail now follows what appears to be a man-made path up the side of the mountain, possibly used for lumbering in the past. Eventually the slope lessens and the footpath meanders through an area characterized by blueberry bushes, moss, occasional glacial erratics, and numerous exposures of bedrock. This terrain is typical of the Precambrian gneiss and granite of the New Jersey Highlands. A slight descent into an area that is sometimes wet brings needed relief, but almost immediately the climb resumes.

Now gaining elevation, the trail passes through laurel and traverses the first of a series of bare rock outcrops contoured with green moss and tall grasses. The first evergreens (hemlocks) are encountered here, and pitch pines appear, often heavily laden with clumps of pine cones. The trail descends slightly into a dense heath forest before it continues, now fairly gradually, up to bare rock and the first of a few small false summits. Look behind you. The views of the Torne, Osio Rock, and beyond are steadily improving. After another slight descent into a laurel depression, the trail winds through scrub pine to the true summit with views to the south, west, and north. There is a real feeling of accomplishment from reaching this heavily glaciated summit. Wyanokie High Point is to the north, and from this vantage point it looks like a small cluster of bare rocks. Beyond it and to the right is Windbeam Mountain. To the immediate west are Assiniwikam Mountain, Buck Mountain, and the Torne.

At the summit look for the yellow markers of the Carris Hill Trail, which begins here and heads east. Follow this trail for a few minutes out over the broad, flat summit of Carris Hill to other viewpoints. Here you'll find pines and a large glacial erratic on bare rock outcrops. The expansive views are to the south and southeast. To the left of the large boulder, follow yellow markers downhill, off the summit. After only 100 yards you will reach yet another viewpoint, this one overlooking the Wanaque Reservoir, nearby Green Swamp Dam, and the more distant Raymond Dam. From here the trail begins a steeper descent. The footing can be difficult until you reach a rock formation not unlike a wall. The trail turns right, following to the right of the wall. If you scramble up the ledge on your left you'll find an even broader view of the reservoir and beyond. Some unique graffiti is also found here. Then head south and down, rather steeply in places. A few cedars line the trail, which winds around a deep and jagged cliff. In sections much care is needed, and careful planning and proper equipment are required in icy or slippery conditions.

Once off the main part of the hill, the going is much more manageable, though still quite steep. Continue following yellow markers steadily downhill over rocky ground. Eventually you will reach a small brook; crossing might be difficult in times of high water. (If it is a problem, keep to the west of the brook and bushwhack downstream to Post Brook, about 0.1 mile from here.) Shortly, the yellow-marked Carris Hill Trail terminates at a junction with the Lower Trail, marked in white. Turn right here, following white markers, with the Wanaque Reservoir fence to your left.

At a rock outcropping near the fence corner, find a trail junction and turn right, now following the white markers of the Post Brook Trail; do not follow the white markers of another trail that lead straight ahead. Soon a crossing of Post Brook is necessary; if this presents a problem, one option is to follow the brook upstream to a rocky area where there is a large fallen tree that you can use as a bridge. If you find this too difficult, you may have to wade across the brook.

A short distance ahead is Chickahoki Falls—a 25-foot sluiceway of water, split in two as the water tumbles into a huge plunge pool. These falls are impressive after a rain. Just below the falls, the trail once again crosses Post Brook and climbs the bank—bearing left and following Post Brook closely—revealing other cascades farther upstream. In just a few minutes you will reach the junction with the blue-marked Hewitt-Butler and the green- and blue-marked Highlands Trails that you encountered earlier (where the climb to Carris Hill began). Follow the blue markers straight ahead, the way you came. Most of the way back is a gradual uphill climb and can be tiring. After about a half hour, turn left, cross over Otter Hole, and return to your car.

BCS

13

Bearfort Ridge

Total distance: 8 miles

Hiking time: 5½ hours

Vertical rise: 1000 feet

Rating: Moderately strenuous

Maps: USGS Greenwood Lake (NY/NJ); NYNJTC North Jersey Trails #21; WB #21; HRM #21B; DEP Hewitt State Forest

This hike is in Abram S. Hewitt State Forest, administered by the superintendent of Wawayanda State Park (PO Box 198, Highland Lakes, NJ 07422; 201-853-4462) as a day-use area; no camping or swimming is permitted. Bearfort Mountain, which this hike traverses, may still even have a few bears—they have been seen in nearby Wawayanda—and it is assumed that this is the derivation of the name.

How to Get There

From the large shopping center (which contains a post office, a 5-Star Value store, and a planned A&P superstore) in Browns (on the southwestern shore of Greenwood Lake where County Route 511 [CR 511] meets CR 513), continue west 0.1 mile on CR 513 to a fork in the road. Take the right fork (Warwick Turnpike) going uphill. Cross a small concrete bridge (marked "#446"), and park on either side of the road just after the bridge. If you go too far, you'll immediately come to another junction (White Road going off to the left).

The Trail

The pathway leaves the north side of the road, just to the right (north) of the bridge. The beginning of the Bearfort Ridge (BR) Trail is clearly indicated by three white paint blazes, a typical start-of-trail marking. Starting uphill through a pretty grove of hemlocks and rhododendrons, it traverses the slope for a short time before heading gently up and joining a woods road. Following the white markers, proceed left along the woods road and, after a short distance, turn left again, uphill and off the road. The main woods road, marked with orange paint blazes, continues northward to Surprise Lake with some significant junctions and wet sections.

The BR Trail is well marked with white paint rectangles. It climbs moderately uphill, with some steep pitches, through a mixed hardwood forest consisting of red, black, and white oak, and some maple, ash, beech, and birch. The forests of this locality were heavily timbered for charcoal production during the area's iron-producing period. This forest is therefore the second—or even third—growth of trees.

After crossing a boggy section in a small hollow, the trail continues ahead along the side of a slope. Except for some road noise from nearby Warwick Turnpike, there is a feeling of isolation in deep woods. As you proceed, gaining elevation, the road noise quickly fades, and the real beauty of this area begins to dominate. Passing through some tall and lush rhododendrons—magnificent in June when they bloom—the climb begins to steepen. After you ascend through some rocks and along the base of a ledge, there is a worthwhile, south-facing viewpoint off the trail to the right. The steep, bare-faced peak across the road is another part of this same mountain in an area owned by the city of Newark (see Hike 15). Continuing ahead and upward, you soon reach the first of the pitch pines that dominate the main part of the hike.

As the trail turns right onto the ledge, a scramble up the large rock on the left of the trail yields a fine view. The water in the distance is a small section of Upper Greenwood Lake. This viewpoint is also a good place to take note of the rock formation that composes much of Bearfort Ridge. A collection of white quartz pebbles imbedded in a red pudding stone, it is considered similar to the Shawangunk conglomerate of the Kittatinny Mountains. These rocks generally make for secure footing, but, as usual, take extra care when they are wet or icy.

Now a little more than a half hour into the hike, return to the trail as it climbs up onto the ledges. The BR Trail now begins a several-mile course along the outcroppings, with several dips back into the woods to cross small hollows and streambeds. The elevation is generally 1300 feet plus, and the climb up has been more than 600 feet. The views from this section of the BR Trail are not as sweeping as those behind you or to come, but the charm of the landscape surrounds you. Note the fine array of mosses along (and occasionally even in) the footway, indicative of the surprisingly light use this tract receives. The boulders strewn along the way are glacial erratics, remaining from the ancient ice sheets as they melted and retreated north. Striations seen on the rock surface can also be attributed to this period. I've always had a special fondness for the pitch pines with their distinctive, thick shingle bark. To me they are like large Japanese bonsai trees. I admire their intricate shapes and the way they cling to life on the otherwise barren rocks.

One of the nicest spots in all of New Jersey is about a half-hour hike along this ridgetop section. Here, a large section of rock has split away from the base, leaving a deep crevice just to the left of the footway. On the far side of the split is an attractive swamp. This spot has long been a favorite of ours for lunch or "elevens" (our traditional, midmorning snack break around 11 AM). The separation of rock here possibly commenced as water seeped into cracks and then expanded with repeated freezings. Time and erosion have widened it to more dramatic dimensions. At first we named this spot the knife edge, but when one companion suggested it was more like a butter knife, we dropped the name and are

0
0.5
1.0 mile
N
SL: State Line Trail (blue)
EW: Ernest Walter Trail (yellow)
A: Appalachian Trail
Bearfort Ridge Trail (white)
Upper Greenwood Lake
West Pond
Surprise Lake
Lakeside
ABRAM S. HEWITT STATE FOREST
BEARFORT MOUNTAIN
Fox Island
WEST MI
TURNPIKE
Green Brook
Cooley Brook

still looking for a more appropriate appellation.

Continuing ahead, pass a rather large glacial erratic. After a while, cross a stream, with the trail then climbing up through a rock notch. The ridge soon becomes less pronounced, with fewer rock outcroppings and rhododendron and mountain laurel reappearing. As the trail gently rises out of the woods, a symmetrical cedar tree dominates the skyline—the first to be observed. Another 40 yards ahead are three white paint blazes on the top of a small rock bump, indicating the end of the BR Trail, about 2.5 miles (and 1½ to 2 hours) from the hike's start.

From this spot you can discern your first good view of Surprise Lake. You will pass this lake later, and the hike route will return to this spot. The view is extensive, with only small traces of civilization evident. Off to the right in the distance is a section of the new Wanaque Reservoir. From here, the hike begins a loop that begins and ends on the yellow-blazed Ernest Walter Trail (EW Trail), named for a dedicated hiker and trailblazer.

This trail, and others in the area, is normally well marked. In the late 1980s, a vandal systematically and repeatedly painted out the blazes of this trail and portions of others in the area. Volunteers of the New York–New Jersey Trail Conference try to keep the trail well marked, but your experience here may depend on which "painter" was on the trail last. If you should find the trail "blacked out," please inform the Conference (GPO Box 2250, New York, NY 10116). The trail has not been rerouted. If the yellow paint marks are not evident, follow the black ones. Once you know what to look for, they are really not that difficult to detect, and the loop you now begin past West Pond and Surprise Lake is worth the small extra effort involved.

The yellow blazes lead both right and left. Proceed left, walking the loop in a clockwise direction. The trail descends 20 feet down a rock face and onto a narrow footpath. Because it crosses against the "grain" on the ridge, the route undulates pleasantly through the woods and outcroppings, soon crossing Green Brook, the outlet stream of West Pond. Shortly afterward, you will see your first view of the pond. The trail wanders above the shore but does not actually go down to the pond's edge. Take a few minutes to bushwhack down to the shore to appreciate its backcountry charm.

The EW Trail continues along the ridge, then crosses the small outlet of a swamp. The trail bends to the right and leaves the ridge, heading down to a hollow where it ends at a T-junction with the white-blazed Appalachian Trail (AT); see Hike 6 for background information on this National Scenic Trail.

Follow the white blazes of the AT, climbing to the top of a 20-foot rock outcropping where the trail veers to the right. Not long after, you will see another view of Surprise Lake before the AT descends to a junction. Here the State Line Trail, a blue dot (or square) in a white field, departs to the right. Follow the blue blazes (again a target of the infamous "black outer") downhill off the ridge.

After about 15 minutes going generally downhill on the State Line Trail, you will encounter another junction. This spot is the other end of the U-shaped EW Trail. Some of the yellow markings may be visible through the woods to the right before you reach the junction itself. Make a sharp right turn onto the EW Trail and climb steeply up to a promontory overlooking

Greenwood Lake.

Surprise Lake is now about 20 minutes away, but the journey may take longer—the views on this rise are super and invite lingering. Much of the two-state area of Greenwood Lake is visible. The large island in the middle is Fox Island, and across the lake are the mountains of the privately owned Sterling Forest. Area hikers are supporting a campaign to bring these lands into the park systems of the two states. New Jersey has already acquired 2000 acres. New York conservationists hope for similar action to acquire at least 9000 acres. If they succeed, and the prospects are still mixed, the hiking lands of this area will be connected with those of Harriman–Bear Mountain State Park in New York; it's likely some new trails will be developed.

Leave the ridge and turn right into the woods, passing a pile of shale ruins. The origin of the ruins is unknown to us. (Any ideas?) Just before the shore of Surprise Lake, there are a few unmarked side trails, so keep a close watch on those yellow markers. Your impressions of this graceful lake may be determined by how many people are there or by what litter and debris they have left. It sees heavy warm-weather use.

Leave the lake, remaining on the EW Trail through a short muddy section. Shortly, the trail enters a splendid section of large rhododendrons and laurels, forming a junglelike canopy over the trail. Walk carefully down a rocky path to a hollow and cross Cooley Brook, the outlet of Surprise Lake. The crossing, on some rocks and root islands, may be a challenge after heavy rains but is otherwise not an impediment.

Ascending steeply onto outcroppings, you will soon reach the Bearfort Ridge/Ernest Walter junction. It was from this point that the loop route began. From here, it is another 2.5 miles to the parking area. Retracing your steps along the white BR Trail takes no more than 2 hours of uninterrupted hiking. You'll be pleasantly surprised at how different the trail looks when you're traveling in the opposite direction.

HNZ

14

Terrace Pond

Total distance: 3.5 miles

Hiking time: 3½ to 4 hours

Vertical rise: 400 feet

Rating: Moderate

Maps: USGS Wawayanda/ Newfoundland; NYNJTC North Jersey Trails #21; WB #21; HRM #36A

This hike in Wawayanda State Park (Box 198, Highland Lakes, NJ 07422; 201-853-4463) is on land called the Sussex Woodlands when it was owned by Fred Ferber, a Depression-era immigrant from Austria. Ferber was not a lover of state parks; he objected to hunting and to such facilities as restaurants, toilets, and campsites, normally part of state parks. His ambition was to keep his property as wilderness, untouched by such facilities. But gradually, as over the years he ran into debt, he sold portions of his land to the state. Bearfort Mountain Ridge, which contains Terrace Pond, was one of the last tracts to be sold, in 1973.

This hike uses the Terrace Pond South Trail (marked in yellow), the White Trail circling Terrace Pond, the Terrace Pond North Trail (marked in blue), and a woods road. The terrain is varied, and all sections are superb. At first the hike is gentle, but the approach to Terrace Pond—the climax of the hike—is reminiscent of a roller coaster. You must also negotiate some wet areas.

How to Get There

The trailhead is on the east side of Clinton Road, which runs north from NJ 23 to Warwick Turnpike. Look for it 1.7 miles south of the junction with Warwick Turnpike, or 7.3 miles north of NJ 23. There is a parking area just north of the entrance to the Wildcat Environmental Center.

The Trail

Cross the road and enter the woods on a steep uphill gradient, following yellow markers. Ignore the blue trail on the left. Instead follow the mossy yellow-marked trail up and over a small hill through mountain laurel and white pine. Shortly afterward the trail winds around a swampy area on the left on bog bridges, then parallels a small stream. You soon move away from the stream to the right and, still climb-

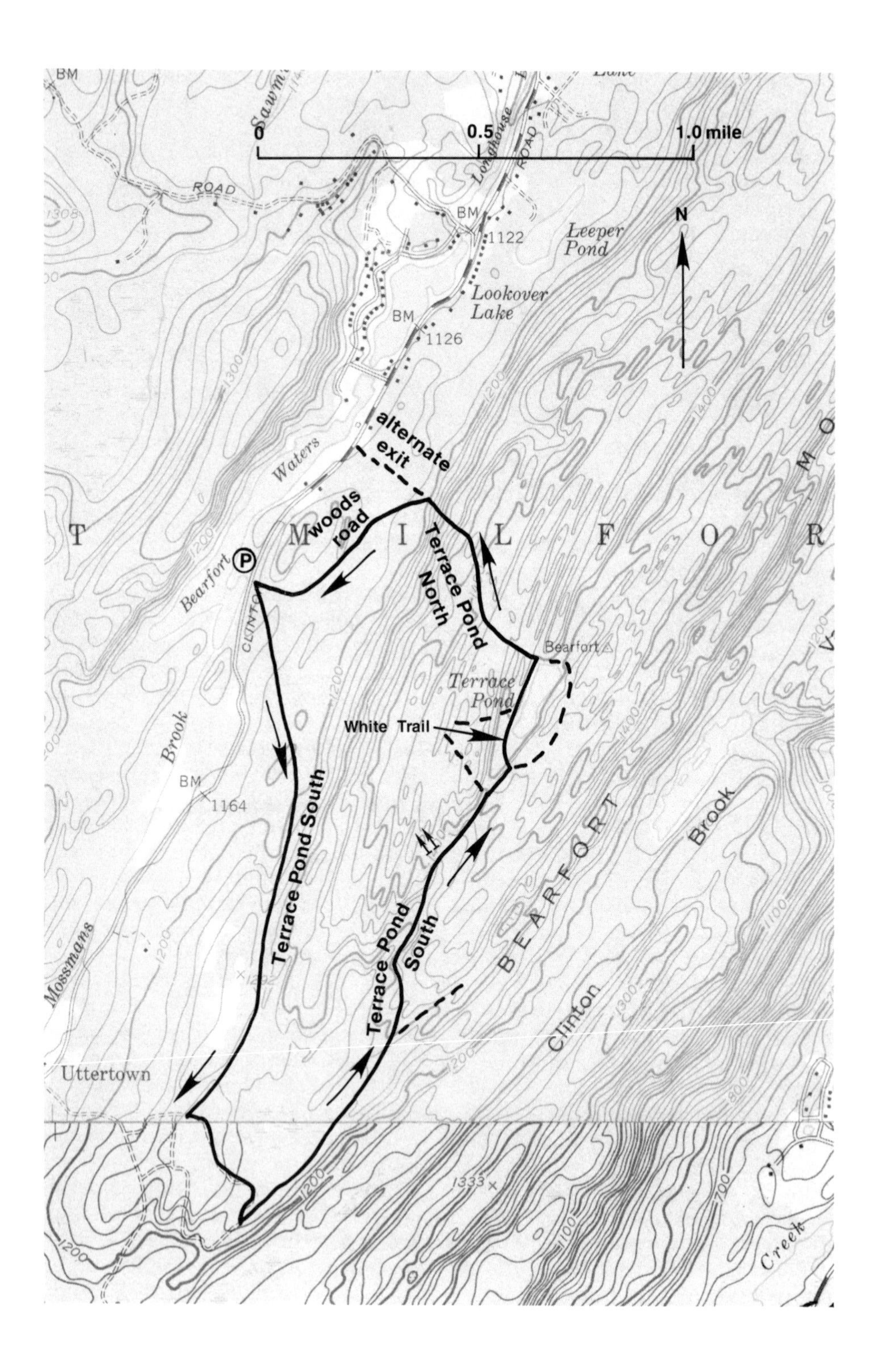
0
0.5
1.0 mile
N
alternate exit
woods road
Terrace Pond North
White Trail
Terrace Pond South
Terrace Pond South
Leeper Pond
Lookover Lake
Terrace Pond
Bearfort
Uttertown
BEARFORT
Clinton
Brook
Mossmans
Waters
Longhouse
ROAD
ROAD
1122
1126
1164
1333

ing, proceed through a piney area and across an interesting rock.

A ridge appears ahead, and eventually the trail meanders along the valley on its right side, winding through white pine and mountain laurel. The trail here is sometimes wet, and there are some blowdowns. Within 30 minutes from the beginning of the hike, you turn left to climb this same ridge. This section of the trail is spectacular. It becomes rockier, travels along the side of the hill with a drop to the right, and follows substantial cliffs on the left that are scattered with huge boulders. A magnificent grove of tall rhododendrons arches completely over the trail. Red paint marks appear on the trees to your right, probably indicating the state park boundary. The trail markers are both can tops painted yellow and yellow rectangular symbols painted on the trees. Pick your way among boulders and blowdowns until you reach the top of the ridge, where the trail levels out through a more open area until it reaches a whale-shaped rock formation on the left. Look straight ahead for a yellow marker on a tree, and walk out to very open terrain through oak trees. Within 2 minutes from the whale-shaped rock, the trail leads right, near the rubble of an old farm wall. Before the wall, there is a pleasant place to take a break on a large rock to the left. This rock looks down over a tiny, elongated lake. At times this area is probably just a marsh, but the rocks to the left make a natural dam to hold back the water.

Back on the trail, walk through larches and remnants of old rock walls and turn left onto an old woods road. There are many woods roads and old walls in this spot. Within a very short time, the trail makes another left onto a woods road, and evidence of another ruined wall is visible. Though trail markers are infrequent, the woods road is very wide at this point, and the route is obvious. After another wall crossing, be sure to turn right through an area of deciduous trees and mountain laurel.

Another 10 minutes brings you to a T-junction. Turn left, descending through a swampy area, then climbing back up until you reach another woods road junction. Turn left again. The swampy area on the left here is drained to the valley on the right by two concrete conduits that cross the road. Shortly, the trail turns left off this woods road. By climbing to the top of the rocks to the right of this junction, you can see the Lookout Tower in the Newark Watershed.

Turn left at the junction—downhill—on the yellow Terrace Pond South Trail. Do not go straight ahead on the Yellow Dot Trail. The trail goes steadily downhill to another swampy area, then climbs again for a short distance. In this section the markers are again a little indistinct, but the trail is wide and you should have no problem making your way until the trail turns left, loses the appearance of a woods road, and becomes rockier. There are many larger boulders to negotiate in this section. The trail climbs up and down quite steeply and crosses another wet area.

Pudding stone is found at the crest of this last rise, and there is a view back through the trees of the Newark Watershed area. Look for a very interesting boulder at the north end of this outcrop. The harder material has resulted in spiderweb markings all over the boulder.

Leaving the ridge, the trail bears left between two banks of rocks and descends, with another ridge immediately ahead. Cross the water at the bottom of this gully, turn right, and

Glacial erratic

walk along what appears to be a streambed with a great deal of sphagnum moss. This section is gloomy, with large rocks looming above the trail and another ridge of rocks close to the left. Markers are not obvious, but there is no doubt which way to go. After 10 minutes in the gully, the still-mossy trail drops down to meet the Terrace Pond Red Trail. Turning left on this trail would eventually take you to the White Trail, but this hike uses a different route.

Continue to follow the yellow trail, which jogs right and immediately left to climb more rocks to another ledge. This section is the hike's roller coaster. The trail appears to be infrequently used—lichen is prominent and slippery when wet. The Terrace Pond Red Trail (which previously joined from the left) now leaves to the right at the foot of a steep, rocky portion. Look up to the left to see a tall rock pinnacle towering above a high rock wall. The trail again follows a damp gully, which shortly flattens out to end at a T-intersection with the White Trail.

The White Trail almost completely encircles Terrace Pond. Turning right here would lead you farther from Terrace Pond, and the outlet of the pond is sometimes difficult to negotiate. For this reason, turn left onto the narrower white-marked trail, which enables you to look down on another stupendous rhododendron grove in the valley below. Notice also the white pines on the other side of this inlet to Terrace Pond. The White Trail at one point splits into high-water and low-water trails, but the way is obvious. Very shortly, the trail descends into the gully (it is much wetter here), and you can look up to see the rhododendrons, now high above you.

Emerge from the gully and walk along the base of a large rock slab to the left. A close watch will reveal where the Terrace Pond Red Trail (ignored earlier in the hike) ends at the White Trail, confirmed by three red markers. Climbing a short way on the Terrace Pond Red Trail is worth the effort for a panoramic view of Terrace Pond. Back on the White Trail, cross the next rock area, which climbs to the right up a jumble of boulders, turns right again, and climbs to another good view of Terrace Pond. Your route is along the west side of Terrace Pond, with many beautiful rock slabs and sandy beach areas, until, at the end of the lake, the White Trail ends at a T-junction with the blue Terrace Pond North Trail, which goes both left and right. Turn left.

The blue-marked Terrace Pond North Trail will take you consecutively over ridges and through wet areas. Stay on the trail until it leads you to a high ridge, which you should climb for a stupendous view of the Wawayanda Plateau.

After refreshing the spirit with the beautiful panorama, continue on the blue trail, which passes alternately through woody, wet areas and rock outcrops. Some of the descents, although short, are steep and slippery. The main direction is downhill, until quite suddenly the trail comes upon the ugly slash of a pipeline. Turn left and follow the pipeline down, keeping to the left of the gash on the hill and looking for the blue arrows to confirm that you are still on the trail. Ignore the several woods roads to the left. Just as the pipeline levels off, you will reach a very distinct, blue-marked woods road. If you miss it, follow the pipeline to Clinton Road, turn left, and walk 0.3 mile along the road to the parking lot. This alternative route should be considered in wet weather.

The blue-marked road is wide, but somewhat damp. Ignore all the other paths and stay with the blue markers. The trail is very low lying, and as you walk, you will be aware of the ridge to the left down which you have just walked. This section is very pretty, passing through white pine, thick mountain laurel, and a dense hemlock grove with large trees. There are several streams to cross, however, and the trail bends left and right to do so. The path parallels the road, finally turning right and climbing, then descending, to the road immediately opposite the parking area.

SJG

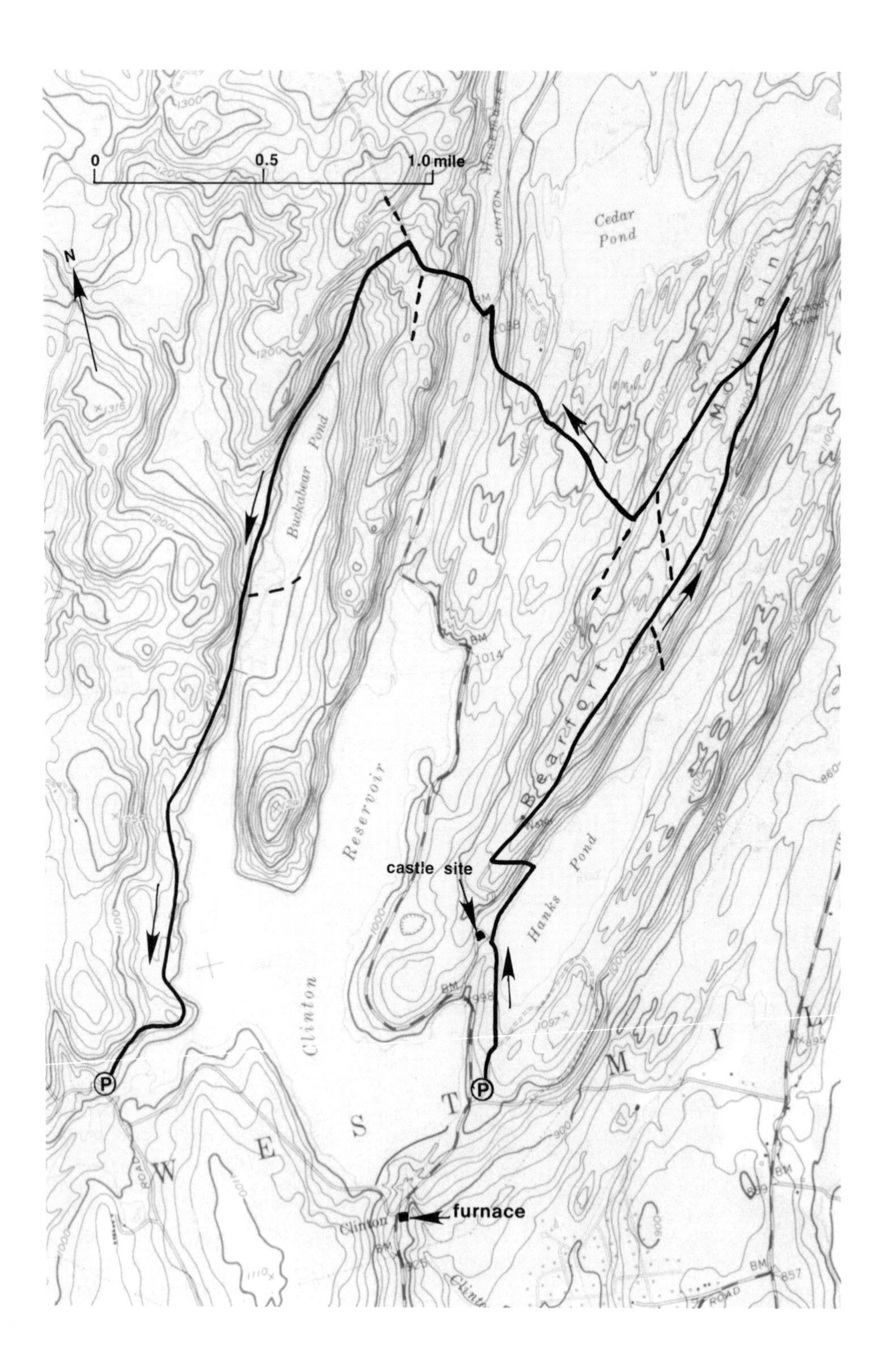
0
0.5
1.0 mile
N
Cedar Pond
Buckabear Pond
Clinton Reservoir
Hanks Pond
Bearfort Mountain
castle site
furnace
Clinton
W E S T M I L
P
P

15

Pequannock Watershed

Total distance: 8 miles (9.5 without car shuttle)

Hiking time: 6 hours

Vertical rise: 400 feet

Rating: Moderately strenuous

Maps: USGS Newfoundland; NYNJTC North Jersey Trails #21; HRM #36A; Pequannock Watershed Trails Map

This outstanding hiking area is named for the Pequannock River. (Pequannock is an Algonquin word said to mean "battlefield.") The river is fed by the streams, lakes, and reservoirs of this mountainous and particularly scenic section of western Passaic County. Owned by the city of Newark, this natural area just south of Wawayanda State Park supplies much of Newark's drinking water. About 30 miles of excellent hiking trails have been cut and blazed in this largely uninhabited area by the Newark Watershed Conservation and Development Corporation (NWCDC), a nonprofit organization, and the land is open for recreational use by permit only (NWCDC, PO Box 319, Newfoundland, NJ 07435; 201-697-2850). You must apply in person at the NWCDC headquarters on Echo Lake Road, on the left about 1 mile north of NJ 23. At the time of this writing, the fee is $8 per year and well worth it.

Originally, all the trails in the watershed were blazed in white, but with the adoption of trail maintenance by the New York–New Jersey Trail Conference, they were color coded. Markings are standard: Three blazes indicates the beginning or the end of a trail, two blazes indicates a turn, and one blaze is simply the route of the trail.

This hike takes you on a grand tour of some of the more scenic and interesting features of the watershed. Though it is long, the walking is not difficult, and much of it is along the shores of ponds and reservoirs. You will traverse some deep hemlock forests typical of this area, and there are a few overlooks as well as the Bearfort fire tower from which you can survey the area. Part of the hike is on the Bearfort Mountain ridge, with its pink to purple sandstones and conglomerates. This ridge, composed of relatively young sedimentary rock, is a geological anomaly—it occurs in the midst of the much older Precambrian highlands formation. Apparently, Bearfort Mountain is the remains of the sand and silt deposits of a long, narrow inland sea or sound that penetrated the older highlands. Notice the distinct change of bedrock as you hike from Bearfort Mountain to Buckabear Pond, the latter being entirely in the highlands with its typical gray Precambrian gneiss, a granitic rock.

Of interest on this hike is the site of the former Cross Castle or Bearfort House, a large mountain estate built by Richard James Cross about 80 years ago. Cross, a native of England, made a fortune in banking and later erected a fantastic but short-lived mansion. The entire 365-acre estate featured a three-story castle with views in all directions, hot and cold running water, numerous fireplaces, stables, carriage houses, guest cottages, and a boathouse on Hank's Pond. The foundations and walls of stone, which survived the dismantling of the mansion by the city of Newark when it was acquired in 1919, were demolished in the late 1980s.

Also of interest is the Clinton Furnace, one of the very few surviving furnaces used during the region's iron-making era. The furnace, located just off Clinton Road near its intersection with Schoolhouse Road, is still in fairly good shape. Iron-smelting furnaces were always built near running water, necessary for the waterwheel-driven bellows. As you would expect, a substantial series of waterfalls is located immediately to the side of Clinton Furnace. Once the furnace was fired up it would burn for months at a time; it was loaded with iron ore from the top. Its location at the base of a sharp drop facilitated this top-loading.

How to Get There

The hike can be done as a circuit, which would include an additional 1.5 miles of road walking, or cars can be parked and a shuttle arranged. The walk on the road is not at all unpleasant and will only add about ½ hour to your hike. If you choose to do the extra walking, park at Parking Area 9 (P9) and walk to P1. If you don't, leave one car at P9 and drive another to P1 to begin the hike.

To find P9 from NJ 23, take Clinton Road north for 1.2 miles and turn left on Schoolhouse Road, a gravel road with good views of Clinton Reservoir. After 1 mile, make a right turn onto Paradise Road; you will find the small parking area on the right in 0.1 mile. After parking, walk or drive down Schoolhouse Road the way you came to Clinton Road. At this intersection, directly in front of you—though it may be obscured by foliage in the summer—are the Clinton Furnace and the falls described earlier. Turn left at the intersection and walk or drive 0.3 mile north on paved Clinton Road to where Van Orden Road (gravel) comes in on the right. This is P1, and you will begin your hike from here.

The Trail

Walk north on the dirt road, which is marked white, heading into the woods. After several minutes, turn left onto a blue-blazed trail. This connector trail leads past some old foundations, crosses the Hanks Pond outlet, and meets the Fire Tower Ridge Trail. Turn right here, now following red/white markers that lead uphill to the former site of the Cross Castle.

After inspecting the site, continue by walking north on the Fire Tower Ridge Trail. Follow the red/white markers, passing the stone water-storage tower that supplied water for the castle, and bear right, following the markers where the trail forks. The footing becomes rockier now, and, after a short rise, the trail swings to the right on what is now a footpath over exposed

Clinton Reservoir

2.5 miles from the start of the hike), you'll come to a clearing, picnic tables, and the fire tower—a good place for a snack or lunch. Take the time to climb the five flights of steps to the top of the fire tower. You will be rewarded by views of the entire watershed.

From the picnic table area, near a stone fireplace, head west for 100 feet and turn left and south on a yellow-blazed footpath, the Fire Tower West Trail. You are now heading south through hemlock and laurel and will soon come out to a viewpoint near a large glacial erratic. Cedar Pond, a natural glacial lake, is below to the north. Continuing, the trail traverses some beautiful woodland with large pudding stone rock outcrops framed with white pine. Soon you will see a trail on the left, and soon after reach another more critical (and obscure) trail junction. Stay to the right here, the way the trail naturally seems to go, and head downhill off the mountain on the white-blazed Two Brooks Trail.

Soon you will come to a small clearing; follow the white markers through ferns and deep hemlocks and then out to a brook, crossing on a recently rebuilt bridge. If you look around, you may find beaver-gnawed trees in this area. After crossing the brook, the trail turns sharply to the right through tall and dense hemlocks. Continue over rocks and pine needles and then out to another brook with a log bridge. After crossing, watch for the trail to turn left and uphill. After a rise, the trail descends slightly through moss, pine, beech, maple, and especially hemlock, which gets thicker as the trail approaches Mossman's Brook. After a

bedrock. White pines, mountain laurels, and an occasional cedar make this section of trail especially scenic. Continue following the red/white markers (a trail comes in on the right in a rocky area) over slabs of glaciated, conglomerate bedrock and downhill over a small stream and into deeper woods. At another trail junction bear to the right and slightly uphill in hemlock and laurel.

As you rise to the broad summit area of Bearfort Mountain, which contains oaks, laurels, and patches of grass, you'll see that the mountaintop is actually a series of parallel, narrow ridges separated by swamp and wet areas. Some of these ridges are well worth exploring. After less than an hour of walking from the Cross Castle site (and about pleasant walk on hemlock needles through a primeval forest along the brook, the trail comes out to Clinton Road at P4. This area is quiet and still. Standing to listen, it is sometimes possible to hear needles falling from the hemlock trees like a light rain.

Make a left on Clinton Road and look for white blazes on the right side of the road. After only 100 yards of road walking, follow the blazes as they turn right onto a woods road. Another right turn comes up almost immediately as the trail heads temporarily north. In a short distance, it swings left and heads steeply uphill. This climb is the longest of the hike (250 feet at most). Notice that the rock in this area is different from that on which you have been walking. Here is Precambrian gneiss, a much older rock than the purple sedimentary sandstones and pudding stone conglomerates that make up Bearfort Mountain. When you reach the top of the rise, you will arrive at a junction. The white markers of the Clinton West Trail turn left here, but continue straight ahead, now following blue markers. Almost immediately you'll come to another junction. Turn left here, following yellow markers south from the main crest of the rise. You should now be heading down toward Buckabear Pond.

This trail, the yellow-blazed Bearfort Waters/Clinton Trail, heads gradually downhill through blueberry bushes growing abundantly below some dead oak trees (decimated by gypsy moths). As the trail descends, more ferns appear, and the land gets damper and wetter. You may need to climb over blowdowns in this remote and little-used section of the watershed. Soon the hemlocks begin to predominate again, until you reach the north shore of Buckabear Pond in a swampy area. Cross a little stream and follow the trail, now an old stone and dirt road that runs parallel and above the west shore of the lake. At about the midpoint of the pond, the trail makes a slight jog to the left where it meets a dirt road used by four-wheelers, but then continues heading south in laurel and rhododendron along the west shore of the pond. Recently a section of the trail was rerouted up the slope to avoid wet or flooded sections near the pond. At the trail junction south of the pond, bear to the right, still heading southward, on the white-blazed Clinton West Trail.

Soon you will see Clinton Reservoir on the left, the largest body of water on this hike. As the trail veers away from the reservoir, it will turn left off the woods road it has been following and then head back toward the reservoir on a footpath. It now hugs the shoreline with good views of water, islands, and hills and again turns left and downhill where a rocky woods road comes in. In this vicinity, on the right and uphill, you will find a number of plaques set in boulders and outcroppings commemorating the lives of hikers and trail builders of the past. Still following the shoreline, the trail passes a cove popular with Canada geese, which frequently forage there. Just a short walk ahead you will emerge from the woods at Parking Area 9 and your car.

Note: Shorter explorations of this scenic but vast area are possible. Consider the following options: Park at P9 and walk along the shore of Clinton Reservoir for a mile or two and then turn back. Park at P1 and explore the shoreline of Hanks Pond. A good 4.5-mile hike starts at P2 and follows the yellow Fire Tower West Trail to the fire tower. You can return the same way or via the red/white Fire Tower Ridge Trail to the Cross Castle site, then turn right following blue markers to the yellow trail. A left turn here will lead to your car.

BCS

16

Pyramid Mountain

Total distance: 3 miles

Hiking time: 2½ hours

Vertical rise: 390 feet

Rating: Easy to moderate

Maps: USGS Boonton; NYNJTC Pyramid Mountain Trails #31; Morris County Park Commission Pyramid Mountain Natural Historical Area map

At 920 feet Pyramid Mountain is not the highest summit ridge in northern Morris County, but it has much to offer the hiker. It is crossed by foot trails that can be steep and rugged in places, has several overlooks, and contains a mysterious glacial erratic that may be part of an ancient Native American calendar site. To the west and below the mountain ridge is Stony Brook and its wetland. Here is found the gigantic Bear Rock, a granite monolith that towers over the brook and swamp. Some of the land containing these wonders is still privately owned, but much has been saved in recent years because of the work of an active grassroots committee, the Friends of Pyramid Mountain, and also the New Jersey Conservation Foundation, the Mennen Corporation, and state and county agencies. Thanks to these organizations and many dedicated individuals, particularly Lucy Meyer, the next generation of New Jersey hikers will find this area as it is today—not developed with condos.

The Pyramid Mountain Natural and Historical Area is a hiker's paradise. Although the area is heavily used at times, there are many trails to disperse hikers. There are actually two trail systems to choose from: the Pyramid Mountain section, a small portion of which is the focus of the hike described below, and the Turkey Mountain section on the east side of County Route 511 (CR 511). Mountain bikes are not permitted in either section. A number of very long loop hikes in the general area are possible, including one around the Butler Reservoir (see NYNJTC map #31, Pyramid Mountain Trails).

While not long, this hike takes in some of the outstanding features of the area. It begins at the visitors center, currently open Friday, Saturday, and Sunday 10–4:30, which contains displays and information about the area and its natural history. An excellent map of the area is also available.

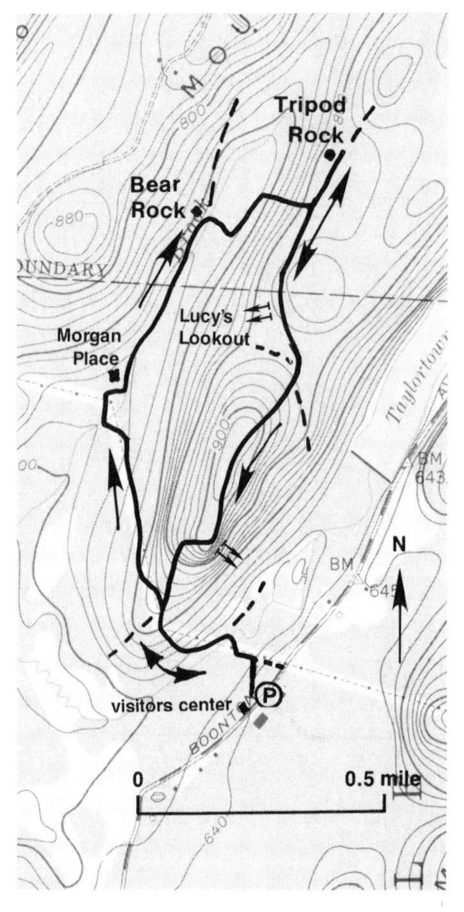

Wildflower lovers will appreciate the first leg of the hike, which passes near a power-line cut. The exposure to the sun allows many species not found in the darker woods to thrive. This section has some wet areas, so wear boots; you should also take the usual precautions against ticks. The two most famous rock formations of the area, Bear Rock and Tripod Rock, are on the walk, as well as two vistas, Lucy's Lookout and the summit of Pyramid Mountain.

How to Get There

From exit 44 on I-287, drive west on Main Street to the center of Boonton and turn right onto CR 511 (Boonton Avenue). The Pyramid Mountain Natural and Historic Area is on CR 511, 3.3 miles north of West Main Street in Boonton (0.8 mile north of CR 511's intersection with Taylortown Road) or 4.4 miles south of NJ 23.

The Trail

Follow the access trail from the parking area. It quickly meets a power-line cut and connects with the blue-blazed Butler-Montville Trail. The trail turns left here and crosses a brook on a long bridge. Next, the trail follows a dirt road, passing a junction with a yellow trail. After a jog to the left, it veers sharply right, leaving the first road, and begins a short but steep climb to the shoulder of Pyramid Mountain. The stone steps leading up the hill are said to have been constructed by the utility company many years ago. The climb ends under a high-voltage tower, which is also a trail junction. Remember this junction. Do not follow the blue markers to the right here or the lane to the left. Look for and follow white markers that lead straight ahead, via a woods road, along the power-line cut or parallel to it.

For the next 0.5 mile the white markers lead through a combination of woods and field near the power-line cut. You will find numerous wildflowers along the route including healall, a member of the mint family (also known as self-heal), and the closed gentian. As the track heads downhill where there are no trees, pay close attention to the markings found mostly on rocks. The trail, which may be wet and muddy in places, will turn left off the woods road, cross a brook on a bridge, then reenter the woods near a high-voltage tower.

Now heading north away from the power lines, the white markers follow an old lane. On both sides of the path are remnants of former occupation.

A foundation is just to the right where the trail first enters the woods, and rock walls parallel the lane as it penetrates the woods. To the right is Bearhouse Brook. According to old newspaper articles, it was the Morgans who once lived here back in the late 18th century. They had a terrible reputation. People knew them as the Tar-Rope Gang that used to make raids into nearby Boonton, robbing people and terrorizing women.

In 0.35 mile from the power lines, you come face to face with Bear Rock. Standing alone in the woods at the edge of a large swamp, Bear Rock has been used as a boundary marker for at least 200 years. Even today it marks the borders of the Kinnelon and Montville boroughs. Although it is difficult and even dangerous to scale, some very old surveying markers can be found near its highest points. Bear Rock is a glacial erratic, plucked from the side of Stony Brook Mountain and dragged several hundred feet by the glacial ice sheet that covered the area 12,000 years ago. To the northwest, about 150 yards away, is a waterfall that cascades over bare rock during the spring and after heavy rains.

From Bear Rock turn right, now following both white and blue markers, to the bridge over the brook and then along the edge of the Sachem Sajapogh of Minising Swamp, also known as Bear Swamp. Along the path are many dwarf ginseng plants, pepperbush, and spicebush. The trail will swing to the left and then to the right, where it begins to climb steeply the ridge of Pyramid Mountain over rocks. The climb, though only about 150 feet of vertical rise, is stiff. Lining the trail are clusters of mountain laurel, which create a tunnel effect in places. As you reach the ridge summit, the trail comes to a T-junction. A left turn here following white markers will lead you, in 150 yards, to Tripod Rock.

Perhaps the most massive perched boulder of its kind in the entire Northeast, Tripod Rock is the focal point of what may be an ancient calendar site. The sheer size and bizarre appearance of it—a 160-ton boulder standing on three medicine-ball-sized rocks—staggers the imagination. If it is simply a chance product of the last ice age, which is what most geologists believe, then it is unique. Others suggest that it was modified by humans. Nearby are two smaller stones partially perched on exposed bedrock. An observer seated on a lip protruding from a piece of bedrock 4 feet high will see, through the gap between these two stones, the summer solstice sunset. The alignment constitutes a simple solar observatory. Whether or not it was used by the early inhabitants of the area is an open question.

From Tripod Rock, retrace your steps to the junction and continue heading south along the ridge, now following only blue markers. This section of trail is overshadowed by tall rhododendrons and mountain laurel, a beautiful sight in winter. Just before the trail swings sharply to the left and meets a yellow trail, look for a small side trail on the right. Marked with blue and white, it leads west in 100 yards to Lucy's Lookout, named for Lucy Meyer, who has led the long crusade to save this beautiful area from development. You will have a view to the south and west over Stony Brook Mountain from this rocky point. Return to the main trail and continue heading south following blue markers (yellow markers share the route for a short distance). Little Cat Swamp, where peepers croak in spring, is off to your left.

After a gradual climb, the blue trail will bring you to the open southern end of the Pyramid Mountain ridge. Here, over bare rock, are expansive views to the east and south, including a view of the New York City skyline when visibility is good. Many years ago a fire tower was located here, but evidence of its former existence is scant today. It is said that on some old maps this summit was labeled High Mountain, though this does not seem to be the case (the next ridge to the west, Rock Pear Mountain, was apparently the one with that name). How the name Pyramid came to be associated with the mountain is a fairly recent story. In the 1920s the *New York Walk Book* directed hikers walking near where the visitors center is today toward the "pyramidal shaped mountain." Indeed, the mountain has a triangular shape when viewed (without foliage) from that direction. Later editions of the book simply referred to it as Pyramid Mountain, and the name stuck. A conflict erupted over the proper name for the peak, and the matter was handed over to the US Geological Survey for a decision. Pyramid Mountain is now the official name.

After taking in the view of woodland, hills, and encroaching suburbia (conflicts over development still rage), head steeply downhill on the blue trail to the power-line cut and its junction with the white trail. You should recognize it as a place you passed earlier in the hike. Bear left and downhill here, retracing your steps, and follow the blue markers east to CR 511 and your car.

BCS

17

Wawayanda State Park

Total distance: 7 miles

Hiking time: 3½ hours

Vertical rise: 200 feet

Rating: Easy

Maps: USGS Wawayanda; NYNJTC #21; WB #21

Wawayanda State Park (Highland Lakes, NJ 07422; 201-853-4462), which covers almost 10,000 acres of forest and water, is located along the Passaic and Sussex County boundary and the border of New York State. The name Wawayanda is, according to one source, the phonetic rendition of the Lenape name, said to mean "water on the mountain"; another source claims it is a Munsee word that translates to "winding, winding water." Despite urban development, the feeling in Wawayanda is that of wilderness, and this hike is delightful in any season. In summer, you are protected from the heat of the sun by the leafy canopy of mature trees and able to cool off in the lake after hiking; in fall, the same trees are a riot of color (although squirrels can bombard the unwary with acorns from above); in winter, these trails are admirably suited for cross-country skiing—gentle and wide—when the snow is deep enough. Because of the high elevation of the plateau, snow remains longer in Wawayanda State Park than in other areas. The terrain undulates and winds in a relaxed way, making for very pleasant and companionable walking. This hike uses the Wingdam, Laurel Pond, Cherry, Old Coal, and Lookout Trails, as well as Cherry Ridge Road, and the hike roughly describes a figure-8.

How to Get There

The park office in Wawayanda State Park is accessed from the northern section of Warwick Turnpike, approached from the north on NY 94 and from the south on Clinton Road. The park entrance is on the west side of Warwick Turnpike, approximately 1.25 miles north of Upper Greenwood Lake. A good road map is an asset. Just beyond the park entrance, stop at the office to obtain the park map and other literature. The hike actually begins at the boathouse area, the second parking lot after the lake. Out-of-season parking is free, but in-season a small

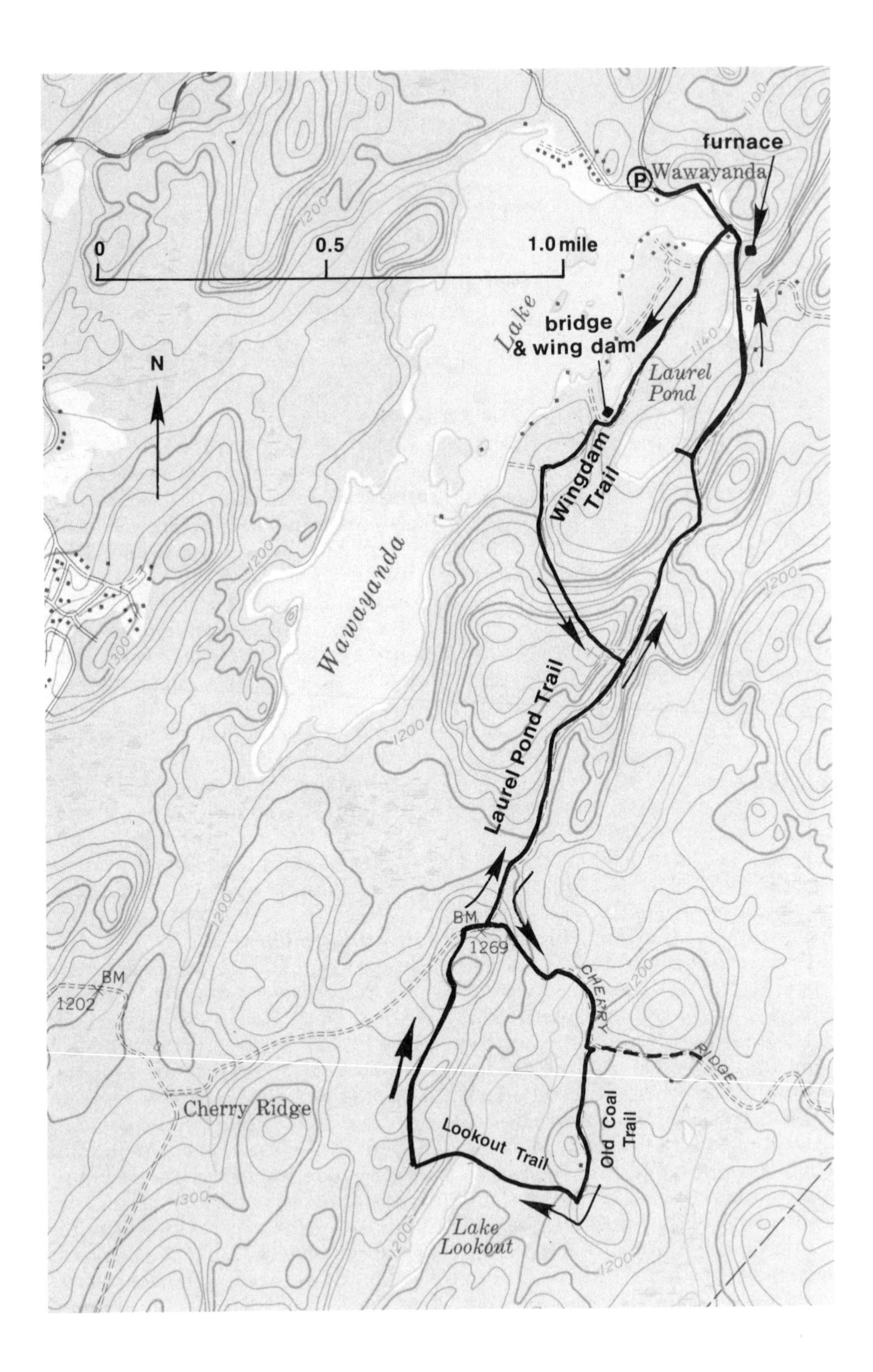
furnace
Wawayanda
0
0.5
1.0 mile
N
Lake
bridge
& wing dam
Laurel
Pond
Wingdam
Trail
Wawayanda
Laurel Pond Trail
BM
1269
BM
1202
CHERRY
RIDGE
Cherry Ridge
Lookout Trail
Old Coal
Trail
Lake
Lookout
1200
1300
1100
1140

fee is charged. During the summer months, it is advisable to arrive before 10 AM to be sure of a parking space.

The Trail

With Wawayanda Lake on your right, leave the parking lot, walk left to a wide gravel road (ignore a woods road), and follow the main road by the side of the lake. Wawayanda Lake was once two separate bodies of water called Double Pond. The narrow strip of land that divided the two areas of water still partly shows on the west side of Barker Island, now in the center of the lake. In winter, when the lake is frozen solid, it is pleasant to walk across the ice to Barker Island and observe the ice fishers.

The stone dam coming into view at the northeastern end of the lake was built in the middle of the last century by the Thomas Iron Company. On the lake, admire the many yellow pond lilies and white fragrant water lilies and note, as you reach the dam, that there are picnic tables and a disconnected water pump. The hike will return to this point. Turn right, cross the dam, walk through the barrier of large boulders, and find immediately ahead the beginning of the Wingdam Trail. You have walked for approximately 10 minutes.

The Wingdam Trail, marked in blue, is a wide gravel road climbing slightly uphill through mature hardwood trees. On the left is an old stone wall, and the road itself is in a dip. After another 5 minutes you can hear the sound of running water, and the trail begins to drop toward a wooden bridge spanning a water spill to Laurel Pond. Just before the bridge—and at other spots—woods roads join the main trail. At present there are still areas of private property in the park. These properties will become state owned eventually. The side roads are often posted and do not merit much attention.

The "wing dam" on the right side of the wooden bridge was constructed by the Thomas Iron Company and, together with the dam you crossed, raises the lake level by about 7½ feet. The water comes over this dam in a wide, swift fall and rushes on its way to feed Laurel Pond, out of sight on the left. Wildflowers abound in this lush area at all times of the year.

Soon after the bridge, you will glimpse Laurel Pond through the trees on the left. The trees become slightly shorter in stature, and rhododendrons begin to appear, hinting of the large stands surrounding this end of Laurel Pond. Soon after you pass a large boulder on the right, another woods road comes in from the same side. This one is worth exploring because it leads to an abandoned home and a derelict walkway across a swampy area on a peninsula, from which a small island in the center of Wawayanda Lake is visible. The boathouse at the northern end of the lake is partially in view also.

Back on the main trail, other home roads come in from the right, some posted with the owner's name. Within about 30 minutes from the start of the hike, the trail grows narrower, begins to climb (with more boulders underfoot), and looks more like a hiking trail. There are a few evergreens as the trail becomes even steeper and rockier and, instead of continuing across the side of the hill, turns sharply right. In another 5 minutes it reaches the crest of the hill and emerges into a rocky, grassy area, with a slight view across the valley through the trees to the left of a tree-covered ridge. This clearing is another pleasant place to pause. The highest point in this part of the park is off the trail to the right, 1375 feet above sea level.

Turn left and follow the marked

trail downhill to a grassy woods road and the end of the Wingdam Trail. This woods road is the Laurel Pond Trail, marked in yellow. Turn right. As you travel slightly downhill, the trees become denser again, and the terrain soon develops into level, pleasant walking.

An interesting section is reached after a few minutes. To the right of the trail a large outcrop of big rocks is split many times, with trees growing in the cracks; farther to the left, another ridge of such rocks is discernible. Even farther down the trail, to the left, watch for a large boulder split completely down the center and fallen apart. This section is a paradise for chipmunks.

The road is wide and distinct and becomes even sandier and smoother. Within 15 minutes and after passing another woods road on the right, you reach the T-junction with Cherry Ridge Road. Turn left here, but do not expect to find markers. In times of heavy rain the road becomes an escape route for excess water. Cross a slowly moving stream within a few minutes on a wooden bridge. Look to the left of the bridge to see "539" etched in nails, a New Jersey Department of Transportation number.

As expected after a stream crossing, the road climbs away, becoming wider and stonier. At the top of this short climb, Cherry Ridge Road goes off to the left. Take the Old Coal Trail straight ahead, marked in red and with a new wooden stake saying OLD COAL TR. Soon the first white pines appear. Within about 5 minutes, at a wide, grassy junction, leave the Old Coal Trail and make a right turn onto the Lookout Trail, marked in white. The three white markers traditionally designating the beginning or ending of a trail can be clearly seen.

Within a few minutes, you come to a small clearing in which a giant hemlock stood until it was brought down by a storm in December 1992. The trunk—at least 9 feet in circumference—still rises 20 or 30 feet in the air, but the rest of this rare old-growth tree now lies to the right of the trail. After 10 minutes of leisurely walking from the great hemlock, you will see Lake Lookout on the left, preceded by a grassy open space. This place is delightful and seldom visited.

Leaving Lake Lookout's peaceful environs, continue straight past the lake outlet and into the woods. The footway is now narrow and a little indistinct but marked clearly with white paint and white metal patches. The trail climbs steeply for a short distance among large boulders wearing hairpieces of fern, then turns right and proceeds north along a valley floor with the heights of Cherry Ridge above on the left. This section is a recent trail relocation winding among large silent fallen trees and through a wet and rocky area dark with mountain laurel. Fifteen minutes brings you out onto Cherry Ridge Road, less than 100 yards west of the junction with the Laurel Pond Trail. Turn right to reach the junction, then turn left onto the Laurel Pond Trail and retrace your earlier steps. When the Wingdam Trail enters, stay on the Laurel Pond Trail to cover new ground.

A visit to the shore of Laurel, an anglers' favorite, is worth the 5-minute detour from the main trail. Shortly after a downhill grade and approximately 10 minutes from the junction of the Wingdam Trail, watch for a yellow marker on a tree to the left. At this point, there is a clear trail that goes left and slightly downhill on a narrow path practically overgrown with tall rhododendron bushes to the top of a rocky outcrop just above Laurel

Pond. If the scramble down to the water's edge is a deterrent, bear left, then switchback right to achieve the same result as climbing down the rocks. If you miss this first access point, there is a second opportunity to reach the lakeshore a little farther down the main trail. As you are sitting on the lake edge, observe that the inlet to Laurel Pond, passed earlier in the hike, is practically opposite. The slope of the opposite bank is much shallower than you would expect given the noise of the water entering from Lake Wawayanda.

After you rejoin the Laurel Pond Trail, parallel the lakeshore for a few minutes, then swing away from it to where, within another 5 minutes, there is evidence that the road was once gated. Here, too, is a yellow-marked tree with the sign LAUREL POND TRAIL. Ignore the gated road coming in from the right and walk toward the open, low-lying area ahead. After heavy rain, this part of the trail is often flooded but usually negotiable. After you cross the wooden bridge at the outlet from Laurel Pond, you will pass the site of the old Mule Barn on the left. The barn was recently burned down by vandals. It once housed the mules used to haul the raw materials required for producing iron in Wawayanda.

Straight ahead is the old charcoal furnace, and on the right is another wooden bridge leading to a group campsite furnished with picnic tables. Pause at the furnace and, with your back to the swiftly running stream, try to imagine the busy scene of yesteryear when Wawayanda was the center of the iron industry in New Jersey. This structure is all that remains of a charcoal blast furnace built by Oliver Ames and his three sons, William, Oaks, and Oliver Junior. William was in charge; his initials, W.L.A., and the date 1846 can still be seen on a lintel in the main arch. Iron ore from local mines was smelted here continuously from 1847 to 1857 when cheap coal became available in Pennsylvania, making it more economical to transport the ore for smelting to those hotter and more efficient furnaces.

In an average day, 7 tons of iron was produced from this type of furnace and poured off twice daily, at noon and at midnight. Wawayanda iron was of such superior quality that it was used to manufacture railroad wheels; during the Civil War, the Ames factories also filled government orders for shovels and swords. During the time of greatest activity, a small village grew up in the vicinity. Nothing remains. The furnace building is currently supported by metal framing and protected from vandals by substantial fencing.

Retrace your footsteps a little to where a sign on the right reads POSITIVELY NO VEHICLES BEYOND THIS POINT. Follow this wide gravel road slightly uphill. It leads past the side of the old furnace and over another old wooden bridge across a mostly dried-up stream. There is evidence to the left of what is believed to have been a waterway from the main dam, which drove a bellows fanning the flames in the furnace. Soon the picnic tables and disconnected pump that you passed on the way out at the northeastern end of Lake Wawayanda can be recognized. Return to the parking lot on the same shoreline path you used to begin the hike.

SJG

18

Appalachian Trail/ Stairway to Heaven

Total distance: 4.8 miles

Hiking time: 3 hours

Vertical rise: 1000 feet

Rating: Moderately strenuous

Maps: USGS Wawayanda; NYNJTC North Jersey Trails Map #21; WB #21; NY–NJ Appalachian Trail Map #4 (Appalachian Trail Conference); DEP Appalachian Trail and Wawayanda State Park maps

The Appalachian Trail (AT) is our nation's first designated National Scenic Trail. It extends 2152 miles from Springer Mountain in Georgia to Mount Katahdin in Maine. The AT is a unique partnership between 14 states, the National Park Service, the US Forest Service, and a network of hiking clubs coordinated by the Appalachian Trail Conference (ATC, PO Box 807, Harpers Ferry, WV 25425). The almost 74 miles of the trail located in New Jersey are managed and maintained by volunteers of the New York–New Jersey Trail Conference.

Entering from Pennsylvania at the Delaware Water Gap, the trail follows the crest of the Kittatinnies to High Point State Park, where it turns east along the New York–New Jersey border. After crossing Wawayanda State Park and traveling through Hewitt State Forest, the trail turns north into New York State just west of Greenwood Lake.

The main part of this hike is on a new section built mostly by volunteers with help from ATC trail crews, local Boy Scouts, New Jersey correctional inmates, and Wawayanda park personnel. The huge 3-year cooperative effort was completed in May 1991. You are about to see, appreciate, and enjoy the results of everyone's labors.

This relocation is a fine example of the concern trail builders now show for the environment. The old trail (about 0.5 mile south) was little changed since it was first built in 1937. It shot straight up the mountain in just more than 0.5 mile. Without a switchback, the climb was an exhausting boulder-hop and rock scramble up an ugly erosion-scarred ditch. The new route, however, loops up the 900-foot elevation gain gracefully. Long

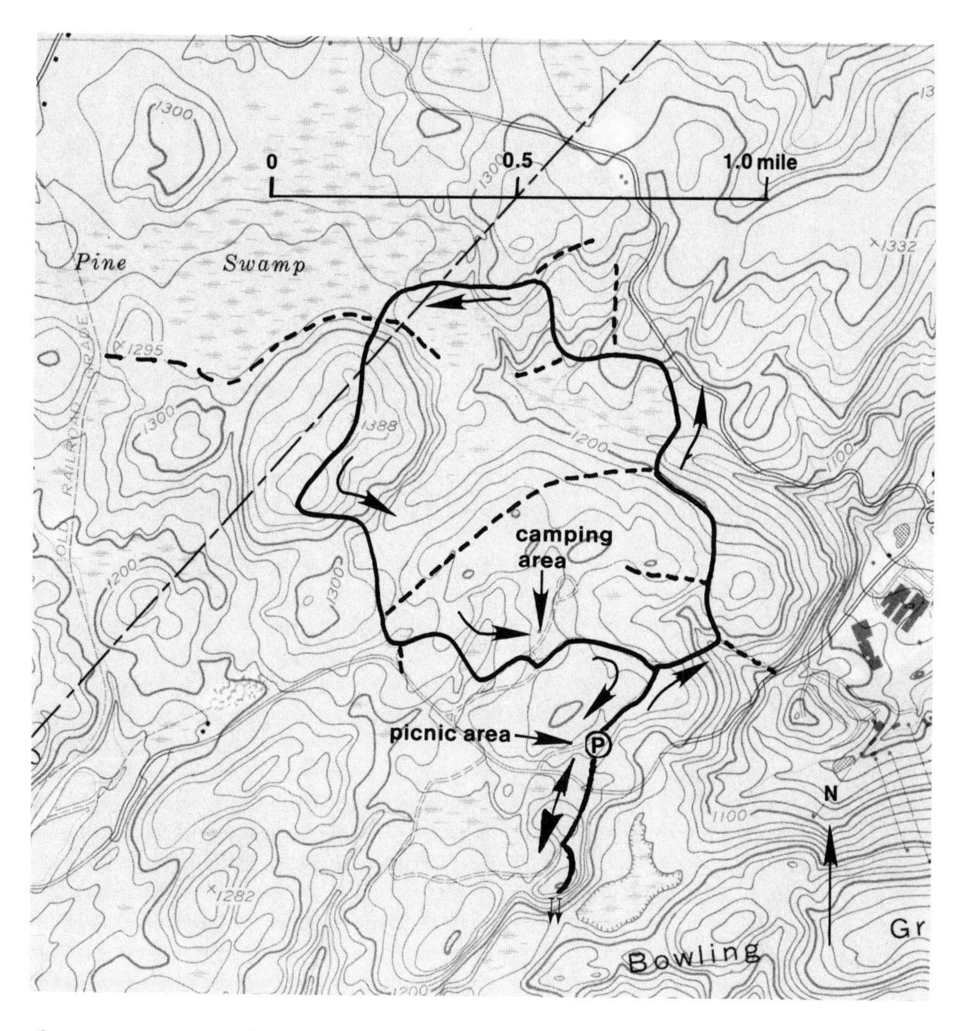

for cross-country skiing, and because the average elevation in the park is 1200 feet, snow remains on the ground longer than in many other areas in north Jersey. Some are open to mountain bikes, and you may encounter them along the way. A section of the 150-mile Highlands Trail (see Introduction) also passes through the park.

Although this hike does not offer sweeping views of the countryside, the change in woodland environments more than makes up for it. Along the route are deciduous forests, rocky scrub growth, damp hemlock groves, laurel thickets, and remote swampland. The reservation is located on a high plateau in the New Jersey highlands province. The bedrock, which is very close to the surface because of glaciation, is Precambrian gneiss, a granitic rock that contains large amounts of iron. There are a few iron mines, long abandoned, in the reservation. Because the park is large and located in the most remote part of Morris County, wildlife, including the red-tailed hawk, many deer, and an occasional bear, make their homes here.

How to Get There

From I-287 (exit 33), take NJ 15 north for 5 miles. Turn right, following signs to Milton and Weldon Road. After a few miles on Weldon Road, you'll see a sign indicating that you've entered the reservation. The road will swing around to the right and pass the large parking area for Saffin Pond. In roughly another mile, you will come to the reservation's three main entrances, the first two for campers. Take the second entrance on the left, which leads to a large parking area, a picnic area, and the trailhead.

The Trail

Walk north on the wide asphalt path past a water pump, a workout station, a picnic area, and a ball field. The access trail you are on is part of the Highlands Trail, marked in turquoise, with some white markers as well. The pavement will soon end, and in just 0.1 mile you will arrive at a junction with the Pine Swamp Trail, a 3.5-mile loop marked in white that passes through the northern part of the reservation. The blue markers of the Highlands Trail share this route for the first third of the hike. Make a right turn at this junction; walk downhill and cross over a small brook. At the next junction, bear left, staying with the white and blue markers. After a short climb, the trail veers to the right at a grassy intersection, heads downhill, then swings to the left through an open forest.

After a short level stretch, the Pine Swamp Trail comes to a triangular junction with the green-blazed Boulder Trail and turns to the right, down a long hill (there is a parallel path here) to a brook. This unnamed brook is one of the principal drainages of the swamp that dominates the interior of the northern portion of the reservation. Notice that the brook's water is a dark color. As in the Pine Barrens, the tannins in the roots of hemlocks and other swamp evergreens color the water. After crossing on a small bridge, be alert for a left turn off the main path onto a cut trail through a corner of the swamp.

In this section of trail, mountain laurel and rhododendron dominate, putting on a display of flowers in June and July. The footing is much rockier here, and there can be a few wet areas that may require some stretching. As you reach the end of this part of the swamp, the trail climbs up a few feet to higher ground, connects with a woods road, and turns left. Because this part of the trail is near Sparta Mountain Road, you may hear an occasional motor vehicle.

After about 0.1 mile, where the white and blue blazes turn to the right, you'll come to a junction with the yellow-marked trail, the Cut-off Trail. Take it straight ahead, following only yellow markers down to and over a small brook, then through a wet area in a hemlock woods. You'll pass another junction, but continue following yellow markers, which now lead uphill on an old logging road. At the end of this climb, the yellow Cut-off Trail meets again with the white Pine Swamp Trail—you have saved some walking and not missed any of the remarkable Pine Swamp.

Turn left on the Pine Swamp Trail, now following only white markers, and enter the area of the Pine Swamp itself. Just ahead on your left, at the edge of a small cliff, look for an area that overlooks the dense foliage of the swamp. This rocky spot is a pleasant place to stop for a rest or to have a snack or lunch. Below you is not a typical swamp of grasses and water, but a pine swamp with tall spruce, hemlock, rhododendron, and laurel.

Continue farther along on the trail, which now heads downhill to the level of the swamp, and get a closer view of this peculiar area. About 0.2 mile ahead, the trail—a woods road and very dry—comes closest to the main swamp itself. Off to your right you can see how wet the area is and how huge boulders protrude from the ground providing drier areas in their cracks for plants incapable of growing in water or very wet soil. You are now in one of the most remote areas of the reservation. On your right, the swamp extends for perhaps a mile into Sussex County. It is virtually inaccessible, because no paths cross it. You get a feeling of wilderness here, broken only by the calls of birds or an occasional aircraft. In fact, some years ago a small private plane crashed in the swamp one May. It wasn't until that November that the wreckage and the bodies were found.

The trail, which travels a high area between two parts of the swamp, continues under tall hemlocks, crosses a small brook, and then begins a climb, leaving the swamp for good. You'll pass a junction with a bike trail on the right marked with yellow tags. For the next mile, you will share the route with this bike trail. Continue climbing gradually to the flat, rounded summit of an unnamed hill that, at 1388 feet, is the highest point in Morris County. There is a resting bench near the summit. Unfortunately, there are no views from this high point, except through the trees during winter.

From the bench, the trail—which in this section is part gravel and used occasionally by maintenance vehicles—swings to the left, then to the right as it descends to lower ground. Follow it through a low area and up a gradual climb. Just before meeting the Boulder Trail, which comes in from the left, you can find a few remnants of iron mining during the last century (mostly pits and rock piles) by exploring the woods to your left and uphill. Just past this junction, the trail turns left at another junction (the bike trail turns right) and heads east on a wide footpath. After about 0.25 mile, you'll emerge from the woods into the middle of the trailer camping area.

Following white markers, make a left on the paved road and bear right near the rest rooms. Walk through the fence opening on your left, cross the field of grass, and reenter the woods on a trail to your right. In about 0.2 mile, you'll arrive at the trail junction you began the loop hike on, marked by signs. Make a right here and walk the path through the picnic area and back to your car.

If you still have energy and would like to take in a vista, the Headley Overlook is less than 0.25 mile away. Follow the blue markers as they leave the parking area in back of the directory across Weldon Road and then out to the overlook. The rocky overlook offers a view to the south and west that includes an arm of Lake Hopatcong.

BCS

20

Allamuchy Mountain State Park

Total distance: 4 miles

Hiking time: 2½ hours

Vertical rise: 110 feet

Rating: Easy to moderate

Maps: USGS Tranquility; DEP Allamuchy Mountain and Stephens State Park map

Allamuchy Mountain State Park, which is administered from nearby Stephens State Park (800 Willow Grove Street, Hackettstown, NJ 07840; 201-852-3790), is mostly undeveloped and not so well known to many New Jerseyites. At present, access to the park is not marked, and the drive to the parking area is over a rough, bumpy dirt road. The effort made to get there is worth it, however, for this park is not heavily used and offers some excellent though gentle hiking and the opportunity to spot wildlife. The trails, most of which are old farm and lumber roads, are graded and are superb for cross-country skiing and mountain biking. Expect to see the latter. Some 15 miles of trail marked with white, red, blue, and yellow paint are shared, about equally, between hikers and bikers.

Allamuchy Mountain State Park is an 8900-acre park that straddles I-80. This hike uses only the portion of the park south of the interstate, a portion that has been designated as a natural area. The large northern section includes historic Waterloo Village and parts of the old Morris Canal. The name of the park is a shortened version of a Native American chief's name—Allamuchahokkingen—which means "place within the hills." It wasn't so long ago that Allamuchy Mountain State Park was part of a large estate owned by the descendants of the famous Peter Stuyvesant, Dutch governor of New Amsterdam, now New York. The acreage, much of which was farmed, was acquired during the 1970s and is slowly returning to a natural state. This park maintains a large wildlife population and may be of special interest to birders and naturalists.

One drawback to the wonderful wildlife habitat found at Allamuchy is the presence of ticks, including deer ticks. Take the usual precautions: Wear light-colored pants with socks pulled over them, use tick spray with DEET around the ankles, and look carefully at your body after the hike.

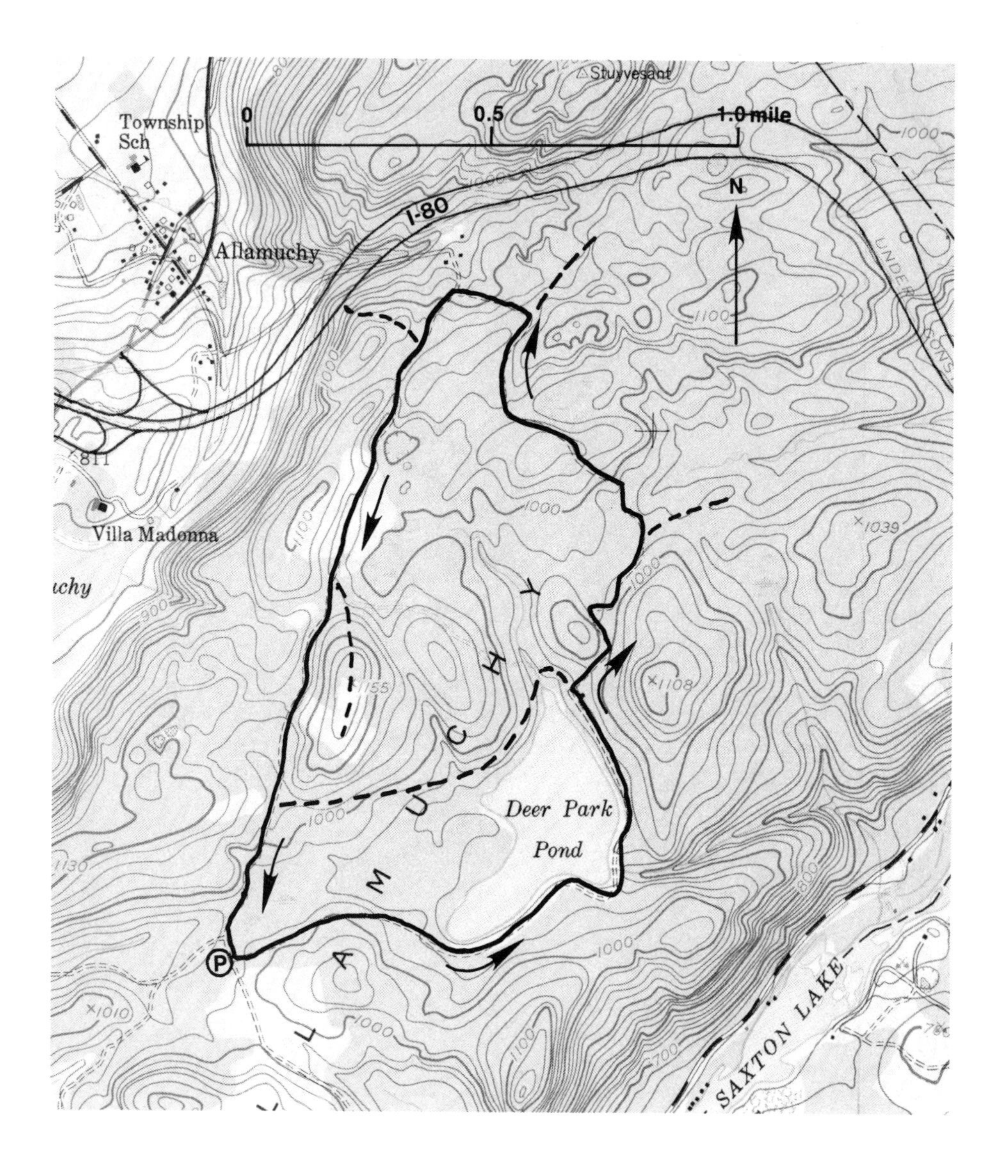

How to Get There

From exit 19 on I-80, take NJ 517 south toward Hackettstown. You'll have to travel exactly 2.1 miles south of I-80 to find the access road to the park, which, at the time of this writing, is not marked. (From Hackettstown this turn is 3 miles north on NJ 517.) The road is on the left near a brick house. There is also a wooden post in the ground at the corner. Turn left here and drive 0.7 mile over small hills and many potholes to the park entrance, where there is a parking area, portable toilets, and a directory. Keep going for another mile, past a residence and through a gate. About 0.5 mile past this gate is a second gate and a large field for parking on the left. Park here. During the winter, the rangers often close the first gate. If they do, park just before it and walk the additional 0.5 mile.

Allamuchy Mountain State Park

The Trail

Walk back to the dirt road you drove in on and follow it through a gate. The road swings right almost immediately, then begins a long, gradual descent through deciduous forest to Deer Park Pond. It's marked with white blazes on trees and easy to follow. Because this trail is the most frequently used in the park, you may encounter a lot of others hiking or biking in both directions. One of the striking things about this section is the openness of the forest. The forest floor is nearly all ferns, particularly on the right, but above that is nothing but open space—right up to the lowest branches of some very large trees. The effect is remarkably expansive for a New Jersey forest.

As you walk on, part of the pond appears through the trees on the left. Deer Park Pond was once part of the estate. Beavers have been introduced to the pond and have established themselves in a few areas. As you get closer to the water, you may spot one of their lodges on the opposite bank. Along with the beavers, you could see some of the birds that nest here, such as ducks, Canada geese, or ospreys.

The white-marked road brings you down to the pond, over the newly rebuilt dam and spillway, and along the eastern shore. There are some beautiful areas here where stands of tall hemlocks and pines border the shoreline. This section is popular with anglers and walkers. When the park was first opened, the public was allowed vehicle access right down to the pond. The amount of litter that accumulated, most of it related to fishing, was staggering. The present 0.5-mile walk to the water has certainly discouraged the worst of this behavior, allowing those who are willing to exercise a little access to a much cleaner park. Today Allamuchy Mountain Park also has a carry-in/carry-out policy for managing trash. You won't find any trash cans at the lake.

At the north end of the pond, where a small clearing leads down to the water, take a lightly used path heading uphill to the right. You will quickly attain the top of the small rise, then walk downhill through deep forest. The trail marked with both white and blue is lined with numerous highbush blueberry shrubs that produce very tasty berries during July and August.

After 0.25 mile or so of walking, you'll come to an intersection near a swamp. Because of its isolation, openness, and water, this area is frequented by deer. Make a left here, following white markers. The trail now climbs gradually on a rockier pathway toward the highest elevation on the hike. Just after the trail levels off and bears sharply to the right, it arrives at an intersection. Keep left, now heading in a ern direction, following the w markers through a series of turns a alongside the remains of old rock walls The highway sounds you hear are those of I-80. The trail will soon turn south, running parallel to a wire fence.

If you care to, walk through fence opening and follow the footpath out to the rest area and vista on I-80. The view out to Kittatinny Mountain and the Delaware Water Gap is quite spectacular. Another option is to visit this spot (accessible from I-80 eastbound) by car after returning from the hike.

Continuing on white markers, follow the path past a large rock wall and then along the edge of former farmland, which is reverting back to woodland. This spot is also frequented by deer and home to many birds and small mammals. Numerous wildflowers may be found here, including wild yarrow. This flower, a member of the sunflower family, is recognized by its clumps of small white blooms at the top of a green, leafy stem. The leaves are delicate and pleasantly aromatic. Yarrow has been used by herbalists in the treatment of fevers and for hemorrhages and bleeding from the lungs. A tea made from the leaves and flowers is said to break up a cold if taken regularly right from the beginning of the illness.

From here, follow the white markers back to your car. On the way, you'll notice a path leading off to the left up what seems to be the open summit of a small hill. You won't find any views there, but you will find a field in transition that contains many sun-loving wildflowers. Farther ahead, staying with the white markers, another road leads off to the left and downhill. The pond is about 0.25 mile down this lane. Past this intersection, which is quite open, the white markers will lead you, in about 0.3 mile, to the gate and your car.

BCS

Jenny Jump State Forest

Total distance: 4.5 miles

Hiking time: 2½ hours

Vertical rise: 700–750 feet

Rating: Moderate

Maps: USGS Blairstown; DEP Jenny Jump State Forest

Jenny Jump State Forest was named for a young colonial girl. As the tale goes, Jenny was out picking berries with her father. Some hostile Native Americans came across the pair and her father yelled out for her to jump from the cliff—if only to save her chastity. Although Jenny was successful in keeping herself pure, the result was her death . . . or so the tale goes.

How to Get There

To reach Jenny Jump from exit 12 off I-80, drive 1.1 miles into the town of Hope. Bear left onto County Route 519. After little more than a mile, turn right on Shiloh Road (near a small pond) at a marked junction. After going another 1.4 miles uphill, bear right at a fork, then right again after an additional 0.6 mile. The state forest entrance road is 0.4 mile farther on your left. After I-80, most of the route is marked with JENNY JUMP SF directional signs, but some are rather small. Stop at the park office (PO Box 150, Hope, NJ 07844; 908-459-4366) for a free map, then drive uphill following the sign TO TRAILS to a new comfort station, several new rental cabins, two small parking areas, and the start of the hiking trails. There is also a trail sign here. Consider combining this short hike with a picnic lunch. There are lots of tables around.

The Trail

You'll begin your hike on the red-marked Swamp Trail, which co-mingles with the yellow-marked Summit Trail for the first few minutes. Trail maintenance responsibility in Jenny Jump was accepted in 1994 by the New York–New Jersey Trail Conference, and the trails show much improvement. All the trails are now marked with standard one-color blazes. Three blazes together mark the start (or end) of a trail; two blazes indicate a turn.

Your trail (red) goes somewhat uphill along a woods road as it turns right and heads toward the crest of the ridge. Pass a few picnic tables as the path swings left. After less than 5 minutes, you will reach a junction. Stay to the left following the red markings. The yellow is the Summit Trail upon which you will return.

The Swamp Trail is wide and proceeds gently through the woods. Continue straight ahead, avoiding a fork to the left. The small gorge off to the right contains some small wet areas that probably gave the trail its name; however, the going is generally dry and easy. As the trail descends into the lower tract, you reach Campsit and a new bathhouse facility. This s forest has many such campsites ava able to the public for a small fee. Res ervations are advisable. There are also eight cabins for rent, with four bunks each and a maximum capacity of six.

Proceed ahead, past the sign to the Summit-Spring Connection Trail and onto the paved road. Bear right, going along the road and passing several more campsites, some water faucets, and another bathhouse. Just afterward, note the large glacial erratic on the left side of the road—as well as the small tree growing right out of the rock. Imagine

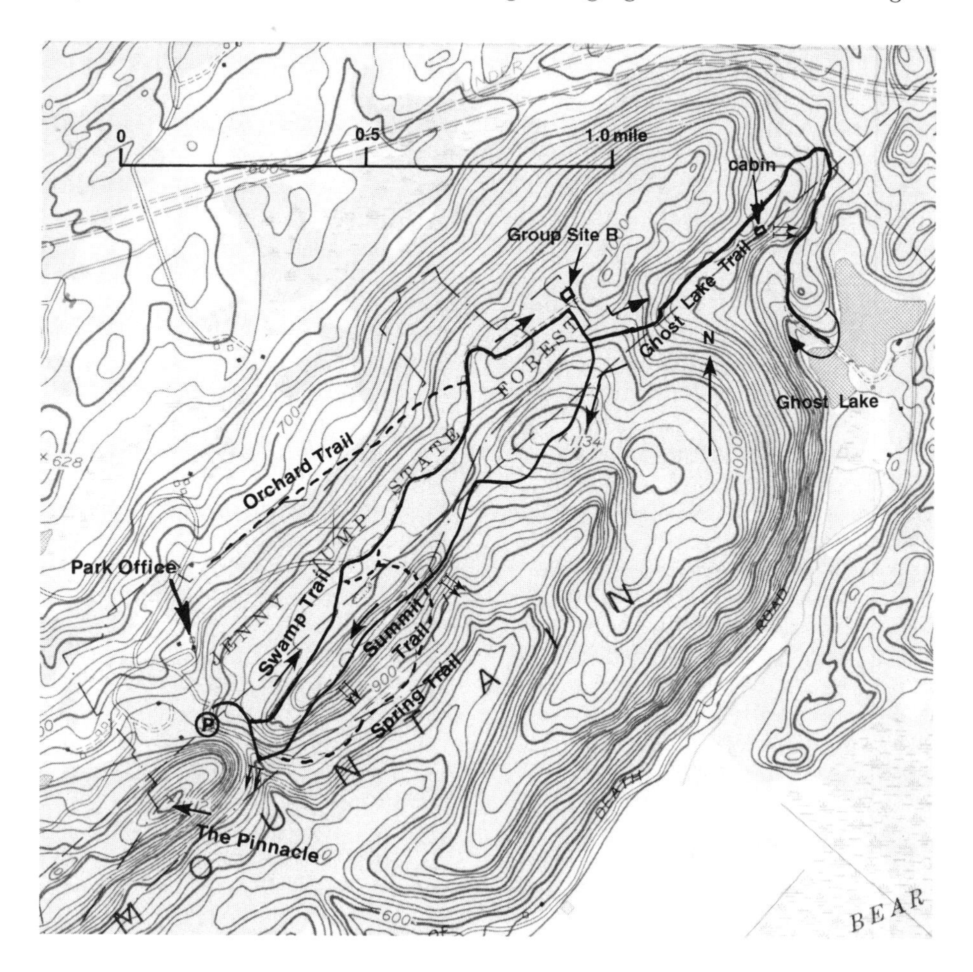

…ce sheet that ripped …en left it here after …ng north. I guess …impressed.

…ad on the road, pass …the Orchard Trail. Keep …g ahead. Just before Group Site B, there is a trailhead sign. Turn right here, onto the Ghost Lake Trail, marked in light blue. This first section co-mingles with the yellow-marked Summit Trail.

Back again in the woods, the course sways gently to the left and back again through a small grove of hemlock trees. After a gentle decent and traverse of a wet area, be alert as the Summit Trail makes a sharp right turn onto a narrower trail. Note this spot for your return trip. Unless you want to really shorten the hike (and forgo a 450-foot up-and-down elevation change), stay on the blue Ghost Trail, which goes straight ahead, soon skirting the side of a hill. For a while, the sounds of nearby I-80 intrude on the solitude, but then the trail begins a rocky descent over some loose rocks. I hope you're wearing your boots.

In a level area, the marked trail joins a woods road, which it will follow the rest of the way to the lake. Shortly after swinging left, the sharp-eyed will notice a cabin roof through the trees to the right. A side trip to the porch is worth the effort. The view east is toward Allamuchy Mountain State Park (see Hike 20) and the Pequest River Valley. The cabin, now unused, is slated for demolition, but the view will still be there. One local insists this is the actual site where Jenny jumped.

Continuing down, the trail passes some house-sized rocks, then the descent moderates as it swings left and parallels a stream. Soon the lake is visible through the trees. The trail ends just before the grass-covered causeway across Ghost Lake, about 45 minutes from Group Site B.

There is some debate on how Ghost Lake acquired its name. One story involves a massacre between two warring Native tribes, the other a mucky prelake swamp where mosquitoes bred and spread sickness and death. The local road leading to the lake is named Shades of Death Road!

From here, retrace your steps to the junction of the Ghost Lake and Summit Trails. Make a left, going south, onto the yellow-blazed Summit Trail. This junction may be hard to spot in the direction you're traveling. If you start seeing both blue and yellow markers together, you've passed the junction; retrace your steps. There was once a trail sign here; the post is still visible on the ground.

You'll follow the yellow blazes for the rest of the hike. The path becomes narrower and woodsy as it first moderately, then more steeply, gains the summit ridge of Jenny Jump Mountain. When the terrain begins to level off and you approach the top, note the mountain laurel off to the right. The path undulates along the ridge, not always on the very top, with some evidence of old yellow blazes. As it approaches the summit and viewpoint, the woodland begins to thin and trees are shorter.

Fifteen minutes of walking from the junction will bring you to a concrete post in the ground (marked NJ 78), probably a park boundary. The park map shows the Summit Trail crossing outside the forest boundary for a short distance. Here a short side trail left will take you to the first of three eastward views. After passing the Spring Trail crossing (blue marked), another side trail to a view is 10 minutes away. This one is signed VIEW and has a nice rock outcropping where you can pause for a final snack or water break. If the conditions are normal or wet, the moss and grass along the trail will be especially lush and green.

Continue ahead. Through trees to the right are some limited views toward Pennsylvania. More people are usually encountered along here. Many take the short hike up from the parking area for the vistas. The hill protruding through the woods ahead is part of Jenny Jump and called the Pinnacle. A microwave tower sits on its top.

As the trail turns right and starts downhill, there is an open area to the left marked VISTA. Walk out to a viewpoint some 30 yards off the trail. This lookout is the best view in the region. To the left is the vista you saw previously (the Hackettstown region), in front of you is the Pinnacle, and to the right are the Kittatinnies and Pennsylvania. Notice, too, the rock surface underfoot. The striations were made by the glaciers during the ice age.

Back on the Summit Trail, proceed downhill through a grove of hemlocks, passing the Swamp Trail junction. Bear left and return to the parking area. I hope the juice machine still works.

HNZ

22

Jockey Hollow

Total distance: 4.5 miles

Hiking time: 2–4 hours

Vertical rise: 600–700 feet

Rating: Moderate to easy

Maps: USGS Mendham; HRM #11; NPS Jockey Hollow Area Trail Map

At just less than 1000 acres, Jockey Hollow is the largest section of the Morristown National Historical Park (Morristown, NJ 07960; 201-539-2085), about 3 miles south of the city of Morristown. The site, operated by the National Park Service, is open year-round, but some of the buildings are closed on Thanksgiving, Christmas, and New Year's, and possibly on a few weekdays, depending on the year's budget. Call ahead to be sure the buildings are open, for they are well worth the visit.

Be sure to allow time for the visitors center. As well as the usual helpful ranger, there is a book nook, orientation film, and "talking" display of a soldier's hut. Simple trail maps are available. For cartographic fans, a very detailed orienteering map is available for $3.

You might also want to visit Wick House, just behind the visitors center. Henry Wick built his house around 1750 and made his living from farming and from his large woodlot. While better off than most, the family was by no means wealthy. During the winter encampment of 1779–80, the farm served as both the Wicks' home and as the headquarters of Major General Arthur St. Clair.

The main building has been restored, and there is usually a ranger in attendance in period dress to explain the fascinating history. You will enjoy visiting Wick Farm in the morning. We have been there on a magnificent fall Saturday yet had it all to ourselves for an hour; but it became crowded with other visitors later that afternoon.

The whole hike, indeed this whole park, is fine for cross-country skiing as well as hiking. Signs are posted at almost every trail junction, and there are scores of junctions. Most have a posted trail map and indicator arrow so you'll always know where you are. Some of the trails have also recently been marked with paint blazes, mostly to indicate various hikes that can be suggested at the visitors center. The trail work, newly coordinated by volunteers of the New York–New Jersey Trail Conference, continues, and other paint-blazed routes may be available by the time of your visit. Additionally, volunteers and NPS staff expect to number all the trail signposts in the park. As of this writing, that has not been done, but detailed plans have been made. Therefore, the numbers in brackets indicated in the text below are taken from the trail plan and may not be 100 percent accurate. If the text and the indicated number conflict, follow the text.

How to Get There

Take I-287 to exit 30B and follow US 202 north about 2 miles to Tempe Wick Road. Turn left on this road and drive 1.5 miles; this will bring you to the entrance and main visitors center. The route from the I-287 exit is well marked with National Park Service (NPS) signs.

The Trail

Leave the rear door of the visitors center and proceed to the NPS sign

Wick House

about the Wick Farm. This sign is about 80 yards behind the center at the end of a graveled path. Turn right and proceed along a wide grass path, flanked by a fence on the left that surrounds the orchard. Crossing a paved park road, continue through the opening in a wooden "snake" fence. A little farther on, take a few minutes to read the NPS sign on Hand's Brigade, and then continue straight ahead on the grass-covered woods road (named the Mendham Road Trail on the park map) that descends slightly.

After about 5 minutes, you will reach a junction marked with a signpost [55]. Turn left and proceed into the woods on the Patriot's Path, now marked with white blazes. This mixed-use trail (no bikes allowed in the national park, but horses can use the trails) is a partially completed linear park, running generally alongside the Whippany River from Mendham to East Hanover.

The trail is now a wide woods road, and the walking is easy. Take time to note the surrounding forest. The huge tulip trees are not typical of New Jersey. Since the park service took over the area in the 1930s (and probably for some time before that), there has been only inconsequential cutting of timber. The result is an unusually mature forest with a lush understory. For 10 to 15 minutes the route ambles through this forest with slight ups and downs on a generally straight course.

After skirting the side of a hill, the path becomes narrower and more traillike and arrives at the junction with the Primrose Brook Trail [33], which makes a red-blazed loop path that you will cross again as the Patriots Path continues. Continue ahead, crossing two streams flowing under wide wooden bridges (the first one with a railing and the second without). Just across the second bridge is a sign [30] and the second crossing of the red trail. Continue ahead toward

TRAIL CENTER (an interior parking lot) as the trail bears left.

You are now about ¾ hour (this time will vary widely) from the start. At the next sign [20], the Patriots Path turns left. You turn right and continue slightly uphill for 10 minutes to yet another signpost [19]. Ahead is a ranger residence, but your route turns sharply left toward the Mount Kemble Loop. A few minutes later you reach another sign [17]. Going straight ahead would shorten the hike by avoiding the loop, but, unless you're tired, make a right as the trail now starts to circle the mountain. The house you might see through the woods is the NPS ranger residence mentioned previously. Stay on the main trail [pass 16]. The sounds you now hear are from I-287—the eastern boundary of the park is close by. Off the trail on the right is a fenced-in enclosure. This one, and four others in the park, was erected in the late 1980s to keep the deer out of these small areas and to study the effect browsing has on the local vegetation.

You will shortly reach an opening in the woods with a view to the east. If you are lucky enough to have a clear day, the tall buildings in the distance are in Manhattan. The tops of the World Trade Center and the Empire State Building are visible, but the rest of New York City is hidden from view by the Watchung Mountains. This area was the camping grounds of Stark's Brigade—New Hampshire frontiersmen who fought at Bunker Hill, Trenton, and Princeton. Take a few moments to read the signs and plaques. This spot is a good one for a break or lunch. The Watchung Mountains are the reason George Washington chose this tract for his winter encampment. Some 30 miles from New York City (and Howe's British troops), they provided a fine natural defense. Lookouts posted on ridgetops could easily spot enemy troop movements toward Morristown or across the plains toward the "capital" of Philadelphia. How easy it is, if you close your ears, to imagine this area as a colonial wilderness.

After about 5 minutes of additional walking, you reach a metal gate and signpost [15]. This area is a little confusing and not well shown on the park map. Go past the metal gate onto the gravel road (private homes on the right) and continue straight on the road—following the blue markers—for about a minute, avoiding the woods road on the left, which heads into a grassy area. Look for a second woods road on the left, which is signed [14] and marked with blue. Make a left, through another metal gate and slightly downhill. You'll know you made the correct move when you reach a sign noting the Mount Kemble Loop [12].

Take the right fork, again following blue markers, slightly downhill. Soon passing by a junction [11], bear left following the blue markers, and cross a small stream running through a culvert. Just beyond the culvert, the blue path now branches off to the left [10]. Your route switches to a white-marked trail going ahead and winding uphill. You go close to the northeastern boundary of the park, where you can see more private residences to your right.

Cross paved Jockey Hollow Road [9] past the metal gates on both sides. The trail, after a gentle downhill, will soon become a moderate climb and then a fairly steep one—but the ascent is short. This section is the only one on which most novice skiers may have to walk.

Another of the many junctions is at the top of the rise [8]. This hike makes a left turn off the white-marked route.

At first the path is level, then it undulates for some 4 minutes until reaching a junction [42] with a yellow trail. Make a right over the hill toward the soldiers' huts. Be alert at this point—stay on the main trail. You can see some NPS informational signs off the trail. Go over and read them, of course, but return to the trail and avoid several left turns, including the yellow trails. You are headed for the soldiers' huts. Note the understory in this area. There are stinging nettles here, which could temporarily annoy those in short pants. The main path comes out behind the soldiers' huts [44], a major tourist attraction.

The NPS has reconstructed five huts as typical examples of those built by Continental troops. The one you come to first was for officers; the 12-bedded ones were for the troops. Some 200 huts lined this hillside during the winter of 1779–80, while perhaps as many as 1000 stood in all of Jockey Hollow. Washington ordered all of them to be constructed alike, in neat lines with officers' huts in the rear. The majority were finished by Christmas, and those for the officers in January and February.

Proceed down and across the open field to the visitors parking area where there are some informative signs explaining the harsh winter spent here.

With your back to the huts, make a left through a grass field with some mature cedar trees. Passing a boulder with a plaque commemorating the war dead buried here, you'll come to a trail post [30] at the edge of the woods with a yellow blaze. The Soldiers Hut Trail, marked in yellow, will take you back to Wick House generally paralleling Jockey Hollow Road. The trail passes through some brush, tall clinging grape vines, and blackberry bushes. The forest floor is especially lush here, and the trail is level and easy to follow.

After about 10 minutes, observe a narrower path parallel to you on the left. Look down. The stone construction with the slate top is a springhouse. The trail described here circles above it and comes to a sign for Wick House [50, 51, 52]. Continue straight ahead, gently upward. Here again are some especially tall trees and a lush forest floor. Perhaps you'll be lucky enough, as were we, to have a deer pause calmly in front of you. The trail soon ends on the paved road just below the Wick House barn [49]. Continue ahead for a few minutes. It will be easy to guide yourself back to the visitors center and the parking area.

The amount of time spent on this hike depends, of course, on the time you spend at some of the many historic areas. You could even combine the hike with a visit to Washington's Headquarters and Fort Nonsense in Morristown, also part of the NPS Historical Park. Do you have time left for another visit to the ranger? You've covered a lot of turf and are sure to have some questions.

HNZ

23

Sherman-Hoffman Sanctuary/Patriot's Path

Total distance: 3.5 miles

Hiking time: 1¾ hours

Vertical rise: 250 feet

Rating: Easy, but with some route-finding

Maps: USGS Mendham/Bernardsville; Sherman-Hoffman Santuary park map

This hike has much historical interest, and it travels through splendid woods and alongside the pristine Passaic River. The hike begins at the New Jersey Audubon Society facility in Bernardsville (11 Hardscrabble Road, PO Box 693, Bernardsville, NJ 07924; 908-766-7775). The Morristown National Historical Park at Jockey Hollow and the Cross Estate property are adjacent. The Hoffman Building, which houses the visitors center, should not be missed; it includes a well-stocked book and gift store and an observation window overlooking a bird-feeding area.

How to Get There

From the north, take exit 30B off I-287 and bear right at the end of the ramp onto North Maple Avenue. At the traffic light by the Old Mill Inn, go straight across onto Childs Road; after a short distance, bear right at the fork onto Hardscrabble Road. The route is well posted with signs reading NJ AUDUBON. The Hoffman Building driveway is on the right, approximately another mile farther on. After a visit to the Hoffman Building—usually closed on Monday, although the parking lot is open dawn to dusk, 7 days a week—turn right on Hardscrabble Road at the end of the sanctuary driveway and drive approximately another 0.25 mile to find the Sherman parking lot on the right.

The Trail

Walk to the bulletin board and look to the left to find the brown sign TRAILS; begin here. Almost immediately the trail splits. Ignore the path to the right and walk uphill on the trail to the left, signed DOGWOOD TRAIL and ENCAMPMENT TRAIL. At the time of this writing, the Encampment Trail is labeled the

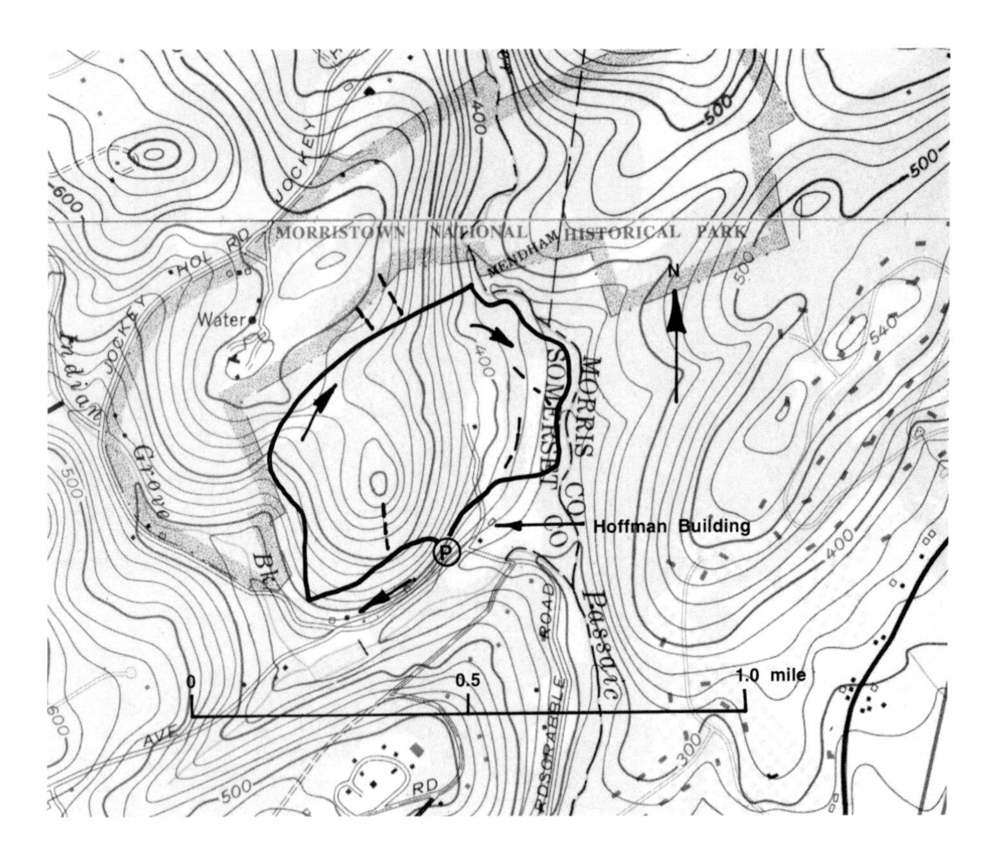

Brigade Trail on the park map, but the map will be corrected in due course.

Within 5 minutes three markers on a tree to the right indicate a junction with the Dogwood Trail. Continue straight ahead, confirming that you are still walking on the blue-marked Encampment Trail. The trail's upward trend continues for about 7 or 8 minutes before it starts downhill. Ten minutes from the start of the hike brings you to a national park boundary sign on a tree to the left. White blazes now join the blue.

A signpost is visible as the trail moves steeply downhill to a junction with the New Jersey Brigade Trail. Walk straight on past the two interpretive signs and turn right at a junction where a post holds a YOU ARE HERE map and the first tree-and-river logo of the Patriot's Path. The New Jersey Brigade section of Washington's army camped here during the winter of 1779–80, suffering greatly from cold, short rations, scant clothing, and late pay, because of roads blocked by winter conditions. It is believed this site was chosen for the iron ore and forge in the vicinity.

The trail, now marked with the Patriot's Path logo, climbs again, following a small stream on the left, and about 30 minutes into the hike reaches a T-junction. Turn right on the Patriot's Path; pass a sign indicating that a right turn would lead you back to NJ Audubon. The trail is narrower here and easy to walk upon, with many chipmunks and tulip poplar trees.

Follow the Patriot's Path past signs for trails to Jockey Hollow, the Cross Estate, and the New Jersey Brigade parking lot. (If you have time to make the detour, the gardens of the Cross Estate are peaceful and well worth a visit.) The trail descends and runs parallel to an old stone wall on the right until it reaches a small wooden bridge over the Passaic River. Two posts (YCC 80 and G7) confirm your position. By now you have been walking for about 1 hour.

Here the Passaic River is an uncontaminated brook, funneled between two hills, tumbling over rocks toward the Great Swamp and to Paterson and Newark beyond. Those familiar with the Passaic River farther downstream where it is polluted and runs through industrial areas will find this aspect difficult to believe.

You will need to do some route-finding now for a short distance, but the navigational skills required are minimal. Follow the faint trail paralleling the river downstream, passing inviting paddling pools, some tributaries, and slightly steeper river banks. Within about 5 minutes you will arrive at a bend in the river with some slabs and a good swimming hole—an excellent place to relax. Continue to follow the river downstream for approximately another 10 minutes until a yellow marker indicates you have reached the River Trail. At the time of this writing, there is a tree with a tortured root system on the near bank of the river just prior to the River Trail.

Continue downstream on the River Trail, noting the National Park Service signs on the opposite bank and a meadow to the right. At one point the trail swings away from the river to avoid a wet area and crosses another bridge sloping uphill, this time offering handrails. Without rest stops, the journey from the bridge over the Passaic River to this bridge takes approximately 25 minutes.

Immediately after this bridge crossing you will emerge onto the Field Loop at a T-junction. Turn left. The Field Loop is wide and grassy, obviously mown, and has some planking over wet patches. To the right there is evidence of old habitation, maintenance buildings, and a tree-identification sign. The trail now uses a shaded and paved road—you have reached the Dogwood Trail. To the right are the two well-kept graves of Tiffany and Gay Pasteur, horses that once belonged to Mr. Hoffman's daughters. The headstones were installed after the property became a sanctuary.

Cross the entry road to the sanctuary and walk back into the woods. A sign will confirm that this trail—the Dogwood—leads back to the parking lot. Down to the left, the sanctuary entry road merges into Hardscrabble Road; 5 more minutes of walking brings you back to your car.

SJG

24

Hacklebarney State Park

Total distance: 3 miles

Hiking time: 1½ hours

Vertical rise: 200 feet

Rating: Easy

Maps: USGS Chester/Gladstone; DEP park map

Call ahead to Hacklebarney State Park (RD 2, Long Valley, NJ 07853; 908-879-5677) for information on hours, which vary with the season. Dogs are permitted provided they are leashed. The park covers 574 acres and contains two feeder streams for the beautiful Black River in its glacial gorge. The river is stocked annually, and trout fishing is a popular pastime. No swimming is available in Hacklebarney, but the park is amply supplied with picnic tables, charcoal grills, and foundations for water fountains (unfortunately, only a few of the latter are working). The tables are concentrated at the main picnic area close to the Black River, but can also be found at many other appealing sites. The fall foliage is spectacular, and autumn is the most popular season in the park. During the 1930s, the Civilian Conservation Corps planted the stands of spruce and white pine you may see. The hiking trail described here has no particular name and is unmarked. However, the route is pleasant and easy to follow. You may need to watch for poison ivy.

There are two possible explanations of how the name Hacklebarney originated. One theory is that it is a combination of two Native American words—*haki,* meaning "ground," and *bonihen,* "to put wood on the fire." The other conjecture is that employees at the local iron mine constantly heckled a quick-tempered foreman named Barney Tracey; over time, "to heckle Barney" evolved into Hacklebarney. Supposition apart, the park is in a delightful section of New Jersey.

There are errors on the relevant topographical maps. The name "Hacklebarney State Park" on the Chester map is printed incorrectly; it should read "Morris County Park." Also, the Black River is wrongly labeled "Lamington River." The latter error is the result of a name change, and the

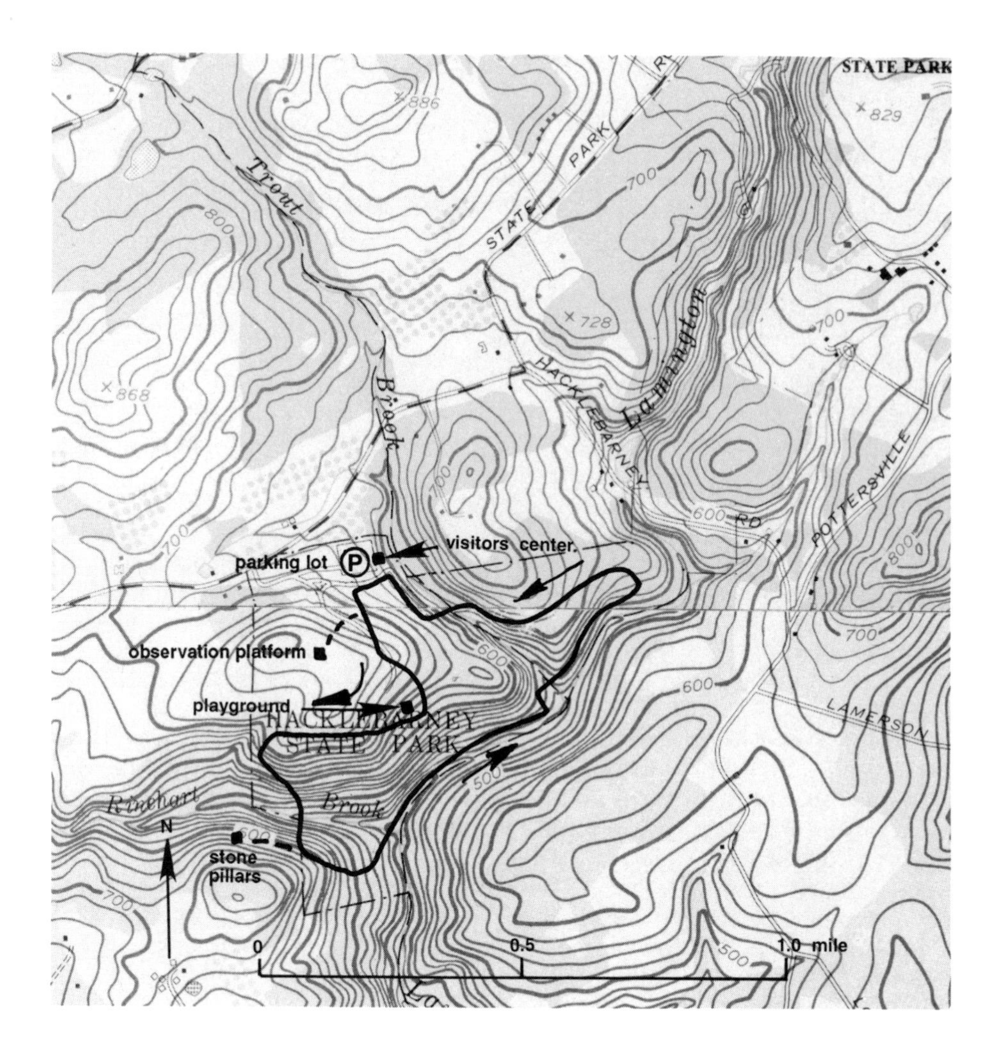

river is throughout this hike description correctly referred to as the Black.

How to Get There

From the north, take exit 27A off I-80 onto US 206 south to the town of Chester. From the south, you can exit I-287 at the Bedminster exit for US 202 and US 206 and drive north to Chester.

In Chester, turn west onto NJ 24 at the traffic light. There is a small sign at this junction indicating the turn for Hacklebarney State Park. Approximately 1 mile from the traffic light, pass the old Cooper Gristmill, cross a bridge, and turn left at the green sign. Immediately there is another sharp left turn onto a road through a pleasant residential area paralleling the Black River. After another 2 miles, the road splits; an apple orchard and farm store are on the corner. Turn right onto paved State Park Road and travel for 0.75 mile until a sign on the left indicates the entrance to the park. You can obtain a park map at the visitors center.

The Trail

Walk to the opposite end of the parking lot from the visitors center, continue on the entrance road approximately a third of the way back to the gatehouse, and turn left on a grassy patch through some large wooden posts. Almost immediately, cross a woods road and an open area with a stand of white pine on the left, and head for the gravel road uphill to the right. About 3 minutes into the hike, at the top of the rise, ignore the dirt road and bear left on gravel. Lettering on the brown sign indicates that the route is to the Black River and playground. Within a few minutes, a side trip to the observation platform is possible by taking the wide, grassy track uphill to the right. This option is new and unsigned at the time of this writing, though there is a wooden post to the left of the entry. According to park management, a sign has been ordered. The observation platform is a sturdy wooden structure and provides a view of the peaceful countryside unobtainable elsewhere in the park.

Return to the main trail and continue walking toward the children's playground. The concrete rectangular block on the left is part of the park water supply. The playground has recently been rejuvenated with new equipment. The open space is furnished with wooden benches and contains a superb cedar tree.

At the lower end of the playground, walk in front of the two benches and proceed to the right along a wide grassy road, which parallels a gravel road for a short distance. Within a few minutes the trail narrows, though the walking is still easy. Signs on the trees indicate that this stretch is in a natural area, and violets and other wildflowers are plentiful in spring. Descending a short way on stone steps, the trail nears Rinehart Brook and within about 20 minutes from the observation platform brings you to a fork. A sign indicates a route back to the parking lot. There is an abandoned water fountain at this junction. Turn right and cross the bridge over Rinehart Brook.

Turn left after the bridge onto a wide trail that climbs slightly above the brook. Within about 4 minutes a similar trail joins from the left. The hike will use this latter trail, but for now proceed straight ahead for a few minutes to arrive at the park boundary, marked by two large stone pillars (probably a relic of the original gatehouse). One is inscribed IN MEMORY OF SUSAN PARKER BORIE 1835–1913 and the other HACKLEBARNEY MEMORIAL STATE PARK. The Black River Fish and Game Club own the adjoining property, and even the river is flagged NO TRESPASSING at this point. Enjoy the view of the Black River, but do not go farther.

Thirty-two acres of land were donated by Adolphe Borie in 1924. The original tract was dedicated to his mother, Susan Parker Borie, and her granddaughter, Susan Peterson Borie. The latter Susan survived the Titanic disaster as a girl with most of her family by boarding the second-to-last lifeboat. Susan's father, Ryerson, donated another 90 acres in 1929, stipulating no camping.

Return to the junction and turn right, walking downhill toward the Black River. After 5 minutes you cross a tributary at river level on wooden planks, then almost immediately cross another substantial bridge over Rinehart Brook. The trail now follows the Black River and is narrow, rocky, and sometimes indistinct. Pick your way for about 10 minutes along the river as it chatters on its tannin-colored way. This bank is very popular with anglers, particularly in the area called Three Pools. After walking up a short rise to the left, continue on a gravel road for a short distance. The sign here indicates that the parking lot may be reached by turning left. Turn right. The trail becomes rockier again, still hugging the riverbank, until it reaches a popular picnic area where rest rooms are available.

Make a left turn at the picnic area. Do not cross the first bridge across Trout Brook to the right, but walk up the wider road for a short distance, seeking an indistinct footpath to the right. Here, head for a picnic table (remember that tables can be moved, so this instruction may be unreliable) and another wooden bridge. Trout Brook is on the right at this point. Cross the bridge and continue along a narrow, rocky trail with the brook on the left. A flight of stone steps leads up to a wider trail. Turn left and, as you top the rise after about 15 minutes, the waterfall and another wooden bridge come into view. This waterfall is another popular spot, and rock-sitting at this attractive place is an agreeable activity.

A sign indicates that a turn to the left would cross the bridge and lead back to the parking lot, but do not follow that route. Instead continue straight ahead on a gravel road. On the way, two plank bridges span Trout Brook, still on your left; a little farther on, rest rooms will be passed on the right. After you make a bend to the left and cross a bridge, a flight of 50 wide stone steps confronts you; there are benches at the halfway mark. At the top of these steps, turn right and walk back to the visitors center and your car.

SJG

25

Merrill Creek Reservoir

Total distance: 8.5 miles

Hiking time: 4 hours

Vertical rise: 150 feet

Rating: Easy

Maps: USGS Bloomsbury; Merrill Creek Reservoir Trail Map

The Merrill Creek Reservoir (34 Merrill Creek Road, Washington, NJ 07882; 908-454-1213) is located on Scotts Mountain in Harmony Township, Warren County. The area is designed and managed specifically for low-impact recreational use—possibly because of the opposition to the reservoir's planned enlargement in the late 1980s.

The present reservoir replaced a smaller one built by Ingersoll Rand to supply water to its plant in nearby Phillipsburg in 1903. Ground was broken for the new reservoir in September 1985, and, because of the workers' long hours—sometimes as many as 20 a day—the reservoir was completed in April 1988. Seven electric utility companies combined their efforts on this project. The 650-acre lake thus formed is stocked with a variety of game fish; it has a maximum depth of 225 feet and more than 5 miles of shoreline. The reservoir stores 16 billion gallons of water for release to the Delaware River during low-water periods to augment the river water used by its generating stations. A 3-mile pipeline, 57 inches in diameter and about 6 feet below ground, links the reservoir to the Delaware. Water is pumped up the mountain from the river by three 8000-horsepower pumps and returned through the same pipeline when needed. The inlet/outlet tower controls water flow. Ports are provided along the tower to permit water to be released from whatever depth best matches the river's temperature.

A 290-acre wildlife preserve surrounds the shore of the reservoir but is only a small part of the 2000 acres of open space surrounding the lake. The visitors center contains an excellent display of the methods used to move the water. Another exhibit uses a unique method to illustrate in sand the tracks left by wild animals. A large collection of animal skulls is displayed in a glass case, and in the back room stuffed birds are suspended from the ceiling.

This hike is easy walking, largely on flat, wide trails, but with a few rocky sections. The trails used are the Perimeter (black) Trail; a bit of the Creek (orange) Trail; parts of the Orchard (green), Farmstead (yellow), and Timber (red) Trails; and almost all of the Shoreline (blue) Trail. Neither bicycles or horses are permitted on the trails, and only electric-motor-driven boats are allowed on the water.

How to Get There

From I-78 take exit 4 (Warren Glen/ Stewartsville). Turn right at the bottom of the exit ramp and drive 1.8 miles on County Road 638 (CR 638) to a blinking stoplight in Stewartsville. Turn right onto CR 638 (Washington Street, then New Village Road). Drive 2.4 miles to NJ 57. Cross diagonally and proceed up Montana Mountain Road for 2 miles. Bear left at a fork. Your destination is signed from this point. Stay on Montana Mountain Road, which makes a left turn after 0.3 mile. The boat ramp is straight ahead, but take the road that veers to the right to the visitors center. You

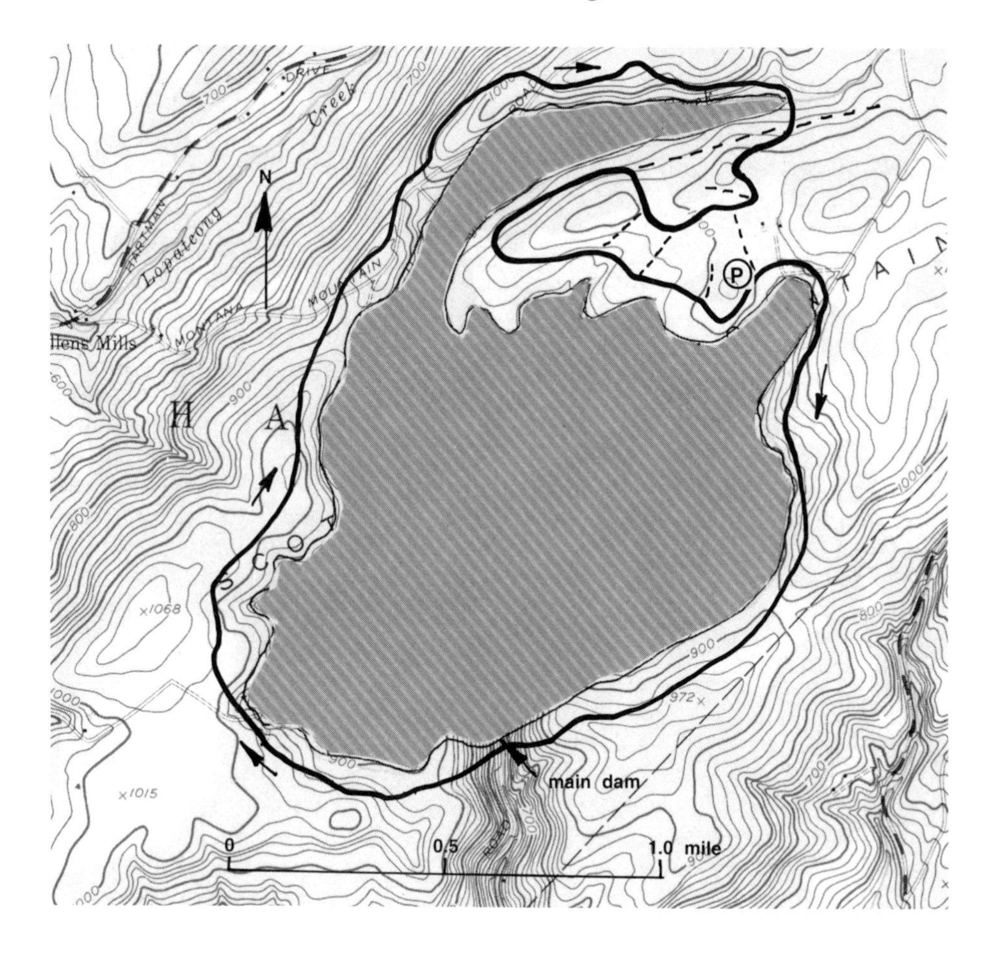

can obtain a copy of the park map here.

The Trail

With your back to the front door of the visitors center (the lake is to your right), proceed toward the hiker-and-arrow sign immediately across the blacktop and to the right. On the first tree there are two markers, one green (labeled MCR), the other black. This first small section of the hike is dual-marked. Do not take the green trail to the left; head downhill to the boat ramp and parking area. Cross the wooden bridge. The route is now marked in black.

Leave the dock and lake on the right, go straight across the paved area toward the DO NOT ENTER sign, find the black marker, pass through the metal gate, and walk slightly uphill on a wide gravel-and-dirt road across a field. Bluebirds, a common sight at Merrill Creek Reservoir, like to nest in the open, and nesting boxes are erected at every opportunity. The first is on a slope to the left of the trail. The two dams that carry the Perimeter Trail are visible. A gentle upgrade, followed by an equally gentle downgrade, brings the Southeast Dike into view. Ignore the trail leading down to the left (it eventually crosses a boardwalk), and walk straight ahead across the Southwest Dike. At the end of the dike the trail heads slightly uphill again and becomes narrower. It is only lightly marked in this section, but continue straight, ignoring any other path coming in from the left or right, until you approach the Main Dam about 30 minutes from the start.

The park map indicates a trail downhill to the left. This trail involves a steep climb back up, however, so to avoid the extra effort, go straight across the Main Dam, wire-gated at both ends. Halfway along on the left is a wooden instrument access staircase, closed to the public. The pipe under the rocks is used to release water from the reservoir into Lower Merrill Creek; the flow is regulated at 3 cubic feet per second.

Ten more minutes brings you to the end of the Main Dam. Go through the gate and turn right at the base of the hill facing you. Black markers lead you through a stand of tall pine trees planted in rows. Poison ivy in vine form covers many of these trees; it is easy to spot because of the furry appearance of the vine. Stay very clear at all times of the year.

Continue walking through hardwoods for approximately another 10 minutes until you reach a T-junction. Turn right, toward the lake. Ignore the trail, passed shortly, that leads to the water's edge. Soon a flat expanse to the right of the trail with some brickwork, a large white pine, forsythia, daffodils, daylilies, and periwinkle denotes the site of an old homestead. The trail is a little rockier here and climbs slightly until it curves toward a parking lot to the left. By now you have been walking for about an hour. The observation deck, a large wooden structure at the water's edge, is a pleasant place to take a break. It can be reached via a side trail to the right that leads downhill to the lakeshore.

Backtrack and continue to follow the black markers gently downhill. In about 10 minutes the trail makes a 90-degree turn to the left and, as it approaches a paved road, turns again, this time to the right. Continue until you have walked across Northwest Dike 1, passing the Inlet/Outlet Tower on the lakeshore to the right. Go through the gate at the end of the dike and walk across the parking lot to admire the views across the reservoir. Here there is a bulletin board and a porta-john screened by a wooden fence.

Follow the arrow on the sign and walk through the metal protective barrier to Northwest Dike 2. The view across the valley to the west includes two gaps. The more northerly is the Delaware Water Gap, and it is through the tunnel under this valley that the water makes its way back and forth between the reservoir and the Delaware River. From this vantage point you also look down on paved Fox Farm Road.

At the end of the dike, watch for a wooden post carrying black markers that indicate a right turn back into the woods on a rockier trail. Skirt a dry creek bed from the left and continue right, close to the lakeshore. In this section a dilapidated deer blind can be seen among the dead and submerged trees, indicating that the water level was once much lower. Look as well for tulip trees with their long straight trunks, a spruce fir stand, and, at the top of a short rise, a large tulip poplar to the right of the trail with a bulbous base and bark that grows in interesting patterns. Naturalists cannot account for the way this tree has grown.

In about 45 minutes the trail splits. Hiking policy indicates that the upper trail, which is the marked route, should be taken, but both lead to a wooden bridge over Upper Merrill Creek. This bridge incorporates seating into its design and is a good place for a lunch break. Within another couple of minutes you will reach the junction with the Creek Trail, marked in orange; the signboard indicates that you have walked 4.9 miles.

Turn left on the Creek Trail and, when you arrive at a junction, ignore both the old trail straight ahead and the orange-marked trail to the left. Walk to the right on the Orchard Trail (green markers). It meanders a little and, after about 15 minutes, emerges onto a gravel road. The trail immediately opposite leads to a substantial wildlife blind. Visit the blind, backtrack, and turn right, following green markers that shortly lead to the ruins of Upper Beers Farm (#5 on the park map).

At the farm's signboard, turn right behind the ruined building onto the Farmstead (yellow) Trail, noting the lilac trees along the edge of the field. If you wish to cut the hike short at this point, follow the green-marked trail that crosses the main entrance road and leads back to the visitors center. Otherwise, follow the yellow markers. Within 5 minutes, turn right onto the red-marked Timber Trail, which crosses the Farmstead Trail. The park has been asked to mark this turn more clearly. At the time of this writing there was neither signboard nor marker to indicate this turn onto the red trail. You can confirm that you are on the correct trail, however, by turning around a few feet from the junction (facing back) to look for a red marker on a tree to the left of the trail.

Within 10 minutes you will reach a junction with the blue Shoreline Trail. The park map does not clearly indicate the color of the trail to the left (trail colors may be changed soon). However, turn right onto a wide and easy trail that leads downhill toward the water, paralleling a rock wall on the left. After another 5 minutes you reach the end of the red trail at a junction with the orange-marked Creek Trail. The red and the orange markers fade to a similar color, and sometimes the orange markers are not labeled MCR. Do not go ahead on the Creek Trail, but bear left onto the blue trail. This section is perhaps the

Looking through the wildlife observation blind

hardest on the hike. Across the water is the trail you used earlier to reach the bridge over Upper Merrill Creek. Trees in this area were deliberately submerged to create a better habitat when the reservoir was scoured and quarried. Northwest Dike 2 is also visible from here. A side trail leads down to the water's edge, indicating that the trails in this area were relocated uphill when the water level rose. This relocation probably accounts for the more difficult walking.

Continuing gradually uphill, emerge into an open field with views of the pumping tower and often geese and other waterfowl. The trail is located close to the trees that border the upper side of the field. Within 20 minutes from the junction of the Shoreline and Creek Trails, a wooden bench provides an enjoyable resting place. The tall post with the nesting platform is intended to attract ospreys.

Walk downhill until, almost at the water's edge, the blue markers direct you left onto a wide woods road. Soon a side trail to the right leads to another wildlife observation blind, this time on the water's edge. It will take about 45 minutes to get from this point back to the visitors center.

A ruined lime kiln (#4 on the park map) stands at the next intersection, one of many in the area. Lime kilns were built on high ground where timber was plentiful and where the elevation caused an updraft, rather than close to the source of the raw materials needed for making lime. The kilns resembled huge stone fireplaces and sometimes served more than one farmstead. A wagon path was built to the top and the kiln loaded with alternate layers of fuel—usually wood—and limestone chunks. When the fire was lit, temperatures frequently reached 2000 degrees Fahrenheit, sometimes breaking up the stone with an explosive bang. The burnt lime filtered down and was used on the fields as a fertilizer. The word *limelight* is thought to have been derived from the light of the kiln when in action.

Continue on the blue trail until the yellow trail joins at the Cathers/Shafer Farm site. The ruins here include the Bank Barn Farm and Farmyard, the Shaffer-Tenant Farmhouse, the Spring House, and, a little farther down the trail, the Cathers House (#3, #2, and #1 on the park map). The pond is a man-made bog created in the 1980s to replace habitat lost in the reservoir construction. The bog turtle is an endangered species in New Jersey and was found in the inundation area. Nonnative grasses, which arrived here along with the soil used to build the dam that created the bog, still need to be eradicated, and studies of the bog turtle continue. Small transmitters are glued to the top of turtles' shells, but tracking their movements is difficult because the animals spend most of their time beneath the mud, only emerging to breed and bask in the May sunlight. The bog is fed by the spring and, because the spring still functions, the trail has been elevated on two sections of boardwalk. Do not leave the blue trail. If you wish to take a shortcut here, the next junction to the left leads to a right turn on the red trail, and thence to the visitors center. Otherwise, go straight ahead on the Shoreline Trail, still following the blue markers, to another bench at the water's edge. From this point the blue markers take you inland where, at the top of a rise, the red trail joins in and the visitors center can be seen immediately ahead.

At the back of the visitors center is a small garden whose plants were chosen to attract butterflies, bees, hummingbirds, and beneficial insects: a pleasant place to unwind after the hike.

SJG

PIEDMONT PROVINCE

26

Palisades

Total distance: 7 miles

Hiking time: 4 hours

Vertical rise: 400 feet

Rating: Easy

Maps: USGS Central Park (NY/NJ); NYNJTC Hudson Palisades Trails #4A; WB #4; HRM #24; Park map (Palisades Interstate Park Commission)

The Palisades Interstate Park Commission was created in 1900, mainly to curb the opening of quarries supplying traprock for the concrete used in building roads and skyscrapers. Most of the 2472-acre Palisades State Park is in New Jersey. The average width of the parkland between the Hudson River and the clifftop is less than 0.2 mile. Apart from the talus at their bases, the cliffs are well wooded with a variety of trees and shrubs, some of them remaining from former estate gardens. The highest clear cliff is 520 vertical feet.

Numerous old woods trails complement the two main trails that run the length of the Palisades. This hike uses parts of the Shore Path, marked in white, and the Long Path, marked in blue. Enjoyment of the Shore Path is enhanced by the sound of lapping water, and on both the upper and lower levels there are many superb views of the river and its boaters.

How to Get There

The hike begins at the administration building of the Palisades Interstate Park Commission (Alpine, NJ 07620; 201-768-1360). Access is east of exit 2 off the Palisades Parkway, approximately 7 miles north of the George Washington Bridge. On weekends you may park in the large lot to the north of the building, but during the week parking may be limited, so check inside with the police department.

The Trail

At the wooden sign near the road with NEW JERSEY HEADQUARTERS PALISADES PARK COMMISSION and the blue Long Path marker on it, walk south. After a very short road walk—Long Path markers are painted in the gutter—turn left, downhill and away from the road, on a wide path signed PATH TO THE RIVER and NO BIKES. There are frequent water bars; a seasonal stream runs on the left.

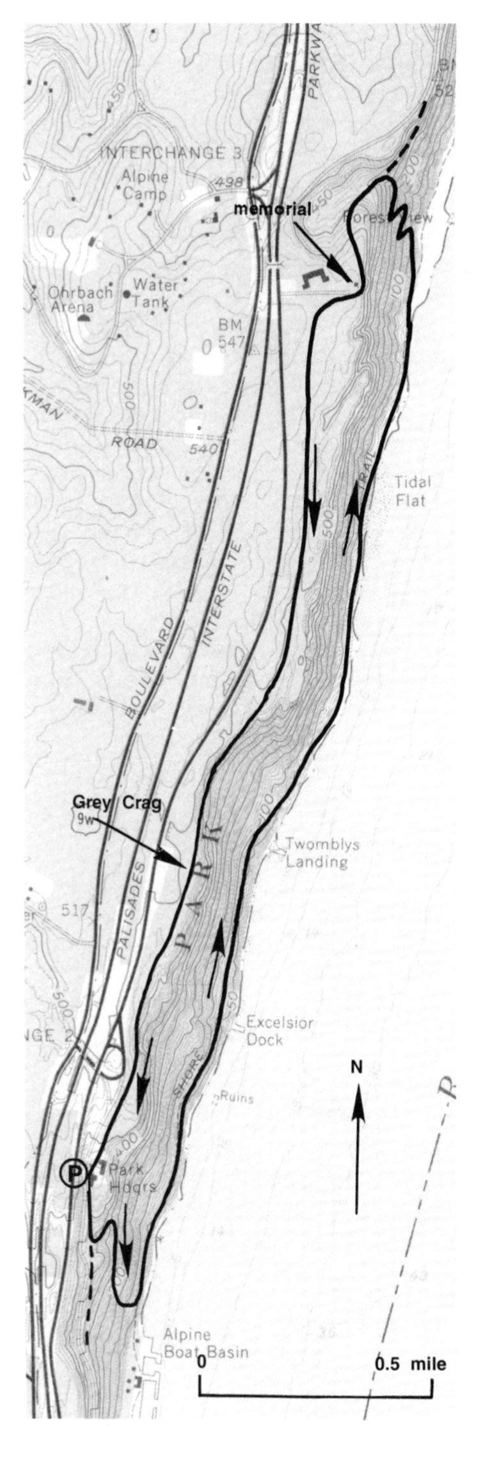

The Long Path turns to go through the stone tunnel on the right, but your trail runs steadily downhill in a gentle zigzag. Passing a stream bridged with concrete on the right, the trail bends left and reaches a T-junction and the first view of the Hudson River. This junction is with the Shore Path, marked by a white blaze. Turn left and pass over a stream with one of many cascades you will notice on your walk. The main cascade is protected by a circular stone wall.

There are several exploratory side trips in this area. The first takes you up two flights of steps to the left of the trail that lead through a gate in a wire fence to two small, rock-constructed buildings. Side trips to the riverbank include one on the right that leads to a small rocky beach with views of the supporting pillars of George Washington Bridge and of Yonkers, immediately across the river.

At the rock signpost, continue on the Shore Path, now protected against erosion by large boulders on the left. The trail runs closer to the water's edge and is very attractive. Opposite Excelsior Dock, 30 steps to the left lead to the Excelsior Flats Picnic Area, which is supplied with picnic tables, fireplaces, and an outhouse. At this point beware of poison ivy, which is widespread.

During the next stretch of the trail there are many signs of human activity. Several streams run under cemented rock covers; two painted-over signs on rocks indicate the way up steps to where buildings once existed. Soon you'll see many attractive lunch sites, each with a natural rock table and chairs. This area features many cascades tumbling over man-made rock walls. It is known as Twombly's Landing, after the man who donated this section to the park. Twombly's Landing is believed to have been a Native American campsite because of the layers of oyster shells found here. Because of the prevalence of *Giardia lamblia* and other pollutants, we do not recommend that you use water from the two places labeled DRINKING WATER. One cookout fireplace is provided at Twombly's.

Moving slightly uphill, the path is again edged on the left by rocks. Soon comes the first view of the cliffs. These outcrops are the two bastions of Ruckman Point, and it is interesting to know that in a little while you will be looking down from them to the Shore Path. Watch the cliffs to the north at this point to get a good view of Indian Head; at river level, observe the Tappan Zee Bridge in the distance.

Shortly after this point, take the steep trail on the left. This path is not signposted, but there is a large blowdown on the river side of the trail, and a second one just beyond. The sections cut from the center of this second blowdown have been left on the right side of the Shore Path. To make quite sure you take the correct path, look for a rock a few feet up the trail painted with orange hieroglyphics.

After climbing a few minutes, you will squeeze past a large rock on the left marked STATELINE LOOKOUT. The cemented rock steps that form the trail climb in a switchback, marked blue on white by the Scout organization, to a trail junction. A stream crossing is ahead; to the right is a Long Path marker on a tree and a boulder once painted with trail directions. Ignore the routes to the state line and river trails and bear left on the trail to US 9W, climbing uphill and south on three short flights of steps. You are following both the Long Path parakeet aqua blazes and the Scout blue-and-white blazes. The trail is called the Forest View, but you may find that the markers are very faint.

The stone lookout memorial of the New Jersey Federation of Women's Clubs is at the top of this climb among mature trees. Shortly after, the blue-on-white Scout trail turns right at a junction and after 5 minutes crosses a stone bridge over the Palisades Interstate Parkway to a small parking area on the side of US 9W. From here, proceed straight ahead on the Long Path, ignoring the woods road to the left. When you see the Palisades Parkway in the distance, the trail veers left and is soon joined by another woods road from the right. There is a broken wall at the cliff edge. This is Ruckman Point. On the cliff edge there is a carving on the rock face dated June 1981; the Shore Path is visible below.

The trail goes slightly downhill to a boggy area with a stream. The damper, rockier section continues until you cross a larger stream on a substantial wooden bridge, then a boardwalk over a culvert. Just beyond, look for a short trail to the left leading toward the cliff edge with a super overlook of a waterfall pouring through a cleft. Take care, as there is no protective fencing. In the spring, drifts of snowdrops bloom here.

Only a short distance down the main trail, watch for a small footpath to the left, leading over a bridge to a secluded lookout called Grey Crag. This section is separated from the main cliff and gives a tremendous feeling of isolation. Again, watch for poison ivy.

Tall maples mark the next section of the trail, which runs very close to the parkway until it finally emerges into a grassy area. Cross this to reach the administration building parking lot and your car.

SJG

27

Watchung Reservation

Total distance: 6 miles

Hiking time: 4 hours

Vertical rise: 500 feet

Rating: Moderate

Maps: USGS Chatham/Roselle; Union County Department of Parks and Recreation park map

Watchung Reservation is a 2000-acre patch of wooded land straddling the first and second Watchung Ridges in central New Jersey. Along with South Mountain Reservation and Eagle Rock Reservation to the north, Watchung has preserved what was for many years a long wall of mountain wilderness overlooking the flat plains that lead toward New York City and the Atlantic Ocean. General George Washington used the long Watchung Ridge as a natural fortification against the British during the Revolutionary War. He planted a number of lookouts along the ridge and kept his troops safely to the west in Loantaka and Jockey Hollow. Much earlier, the Watchung Ridge formed the eastern rim of the basin that contained glacial Lake Passaic, a 30-by-10-mile lake of which the Great Swamp is but a remnant.

Although it sits in the middle of suburbia, Watchung Reservation is large enough for a good workout and also contains a number of interesting features, most of which you will see on this hike. Not that long ago, the construction of I-78 on the boundary of the reservation made access easier for many hikers not from the immediate area. More recently Watchung has been the scene of user conflicts. Mountain bike users loved it so much that they seriously damaged the trails. Today bikes are not permitted on trails in the reservation.

Watchung Reservation is laced with wide lanes and horse trails. Several shorter marked trails are found in the vicinity of the Trailside Museum. The longest trail is the white-blazed Sierra Trail, formerly marked with Xs, now with white squares. It is 10 miles long, has many ups and downs, and passes near just about every interesting feature the reservation has to offer. You will use a large portion of this trail for your hike.

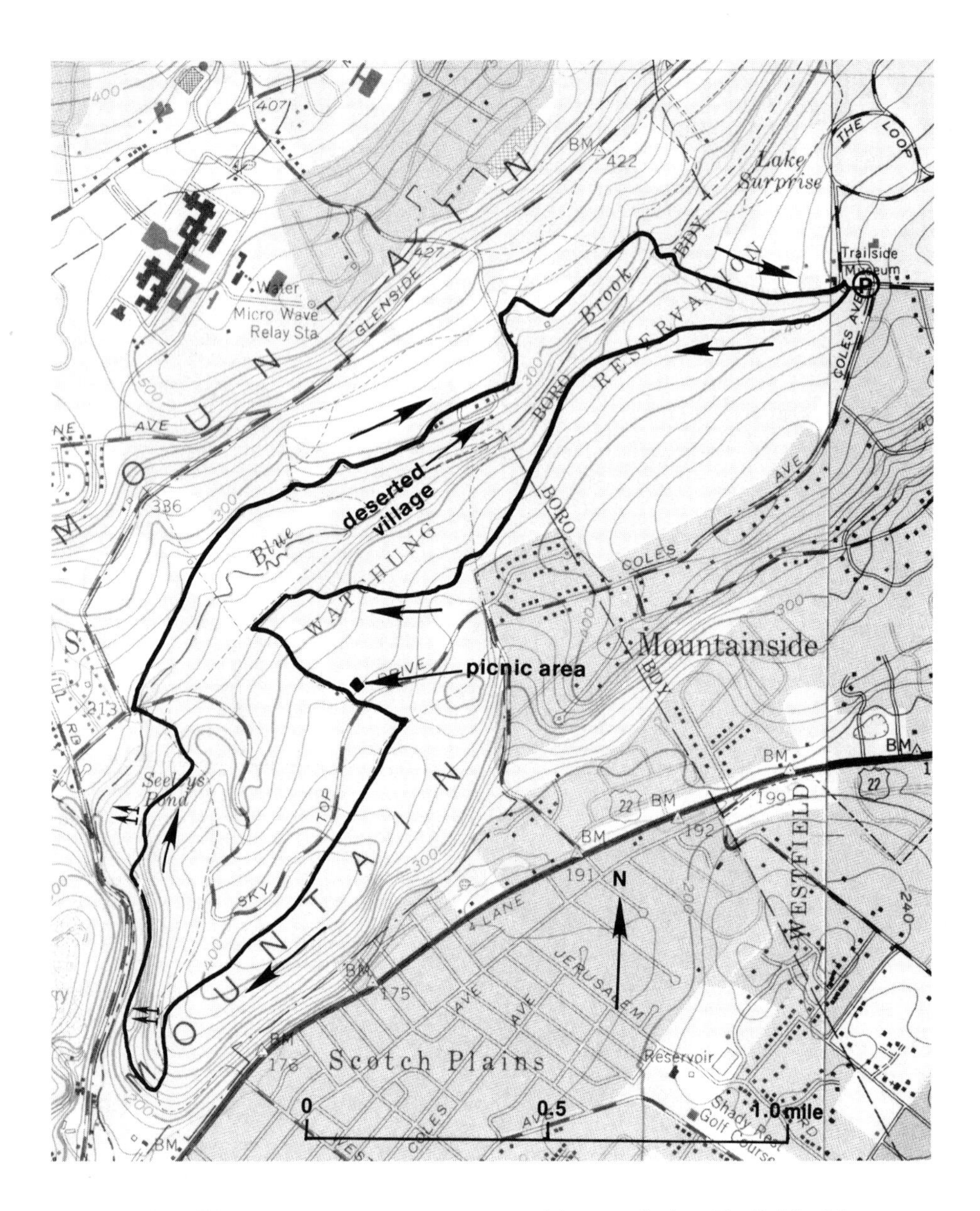

How to Get There
From I-78 eastbound (exit 44), turn left at the traffic light onto Glenside Avenue. In 1.2 miles turn right into the reservation (County Road 645), passing Lake Surprise and some picnic areas. At the circle turn right onto Summit Road, then right onto New Providence Road. Directly ahead is parking and the Trailside Museum. Sketch maps of the reservation are available at the museum and also from a box near the parking area.

The Trail
The trailhead, marked NATURE TRAILS, is located on the left side of the paved road that passes the museum. Begin

your hike on the Sierra Trail, marked by white squares painted on trees. In addition, a green trail begins here and runs concurrently with the Sierra for a short distance. As you cross the brook on a very well-made bridge, note the exposure of bedrock in the streambed. These rocks are basalt, or traprock, which has been quarried extensively throughout the Watchung Mountains.

Once over the brook, bear right following the white markers. Pay close attention to the markers in this section. There are numerous paths, and it is easy to lose the correct one. The trail heads gradually downhill after this turn and then bears to the left through an area that is sometimes wet. Watch closely for markers (ignore the orange markers) as the trail makes a subtle jog to the right.

The Sierra Trail takes you along the rim of a small glen quite beautiful in any season. On the left, the brook is eroding the red shales that overlay the basalt. You will soon encounter exposed basaltic bedrock, and—as the glen widens—hemlocks. In this section, a blue-marked trail co-mingles with the white trail for a while.

After descending through the hemlocks in this beautiful section of the reservation, cross the brook, still following white markers, and begin to climb. Below, Blue Brook makes an oxbow bend as it snakes through the drainage between ridges. As you climb, watch the markers carefully. There is a steep climb at one point, which then levels off in a pleasant mixture of deciduous trees and hemlocks. Farther along, the Sierra Trail comes to another smaller glen with some fairly large boulders and even a grassy area. This spot is good for a break and perhaps some exploration. Deer are plentiful in this reservation—perhaps you've spotted one already.

Still following white markers, cross the brook and climb the opposite bank. After this small climb, the trail levels off and, as it swings to the right, passes a residential area. Next, cross a gravel road, head back into the woods, and begin another long, gradual loss of elevation. There are no hemlocks here, and the ground is higher and drier. Notice on the descent that where the trail has been deeply eroded there are some exposures of shale and sandstone, hardened mud, and silt deposited during the Triassic period. Later, volcanic magma intruded into these shales, forming the erosion-resistant, basaltic Watchung Mountains. At the bottom of the descent, the trail comes to a dirt road and turns left. Tall cedars line the west side of this road, which was once a driveway. Within a few hundred feet, the trail turns left and cuts back into the woods in a pine plantation, heading uphill once more.

Look carefully for the markers here; the trail jogs slightly to the right and then heads straight through a row of tall pines. This is a peaceful environment. Little patches of sunlight decorate the uniform brown carpet of pine needles. These red pines were planted in the 1930s as part of a Civilian Conservation Corps project, and though some are shorter than others, all are the same age. If you are lucky, you might spot one of the owls that nest here. Too soon the trail emerges from the pines, swings to the left, and, after crossing a small bridge, enters a picnic area with a shelter. The trail leads through this cleared area on a gravel service road, crosses Sky Top Drive, and reenters the woods on a dirt road.

At the first intersection, bear right and begin a long, nearly level walk on a dirt road that parallels Sky Top Drive. Along with white markers of the Sierra Trail are some cross-country ski markers of green and white. You will cross several intersections before you

Pine plantation at Watchung Reservation

arrive at a section very close to the actual summit of the first Watchung Mountain. Bushwhack to the left to obtain a glimpse of civilization through the trees. From here the trail begins to head downhill, and, after another 10 minutes of walking, you will come to a small overlook to the south and west. Here you can see—and often hear—the effects of quarrying in the Watchung Hills during the week when the quarries are operating. Traprock, the popular term for basalt gravel, has been used for years to pave New Jersey's roads and highways.

At the overlook, the trail swings to the left and heads down the mountain. Now the sounds of civilization are more apparent. The trail makes a sharp right at the bottom, just before a house, and may not be marked very well. This section of trail is washed out in places and tends to be clogged with leaves and branches washed down by the rains. Soon you will see Green Brook on the left and, beyond that, New Providence Road. Green Brook is a stocked trout stream and attracts many anglers. As the trail heads north along the bank of the brook, it becomes rockier. The trail, the brook, and the road all pass together through a gap in the long wall of the Watchungs.

Above you, you will see some outcroppings of basalt on your right. Look closely at the rock and observe the way it forms hexagonal columns much like the Palisades of the Hudson, only on a smaller scale. Next you will reach the remains of an old mill foundation. The mill that once stood at this site used the power of the brook to make paper; later it held a 10,000-gallon still operated by bootleggers whose product is said to have been world renowned. The brook drops quite a few feet in a short distance here and once was diverted to turn a mill wheel. Look around to find where the water was channeled away from the brook and over to the mill. The trail, which is not well marked here, swings to the right and steeply uphill after leaving the ruins of the mill.

At the top of the climb, another rock outcrop offers more views to the south and west. I-78 is clearly visible. During the late 1970s and early 1980s, many conservation-minded people tried to prevent the construction of I-78, which planners had routed through the western and northern section of the reservation. It was a major regional issue that was finally settled by replacing the land used for the highway, which totaled about 70 acres, with land from a nearly adjacent rock quarry. With the deal came $3.6 million for the upkeep and development of the reservation. The highway was also built low in the ground and is flanked by walls that muffle the sound somewhat. In one place, a cut-and-cover structure (a 220-foot-wide bridge with soil and plants) allows animals to cross the highway safely; we were told that it didn't take the large deer population long to find the way across.

From this overlook, the trail turns right and heads back toward the woods into a grove of old hemlocks. Now following a woods road, the trail bears to the left heading gradually downhill. Just before reaching Sky Top Drive again, the markers lead to a shortcut on the left, ending at the paved road near a bridge at Seeleys Pond. Head toward the bridge.

Cross the bridge and immediately bear right to find the trail that heads back into the woods. This point is at the edge of the reservation, and suburbia is just across the street. The trail soon becomes a footpath in some fairly dense vegetation. In places it is crowded by wild roses; you will find violets and spring beauties where an occasional spring keeps the ground moist. Watch for poison ivy in this section, both as a vine on trees and as a bush.

After a few minutes you will come to a quiet spot where some large hemlocks dominate the land between two small brooks. The trail next crosses the second brook and makes a left on a badly eroded path. Almost immediately, at a small clearing, the trail swings sharply right and heads back into the woods, crossing several small streams that run only in the spring or after a rain. As the trail gradually gains elevation, it also becomes wider and more badly eroded.

Continue on this eroded path, heading gradually uphill. At the right turn just before the trail passes a hemlock grove on the right, you will find a partially exposed conglomerate boulder. This stone, which technically is Shawangunk conglomerate, is not native to the area—it was dragged south by the glacier for a distance of more than 20 miles.

Suddenly you will see a large building facing you—you've entered Deserted Village, also known as Feltsville and Glenside Park. From 1845 to 1860, David Felt owned and operated a paper mill on Blue Brook. Feltsville was a factory town then, but when the mill closed, it became Glenside Park, a Victorian retreat with lawn tennis and pure water. Some say there is a salt brook and a magnesium spring in the vicinity, which may have been why the area was made a miniresort between 1882 and 1916. In 1991 a New Jersey Historic Trust grant was awarded for the preservation of Feltsville as a unique resource.

After passing the last two houses (one with a wooden tower attached to it), the trail bears right, turning off the road and onto a dirt road. It immediately turns again to the right and onto a footpath. In a few hundred yards is a small Revolutionary War cemetery where members of the Willcocks family, the descendants of the original settler Peter Willcox, are buried. William Willcox was a judge and advocate of the Revolutionary War, and he died in 1800. Joseph Badgley was a private in the First New Jersey Regiment and died in 1785. John Willcocks, Sr. died on November 22, 1776. He was in the Light Horse Company of the New Jersey militia.

Leaving the gravesites, continue along the footpath, following the white markers as the trail snakes through the woods at a nearly constant elevation. Soon the trail begins to descend, then meets a horse trail. Your trip on the Sierra Trail is over. Turn right here and cross the bridge and Blue Brook. Where the road swings to the left, bear right onto a footpath that leads to a log bridge and blue markers. Do not cross the bridge; follow the blue markers upstream, keeping the brook on your right. After a short distance, the blue markers change to orange. Continue uphill and keep the brook to your right. After a few more minutes you will reach a gate and a paved road. Bear right here and walk uphill. The museum and then the parking area will be on your left.

BCS

28

Great Swamp

Total distance: 4 miles

Hiking time: 2½ hours

Vertical rise: None

Rating: Easy

Maps: USGS Chatham; Great Swamp NWR (US Department of the Interior, Fish and Wildlife Service)

The Great Swamp National Wildlife Refuge (NWR) (RD 1, Box 152, Basking Ridge, NJ 07920; 201-425-1222) was established in 1960 following a successful battle to defeat a proposed jetport. It was this controversy that enabled a local committee of the North American Wildlife Foundation to raise more than $1 million to purchase 3000 acres, which now form the heart of the 6818-acre refuge. In 1968, the eastern half of the NWR was designated by Congress a wilderness tract. The hike described here is within this 3660-acre wilderness, where only foot travel is permitted. Poison ivy is present in the area, as well as ticks carrying Lyme disease (see Introduction).

For a maximum chance to see wildlife, a small group of hikers is advised. The trails are easy to follow but not well marked. They are also often very wet. In fact, this may be the wettest hike you ever take! In spring or fall, waterproof footwear is a must. In winter, much of the surface may be frozen but icy. Even in summer, expect wetness and have a change of footwear ready in the car for your return. Once you've decided you're going to get your feet wet anyway, you can just begin enjoying the area. Of course, stay on the trails for safety. Bug repellent is a good idea. With the right conditions, these trails are fine cross-country ski territory.

The Great Swamp is a relic of post-glacial Lake Passaic, an immense lake some 30 miles long and 10 miles wide. The lake existed some 5000 years ago. It formed when the terminal moraine of the glacier blocked the exit of the Passaic River through Short Hills and a bowl behind the Watchungs filled with water. The water eventually drained out, at first near Far Hills, then near Great Notch, and finally at the present-day falls near Paterson.

How to Get There

To reach the wildlife refuge from exit 30A of I-287 near Basking Ridge, take

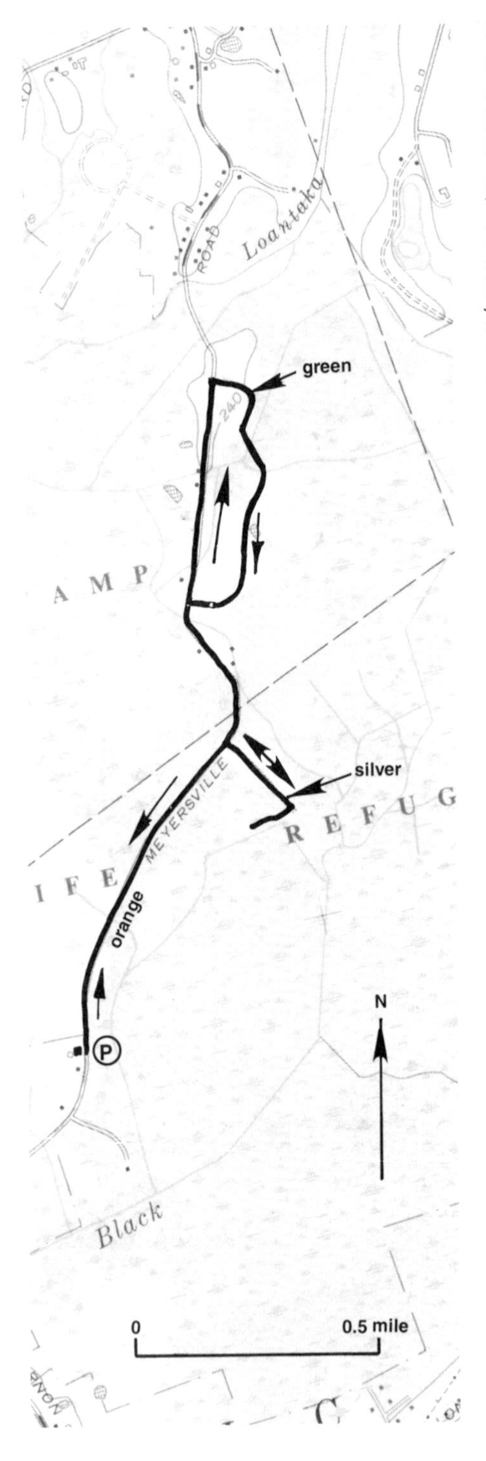

Maple Avenue south through the town of Basking Ridge to Lord Stirling Road, a distance of about 2.5 miles. Make a left onto Lord Stirling Road, which becomes White Bridge Road after it passes the junction with Carlton Road. You will also pass Pleasant Plains and New Vernon/Long Hill Roads before you dead-end at a large parking area, just less than 3 miles from Maple Avenue. The route to this particular trailhead area is unsigned, and the trails here are likely to be yours alone.

En route to the parking area, you'll pass roads to some places of interest. Along White Bridge Road, the refuge office is located a short distance left (north) up Pleasant Plains Road. It is open weekdays 8–4:30. Maps and flyers are available there. A wildlife observation center is located about a mile left (north) up Long Hill Road, as is another trailhead area. Here there is an information kiosk, blinds for wildlife observation, short trails, and rest rooms. Also in the area, on Lord Stirling Road near Maple Avenue, is the Environmental Education Center operated by the Somerset County Park Commission. The center, with more than 8 miles of trail, has a program of courses and field trips (201-766-2489).

The Trail

The trailhead is at a signed wooden gate where park officials have posted a copy of their hiking map. Your trail goes along an old woods road through the high grass and swings gently right onto a more gravelly surface. There are orange plastic disks (three together indicate the trail's beginning) and occasional splashes of paint as a guide.

Almost immediately, you will begin to notice an abundance of bird sounds. Because the hike is short, there is lots of time to stop, look, and listen, for this area is not the typical woodland environment of most northern New Jersey hikes.

After 20 minutes or so, you'll pass by a silver-marked trail going right. If you notice it (and you may not), mark this junction in your memory because a side trip down this fork is recommended later. For now, continue straight ahead. Ten more minutes brings you to a crossing over a still stream on a recently constructed, boardwalk-style bridge. On the far side, the grass closes in and makes the trail narrower. A few minutes later, there is another junction with a marked trail going to the right. There is a metal post here with no sign. This is the southern end of the green trail upon which you will return. Still, it's worth a short detour now onto the dry boardwalk—you'll get a good open view of the swampland and see if any waterfowl are around.

The orange trail continues ahead, passing some unusual open water. Notice a long row of large conifers on the left? Before the wildlife refuge was created, people lived along this road. This planting was associated with one of those houses. The main trail is, in fact, the route of Meyersville Road before it was closed by park authorities. Now keep your eyes peeled for a junction, in a wide area of the trail, with the green-marked trail. If you cross over a second boardwalk bridge (or come to the trail's end at the Meyersville Road parking area), you've missed it and will have to retrace your steps for a few minutes.

This green trail is a 0.75-mile loop. It leads through hardwoods with fine ground cover (note the lush areas of ground pine and ground cedar) and some open water. The area has a distinct feeling of the jungle, with many different birds adding the "right" sounds. There is but one turn that might confuse you. If you lose the markers in a grassy area, jog very slightly to the right (back into the woods), and you should pick up the trail again almost immediately.

The NWR trail map shows a junction halfway along the green trail with a 0.5-mile, beige-marked spur trail to the "shore" of Black Brook. While I did not spot it, perhaps you will. After skirting a large open water section, the final segment of the green trail goes across a long boardwalk. This is fairly new. Back in 1988, not wanting to go for a long wade, we had to retrace our steps at this spot. Your chance of seeing waterfowl here are excellent.

Back at the previously passed junction with the orange trail, turn left back toward your car. Twenty more minutes brings you back to the silver trail junction you passed near the start of the hike. It may be easier to spot from this direction. It is in an open, wide area of the trail. The route is easily seen, but the silver disks blend into the tree bark. Turn left down this spur, the beginning of which shows evidence of having once been paved. It soon becomes grassy, skirts the edge of a field, and reenters the woods. While most of the trail is dry, it gets quite wet and overgrown toward the end (about 7 minutes in) as the route goes along a wide area of stagnant water. This is the shore of Black Brook. Find some dry ground (if you can), sit, and enjoy the peace of this wild domain before retracing your steps to the main trail and your car.

HNZ

29

Lord Stirling Park

Total distance: 3.5 miles

Hiking time: 2 hours

Vertical rise: Minimal

Rating: Easy

Maps: USGS Bernardsville; Somerset County Park Commission trail map

The Somerset County Park Commission is the steward of Lord Stirling Park, a section of the Great Swamp that offers the hiker many fine trails. The park commission's Environmental Education Center is also located here. The Great Swamp is what remains of the former Lake Passaic, a huge 10-by-30-mile glacial lake created during the previous Wisconsin Ice Age, which shaped much of north Jersey's topography 12,000 years ago. The lake was formed by meltwater from the retreating glacial ice sheet and was blocked by the long wall of basalt that is the Watchungs. Today, all that remains of the lake is an extensive series of wetlands along the course of the Passaic River.

Lord Stirling Park (190 Lord Stirling Road, Basking Ridge, NJ 07920; 908-766-2489) derives its name from William Alexander, who was the Lord of Stirling. He served as a general in the Continental Army and was the owner of vast land holdings. The area that is now the park is only a small portion of the original estate. He also held title to the land that is now Island Beach State Park (see Hike 41).

It may be hard to imagine, but if it weren't for the efforts of some very concerned residents, this wilderness could have been an international jetport. In the 1960s, plans for the construction of such a jetport in the Great Swamp were halted by a grassroots effort of concerned citizens. Marcellus Hartley Dodge managed to get the cooperation of many local and national figures and took on the Port Authority itself. In the end, 6100 individuals contributed toward the purchase of the original 3000 acres, which were then donated to the Department of the Interior.

The 400 acres of the Environmental Education Center at Lord Stirling Park adjoin the holdings of the Department of the Interior (the Great Swamp National Wildlife Refuge) and, farther north, the Morris County Park Commission. Combined, these contiguous parks and refuges make north

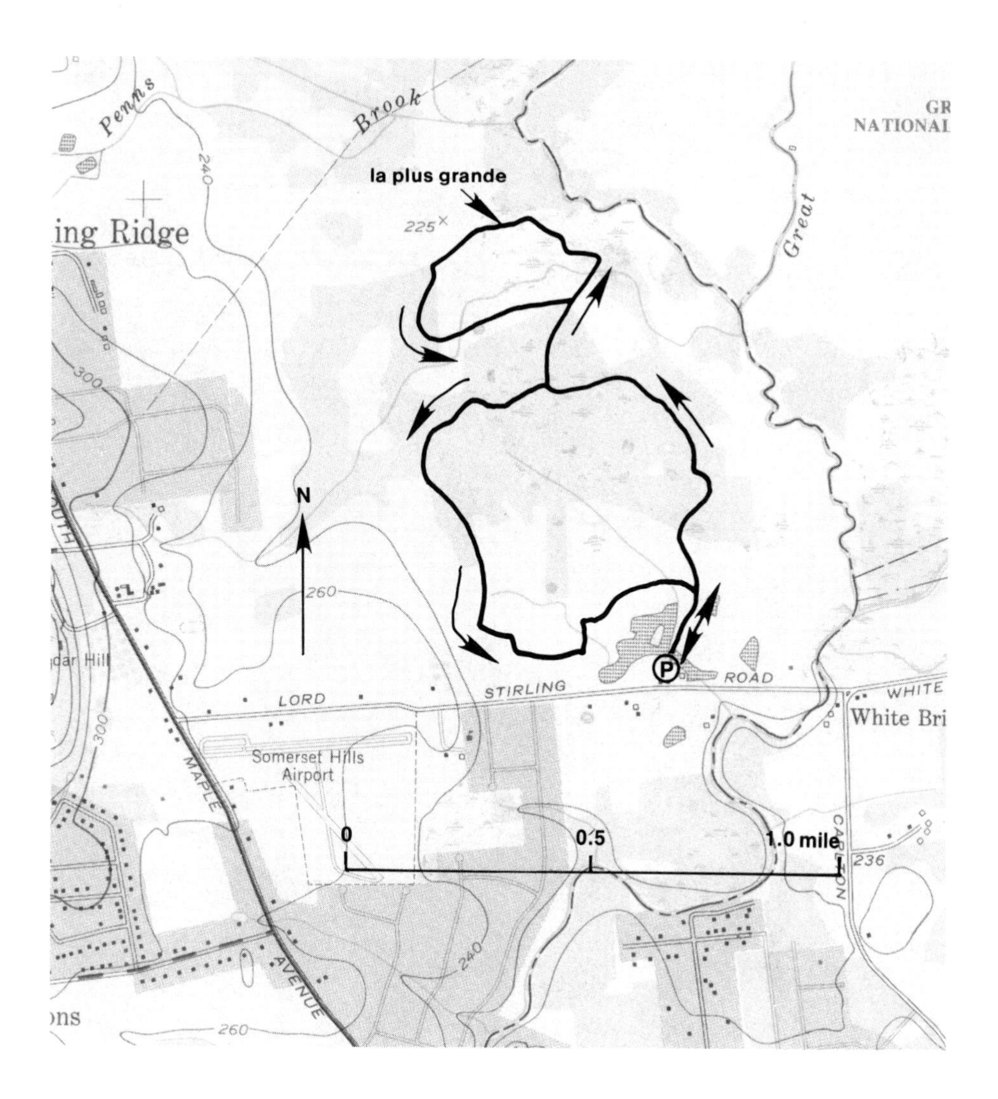

Jersey's largest protected wetland. Within this area are a number of diverse plant communities and habitats of special appeal to naturalists and birders. About 9 miles of 8-foot-wide trails and boardwalks and two observation towers permit exploration of this southernmost section of the Great Swamp, a true relic of the ice age.

The center itself is a large building that serves many purposes. Offices, meeting rooms, and classrooms are part of this solar-heated and -cooled building, as is a new permanent exhibit called "Secrets of the Great Swamp." This exhibit features 15 displays that describe the swamp, beginning with its geological origins and moving through the colonial era and up to the present-day environmental threats.

How to Get There

From I-287, take exit 26A to North Maple Avenue. The road veers to the left at the town of Basking Ridge and becomes South Maple Avenue. After

La Plus Grande freshwater swamp

a total of 2.5 miles from I-287, make a left onto Lord Stirling Road and go 1 mile to the Environmental Education Center on the left.

The Trail

Before your hike, stop in at the center, sign your name in the register, and request a free map of the trails. Then follow the trail that begins to the right of the building and heads out along the north side of Brant Pond, a man-made lake. A split-rail fence along this trail is marked with red reflectors attached to posts. This area was once an operating sheep farm. Notice the yellow markers turning off to the right at the end of the pond, and continue straight ahead following red markers. You will soon reach an intersection, and the red trail bears to the right over a small bridge. Stay on this trail, which is 8 feet wide and generally quite dry considering that it travels through a very wet area. An occasional bench along this trail provides you with a convenient resting place—hard to come by in this swampy, rockless environment.

This section of trail passes through a wet forest of white oak, beech, and shagbark hickory. Notice that the roots of the trees are very close to the surface because of the overabundance of water. You will actually see some tree roots above the surface of the ground, spreading out in all directions. The instability of this situation is evidenced by the number of fallen trees in the woods. After about 15 minutes, you will reach a junction with a boardwalk. Keep to the left here, staying on the red trail. At the next junction, near the frame of an old automobile, turn right on an unmarked trail that soon becomes a series of boardwalks. The woods now become wetter, pin oaks predominating among hummocks of sedge.

After just a few minutes, you'll come to a triangular intersection of boardwalks. Make a mental note of this junction. There are no markers here, but you will need to recognize this intersection on the way back. From here, turn right and walk a loop almost entirely on boardwalk, bearing left at every intersection. After passing two more intersections (bearing left at each one), the boardwalk will lead into the heart of a freshwater swamp named La Plus Grande, an open section of the Great Swamp. All around are cattails, buttonbush, swamp rose, and sedges. The birds are active here, even in winter. Sparrows flit from bush to bush, and you may even see a pair of cardinals.

After leaving the open area, the trail reenters the woods and alternates between boardwalk and some very wet and muddy sections of trail. Deer are abundant here, and the red-tailed hawk is frequently spotted. After a few more minutes of boardwalk hiking, look for the triangular junction on which you began this second loop. Bear right here onto the red-marked circular trail.

Soon, at another junction, the red trail swings to the right. Look around and notice a number of hollows in the ground here. These sites are where trees were removed during the early 1900s, when lumbering was beginning to alter the natural appearance of the woods. Soon you will reach another section of boardwalk that skirts a very wet and open area full of dead trees, and farther on, you'll cross a bridge over a small running brook. Notice the straight ditches of water in this section. These trenches are the remains of man-made attempts to drain the land when it was being farmed as recently as the 1950s.

The red trail bears left at a field and begins to swing back to the Environmental Center. These abandoned farm fields were once used for sheep grazing. Here the land is in transition, reverting back to its natural wooded condition. The red markers lead over a bridge over another drainage ditch constructed by farmers of the past. Soon the center will come into view. Before reaching it, the trail swings around the ponds and past a large bird blind before connecting with the yellow trail. Return to the center along the same path on which the hike started.

BCS

30

Round Valley Recreation Area

Total distance: 10 miles

Hiking time: 5 hours

Vertical rise: Approximately 400 feet

Rating: Moderate

Maps: USGS Califon/Flemington; DEP park map

Round Valley Recreation Area (Box 45D, Lebanon/Stanton Road, Lebanon, NJ 08833; 908-236-6355) is in a natural, horseshoe-shaped basin surrounded on three sides by Cushetunk Mountain. The reservoir covers more than 2300 acres, holds 55 billion gallons of water, and has an average depth of approximately 70 feet—one of the largest and deepest lakes in New Jersey. Fishing, swimming, and boating are permitted. It is recommended that this hike be walked out of season, when the area is not as heavily used. During the summer months, a special permit is required to use the wilderness camping area.

Hiking is limited to one long, multiuse trail circling the lake, at first through open terrain and then through densely wooded areas. There is not much evidence of horse riding, but mountain bikers use the trail extensively, which results in some muddy, eroded sections, particularly at the beginning of the trail. The route mostly is marked with a horseshoe and a footprint, but in some sections a yellow-painted metal disk is used. Ignore the occasional wide, mown grassy tracks.

How to Get There

Round Valley Recreation Area is accessed from US 22, 8 miles east of Clinton and 4 miles from Whitehouse. US 22 can be reached from the north via exit 20A off I-78, or from the east via I-287. Half a mile west of Lebanon, there is a sign to the park. Turn onto the park access road (which soon merges with County Road 629 [CR 629]) and travel for 2 miles. Pass the road to the boat launch and, after approximately 1 mile, turn left into the Round Valley entrance. After you reach the visitors center, drive through the gate and take the first right to the parking lot for the boat launching area.

The Trail

Away from the lakefront is a large green trailhead sign with a hiker and an arrow. Ignore the arrow, which points to the Pine Tree Trail, and begin walking

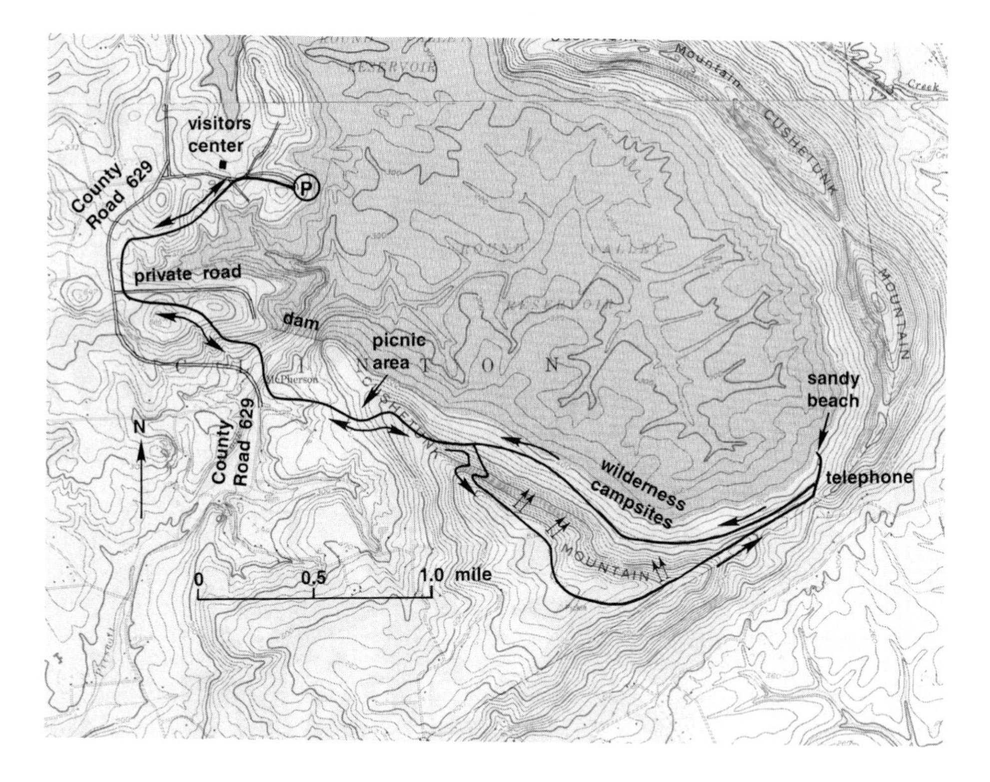

uphill through an avenue of white pine. To the left are many dogwood trees; the area is a dogwood lover's delight, especially in spring and fall when these trees are at their most colorful. Momentarily, the trail parallels the road, but almost immediately signs indicate that it turns away from the road to the left on a bare, stony track. These signs are closely followed by a board announcing that the trails are marked by Boy Scouts. Look left to admire the broad sweep of the reservoir and to enjoy the boating, scuba diving, and fishing activity usually in evidence.

At the top of the hill you can see the visitors center to the right as the trail descends toward the lake. Here again are many dogwood trees. The trail becomes narrower, paralleling the lake and rolling gently until it goes under a power line, the maintenance of which requires the usual massacre of surrounding shrubbery. After approximately 20 minutes, a fence protects you from CR 629. Pass through a chain-link fence and cross the private access road to the dam.

After a short distance in the woods, the trail emerges into the open, with the chain-link fence on the left and the power line on the right. After descending quite steeply, you will get a superb view of rural New Jersey ahead. The old trail continues downhill, but where a new piece of chain-link fencing has been installed at a right angle, turn sharply left through the gap in the old fence and proceed downhill on a steep soil slope toward another section of chain-link fence protection from the road. The reservoir dam rises behind a second fence to the left, and it is common to see deer congregated here on the slope, particularly at dawn or dusk. This section is grassy and open, and the route is between the two fences. Walk across a second dam access road at the bottom of the hill, keep to the upper side of the bushes and the ditch near the main road, and cross over the stream on a bridge. Watercress grows abundantly in the stream.

Climb the muddy, eroded bank on the other side of the stream, noting the trail signs at the top, and walk alongside the chain-link fence on a newly cut section of trail. Cross another official vehicle entry point to the dam and walk straight ahead. The trail gradually moves away from the dam and into the woods. The direction of travel to this point has been southerly, but you now head east. Markers and a signboard for the Round Valley Youth Center are installed at the point where the chain-link fencing makes a turn to the left.

Halfway up the hill is an oddly shaped building foundation. Eighty-seven of Round Valley's acres are not administered by the state of New Jersey but leased to a nonprofit organization for group use; this pseudo-building is part of its facility. Shortly beyond, a red arrow indicates a 90-degree turn to the left, and the trail leads slightly uphill and straight ahead to a picnic area. The walk so far has taken approximately 1 to 1½ hours, so the large, open, grassy spot is a natural place for a rest. The short distance to the picnic area, marked with a NO BIKES sign, is not included in this hike's mileage, but the view of the reservoir and a ridge of hills at the open picnic site is worth the extra few yards. There are comfort stations at the picnic site as well as picnic tables and makeshift grills.

Return to the main trail and climb through mature maples and oaks. About 30 minutes from the picnic area and at the top of the hill, you have a choice. Taking the marked trail downhill will eventually bring you back uphill to join the alternative trail, so it is suggested that you take the right-hand path, passing rocks piled in the footway.

The trail continues its climb to the top of the ridge, levels out, follows the ridgeline of Cushetunk Mountain right on the boundary between private and state property, and finally begins to descend. The trail is narrower and less well maintained in this section, but wooden seats are provided at intervals. Soon you will be aware that the marked trail you ignored a little while ago joins your path from the left. Continue straight ahead until you reach two wooden posts, then take the trail downhill to the left. (The trail ahead is a dead end.) Turn right within a few minutes onto the fire road, passing several water pumps and rest rooms, until you see the lake on the left. The small sandy beach, reached by crossing an open area, makes an inviting lunch and swimming spot. The lake is shallow here and the water cool.

The beach is the end point of the hike. Return along the gravel fire road, which takes you through Round Valley's wilderness camping area. For novice backpackers and for hikers wishing to test their abilities or new equipment, this area is ideal. The campsites are widely spaced and provide the feeling of isolation expected in a wilderness area. All are well hidden from the access road and plentifully supplied with comfort stations and water. There are many tulip trees.

Within 30 minutes, the fire road dips closer to the lakefront. At a crossroads, the Round Valley Wilderness regulations are posted on a sign. Take the trail straight ahead (not the one to the left); it is marked with a footprint and yellow disks. Climb on a steep, rocky path until you reach the junction with the pile of stones. From here, it is only necessary to retrace your footsteps to the parking lot.

SJG

31

Bull's Island to Prallsville Mill

Total distance: 3 miles (or 6 miles using one car)

Hiking time: 2 hours (or 3½ hours)

Vertical rise: Minimal

Rating: Easy to moderate

Map: USGS Lumberville/Stockton, DEP D&R Canal State Park

The 22-mile-long feeder to the main Delaware and Raritan Canal is part of Delaware and Raritan Canal State Park. The towpath in this section was used by the Belvidere and Delaware Railroad and is surfaced today with fine stone chips. From Bull's Island to Stockton at the Prallsville Mill, the railroad bed is located on the east bank of the Delaware River. At Stockton, it swings over the canal to the towpath, which separates the canal from the river. Containing a large campground, Bull's Island is the main developed section of the state park and invites exploration. The Prallsville Mill, 3 miles to the south, is a restored historical area scenically located on the canal and overlooking the Delaware River.

Bull's Island is an artificial island created by the construction of the canal. Richard Bull, one of the original owners, gave his name to the island and also to Bull's Creek, displaced by the canal, which separated it from the mainland. In 1832 work on the Delaware and Raritan Canal was started, and by 1834 the Delaware River Dam, which is used to divert water from the river to the canal, was completed. Here, the Delaware River water enters the canal and begins its long journey south to Trenton. This section, known as the canal feeder, was not only a source of water for the main canal but also a navigation channel that competed with the Delaware Canal on the Pennsylvania side of the river. The feeder meets the main canal at Trenton, where the canal turns north and, following first the Millstone then the Raritan River, terminates at New Brunswick. Along the way, the water level is maintained by a series of locks. A 24-acre state-designated natural area is located on the southern portion of the island. A trail through the area begins near the park office and provides views of both the canal and the Delaware River.

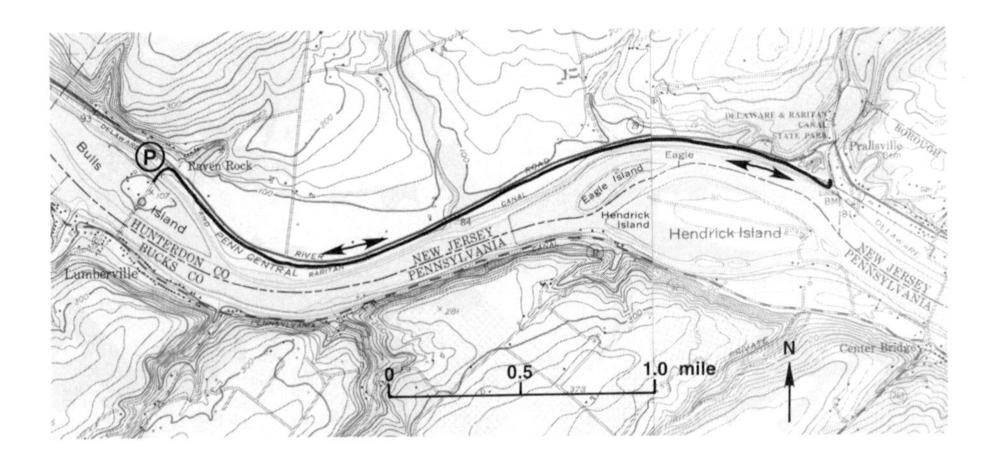

How to Get There

From its junction with US 202, take NJ 29 north for 6 miles to the Bull's Island section of Delaware and Raritan Canal State Park (2185 Daniel Bray Highway, Stockton, NJ 08559; 609-397-2949). The park, which offers car and tent camping, is located on a densely wooded floodplain of the Delaware. Park in the large day-use parking area, which will be on your left.

The Trail

You might want to begin by hiking past the ranger's house toward a long suspension bridge for pedestrians that crosses the Delaware and allows access to Pennsylvania. The views of the river from this bridge are outstanding.

Go back toward your car and the entrance road. Just before reaching NJ 29 (which the hike will parallel), find the abandoned Belvidere and Delaware Railroad bed, now a 17-mile multipurpose trail suitable for walkers, joggers, and bicycle riders. Pass around the gate and begin the 3-mile walk to the Prallsville Mill.

As you walk east along the railroad bed, the woods will be on the right and NJ 29 on the left. After only 0.5 mile, you will see the canal far below. Throughout most of Delaware and Raritan Canal State Park the actual towpath, which lies between the canal and the river, is used as the recreational path. In this section, the towpath is cut by unbridged overflow points that present major obstacles for the walker. The railroad bed, covered with a fine gravel, therefore serves as the main path until you reach the first lock at the mill. Occasional piles of old railroad ties lie along the route, which is quite straight and, of course, very flat.

On the way to the mill, the walkway takes you through a mixture of sun and shade, field and woods. At about the halfway point, cross over an inlet leading to the canal on a high bridge. Here, 50 feet or more above the canal, you will see a break in the towpath out to the Delaware.

Farther along, the path becomes more shaded and crowded in with honeysuckle and other vines. A rock embankment, which separates the path from the road, appears. The stone, the Stockton Formation, is better known as brownstone and is quarried locally. This stone has been used in the construction of many historic buildings in New Jersey, including some at Princeton and Rutgers Universities.

Ahead on the path, a bridge over a brook flowing into the canal is particularly picturesque. On a clear summer day you can look over an expanse of water to wooded islands, banks of purple loosestrife, and the mighty Delaware River. Ahead are the first locks on the feeder canal, and to the left are the buildings of the Prallsville Mill.

Located just north of Stockton, the mill is named after John Prall who, though not the original owner, bought the property in 1794. He enlarged the original gristmill and sawmill operation by adding a stone building used to mill linseed oil and plaster. In 1874 the original gristmill burned, ignited by a spark from a passing steam engine on the B&D Railroad, but the mill was rebuilt on the old foundations 3 years later. After milling came to an end in the late 1940s, the entire complex of seven buildings was acquired by the state and gradually restored by the Delaware River Mill Society, which leases the site. What makes the Prallsville Mill unique is that it is the only historic multiple milling operation remaining in the state.

Today, the displays at the restored mill include an industrial herb garden, an exact-scale model of the mill built by the last mill owner, and a crafts shop, along with the restored buildings themselves. Near the old sawmill is a picnic table, a good place to have lunch or a snack after the walk from Bull's Island.

After visiting the mill, head back to Bull's Island the way you came—or leave from here if you have arranged a car shuttle.

HNZ/BCS

Prallsville Mill

32

Washington Crossing to Scudders Falls

Total distance: 6 miles

Hiking time: 3 hours

Vertical rise: 100 feet

Rating: Moderate

Maps: USGS Pennington; DEP Washington Crossing State Park

Washington Crossing State Park (RR 1, Box 337, Titusville, NJ 08560; 609-737-0623) is #13 on the state's historical site listing, and this hike is a combination history lesson and long walk on a towpath. On the towpath you will be exposed to much sun—a blessing or curse depending on the season or the weather. In all, the park boasts 13 miles of walkway and trails. Other hiking possibilities include footpaths through a 140-acre natural area with an interpretive center.

The park's visitors center (open Wednesday through Sunday) contains a large collection of Revolutionary War artifacts, maps, and descriptive brochures, and a short slide presentation on the history and offerings of the park. It will give you a feeling for the momentous event that justified the creation of this park. The importance of what happened here in 1776 cannot be overestimated. This was the site of probably the single most important offensive in Washington's military career. At the very least, it kept him and the country alive during the early days of the American Revolution.

Since independence had been declared, the Continental Army, led by Washington, had not scored a point against the British. Washington and his men had tried to stop the British invasion of Long Island (Brooklyn) but were driven back to Manhattan and then to New Jersey. Denied adequate troops and supplies to meet the threat, Washington had no recourse but to retreat across the middle of New Jersey, across the Delaware, and into Pennsylvania. Although the situation appeared to be cause for extreme depression, Washington took a risk and won, and in the process stirred hope for the revolutionary cause.

On the night of December 25, 1776, he ordered three divisions of troops to attack the Hessian garrison at Tren-

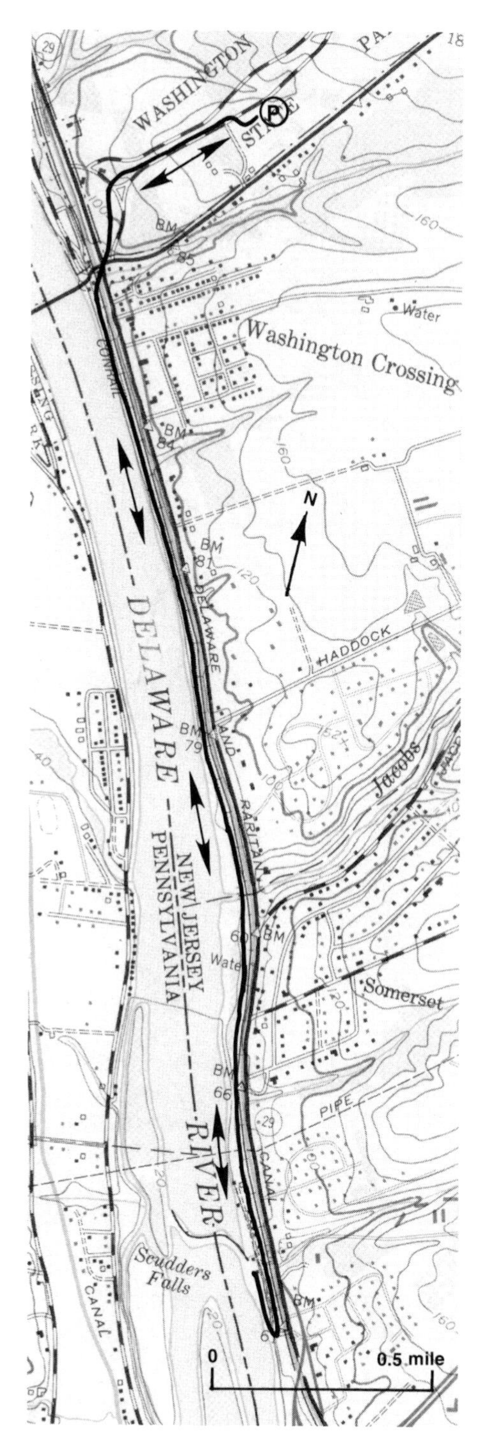

ton. The plan called for each division to cross the Delaware at different points and then converge on the enemy by surprise. Washington himself and 2400 men crossed the river in ferryboats at the site of the present-day park. After a difficult crossing in the ice-choked river, he and his men marched south to Trenton, caught the Hessians by surprise, and won the victory. The other two divisions never made the crossing that night because of river ice. Washington immediately followed up the victory with a successful attack on the British at Princeton. Having pushed back the enemy halfway to New York, he took shelter for the remainder of the winter behind the long, curving natural wall of the Watchungs in central Jersey. These two battles marked a major turning point in the war, and they kept Washington in place as commander in chief.

How to Get There

You will see signs for Washington Crossing, including the number 13, as you approach it from any direction. From I-95, take exit 1 north (the last exit in New Jersey) to NJ 29 north. About 3 miles from the exit, make a right turn onto County Road 546; you will find the main entrance to the park on your right in about 0.5 mile. Alternatively, take exit 3 and follow signs to the park entrance. Between Memorial Day and Labor Day there is a $3-per-car entrance fee on weekends only. Pass the toll gate, follow signs to the visitors center, and park in the large lot just to the north of the center. (Parking is free just north of the Nelson House near the river. You may wish to park here and walk back to the visitors center to see the museum's collection of artifacts or simply walk south along the towpath as described below.)

The Trail

After a visit to the center, walk over to Continental Lane, the grassy walking path about 100 yards due west (in front) of the center. You'll find it between a long line of trees and other plantings just across the paved road. Turn left onto the lane and head toward the Delaware River. Continental Lane is a pleasant, tree-lined walkway between park service roads. Ashes, oaks, white pines, and cedars line the path on either side. After a few minutes, you'll come to a few colonial buildings. To your right is an old barn that now houses rest rooms and a flag museum. In front of you is the Ferry House, fronted with an herb garden. You may wish to explore these buildings now or perhaps on your return. At the terminus of Continental Lane, bear left for just a few feet on the paved road and turn right onto a paved path heading south. This path will lead you past a walled-in overlook (overlooking NJ 29 and the Delaware) and out to a pedestrian walking bridge over the highway. This area is part of the memorial arboretum, and the varied plant life here may be of interest. Take the pedestrian walking bridge over NJ 29. Make a left, crossing the road leading to the bridge, and head south (through the gate) on the canal feeder towpath. En route you'll pass two stone markers commemorating the crossing.

The towpath, which was used for a time as a bed for the Belvidere and Delaware Railroad, is very flat and is surfaced by a very fine, though loose, gravel. It gets much use from joggers and bikers as well as walkers. To the right and quite a drop below is the Delaware River. To the left is the feeder canal and, beyond that, NJ 29. It is unfortunate that the highway is so close, but that is an unavoidable reality in such a densely populated area. This section of towpath is very exposed to sunlight and, during hot summer days, it may be advisable to hike in the late afternoon when the shade of the taller trees on the west bank covers the entire path.

As you walk along the towpath, you'll see vegetation very different from that of the highland mountains or the Pine Barrens. The plants—weeds actually—are more typical of highways, urban vacant lots, and other places that receive much sunlight. Don't be put off by this; some of the most valuable medicinal herbs are found in such environments. For example, you'll see thistle, with its prickly leaves and round flower heads, which is used for fevers (it produces sweating). The common mullein, the tall, spikelike plant commonly seen along the roadside, is also found here; a tea made from its leaves and flowers is used for lung complaints and asthma. As for flowers, you'll find purple gentians, black-eyed Susans, goldenrod, and wild carrot (better known as Queen Anne's lace). Poison ivy is in abundance here as well, though it doesn't encroach upon the path. Pokeweed, edible as a young shoot but poisonous fully matured, is found here also. You'll find the staghorn sumac with its red berry clusters that, when soaked in cold water, make a lemonadelike drink. At the edge of the dense woods that separates the towpath from the river are flowering dogwoods and even a few catalpa trees with their large heart-shaped leaves and long, beanlike pods.

Where the canal curves slightly to the east, notice the outcroppings of red Brunswick shale, also known as brownstone, on the opposite bank. This rock is the primary bedrock throughout all of central New Jersey, except for the igneous intrusions that make up the Watchungs, Cushetunk

Mountain, Sourland Mountain, and Rocky Hill. A little farther ahead, Jacob's Creek passes under the canal and empties into the Delaware. There's a nice view of this wild and rocky confluence from the towpath, which stands 50 feet above it. Blue herons may be wading in the shallows, where they are safe from intruders. Don't be surprised if you see deer hoofprints on the towpath; they've got a dense woods to hide in during the day.

After passing a flood-control structure, which allows the canal to drain into the river if necessary, you'll see a bridge across the canal ahead of you. Bear right here and head downhill on the paved road. Take one of the pathways to your left down to the river, and you'll come out near Scudder's Falls, a Class II set of rapids on the Delaware. At the time of this writing, the best path to the falls was directly opposite a parking lot off NJ 29.

Scudder's Falls was named for the Scudder family, whose 18th-century farmstead and mill were once located in the area. One well-known member of the family was Amos Scudder, one of Washington's scouts at the Battle of Trenton. John Hart, one of the signers of the Declaration of Independence from New Jersey, was married to a Scudder. Unfortunately, nothing is left of the original house.

Notice the huge sections of concrete on the island just across from the falls. A structure located here once utilized the immense power of the water, which drops several feet in a short distance. These falls, more like a channel or chute between shoreline and island, are popular with kayakers. If you are here during high water and on a weekend, you will no doubt be treated to a display of paddling skills. The area, also heavily used by anglers and partygoers, is quite pleasant and very interesting, making it a good spot for lunch. You can sit on some of the big rocks near the river's edge, listen to the roar of the rapids, and gaze out toward Pennsylvania, far off on the other side.

After watching the rapids, return to the towpath (or follow the road along the river to a gasline and then scramble back up to the towpath) and begin the long walk back to Washington Crossing State Park. The benches placed about every 0.25 mile can provide a welcome rest should you need one. Before taking the pedestrian walkway over NJ 29, you may wish to take a look at the Nelson House just below it toward the river. There is a portion of the original tavern here at the ferry dock. The building contains a large collection of period pieces, a flag collection, and, adjacent to the building, a reconstruction of one of the original ferryboats that took Washington and his men across the frozen river on that cold December night.

From the Nelson House, take the pedestrian bridge across the highway and bear left through the walled overlook. Continue retracing your steps toward the Ferry House and flag museum to find Continental Lane that, in 0.3 mile, will bring you to the visitors center and parking area.

BCS

33

Sourland Mountain Preserve

Total distance: 3.3 miles

Hiking time: 2 hours

Vertical rise: 360 feet

Rating: Easy to moderate

Maps: USGS Rocky Hill; Somerset County Park Commission trail map

Sourland Mountain is really a 10-by-4-mile sheet of Triassic traprock, similar to the Palisades, Watchungs, and Cushetunk Mountain (see introduction). Here a portion of a buried igneous intrusion was tilted, with its eastern edge leaning up, then uplifted. Erosion left the harder igneous rock exposed, and it now looks over the surrounding plain. The highest elevation on the mountain, attained in two places, is 586 feet. Contrast this with the 120-foot elevation of the eastern plain and you have one of the steepest gradients in central New Jersey. It is on this eastern edge that the hiking trails are located. The western portion of the mountain slopes off into the plain more gradually.

Two factors have allowed Sourland Mountain to remain mostly undeveloped. The first is the fact that the land has never been of much agricultural or commercial worth—something that seems to be reflected in the name. Sourland may have stemmed from the German term *sauerland,* meaning land that is not sweet. It is true that the soil is rocky and acidic and that there is little groundwater. The name may also refer to the reddish brown ("sorrel-land") color of the soil found on the plains beneath the mountain. In some old records is the name Sowerland.

The second factor is that Sourland Mountain is far from any major thoroughfares. It has served as a retreat for many, including Charles Lindbergh, whose child was kidnapped there. The broad, flat top of the mountain is quite rocky, mostly wooded, and includes about 400 acres of old growth. Many historical buildings still stand along the several quiet country roads that cross over it. But developmental pressure in New Jersey is relentless and many have become concerned. One such voice is the Sourland Regional Citizens Planning Council, which has pushed for preservation of

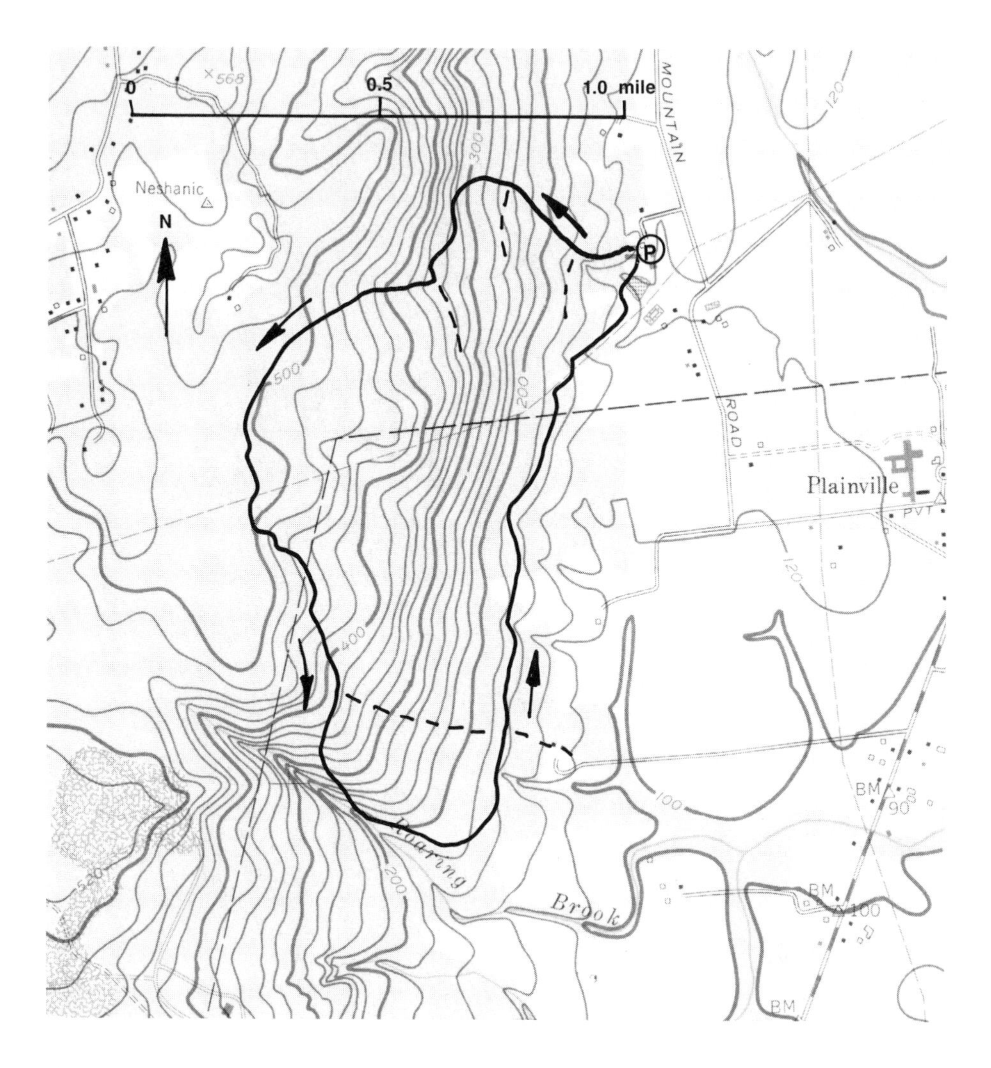

the area since 1989. The matter is complicated by the fact that portions of the mountain fall in Mercer, Hunterdon, and Somerset Counties. To date, only Somerset has established a public reservation.

The Sourland Mountain Preserve is one of the newest components (opened in June 1995) of the Somerset County Park Commission (PO Box 5327, North Branch, NJ 08876; 908-722-1200) and now totals more than 2000 acres. One interesting feature near the preserve not currently accessible from the marked trails is the Roaring Rocks boulder fields, an area of large traprock boulders. Ask a naturalist or ranger about this area (naturalists are present on Saturdays and lead walks at 10 AM and 2 PM).

How to Get There

From the junction of US 206 and US 202 at the Somerville Circle, drive 8.6 miles south on US 206 and turn right onto County Road 601 (CR 601) South.

(This turnoff is 2.7 miles south of where Amwell Road/NJ 514 crosses US 206.) Drive 1.2 miles on CR 601, then turn right on East Mountain Road. The Carrier Foundation buildings are located at this corner. Follow curving East Mountain Road for 1.1 miles to the entrance to the Sourland Mountain Preserve. Turn left here and drive to the large parking area.

The Trail

There are three marked trails in the Sourland Mountain Preserve marked with symbols and numbered junctions. They were designed to meet all needs: an easy trail of 0.5 mile, a moderate trail of 1.1 miles, and the trail that you will take, the 3.3-mile Ridge Trail. The trails in the preserve were built by groups of volunteers that included the Boy Scouts (Troop 46), the Sourland Regional Citizens Planning Council, and the federal Youth Conservation Corps. Unlike other large tracts of land that become open to the public and only later develop trails, the preserve sprang into being with a trail system in place, including bridges, boardwalk, and water-control features. At the time of this writing, mountain bikes are permitted to ride the trails. This may change in the future as a separate trail for bikes is being planned.

From the parking area, walk past the directory/booth to the single trailhead for all trails in the preserve. Follow the footpath as it enters the woods and crosses a bridge. The trail follows a small brook for a distance, crossing it again before entering a section of boardwalk. After this boardwalk, a sign will direct you to turn right. At this point the concurrent trails begin to divide. Here the Pondside Trail, marked with a circle, turns off, leaving you now following only the Maple Flats Trail (triangle) and the Ridge Trail (rectangle). The path begins to climb. At the next intersection the triangular trail diverges; keep right, staying with the Ridge Trail and still heading uphill.

When you arrive at post #4, which is a junction, turn left. After a few more minutes you should arrive at a pipeline clearing and post #5. The cleared pipeline is the Texas Eastern Gas Transmission Corporation right-of-way. If you turn left onto the pipeline clearing and walk a short distance up the slope, you'll come to an expansive vista that looks out to the east. This is also the high point on the hike.

To continue with the hike, return to post #5 and continue downhill on the pipeline path, cross a small brook, then immediately turn left into a small field of tall reeds called phragmites. These, the reeds of the Bible, are not native to the Americas but they seem to be found everywhere in New Jersey. Follow the trail here, which brings you to the other side of the pipeline cut and back into the woods.

Back in the woods the trail crosses a bridge, then follows a rocky path that snakes its way between a convergence of small streams. After passing this wet section, the path swings to the right onto a boardwalk. When you reach post #6, located near a fence, turn left and head steeply downhill (be careful—this area can be quite slippery when wet). The pathway widens as it reaches post #7. Bear right here. Next you'll pass through a wet area and arrive at post #8, which marks the point where the Ridge Trail comes closest to Roaring Brook, the largest brook on the hike.

The boulders in Roaring Brook are typical of the main rock type on the mountain. This igneous rock, called diabase, is mined by the 3-M company located nearby. The rock is ground down to make the abrasive coating on asphalt shingles. Farther upstream and in other parts of Sourland Mountain are large boulder fields where these rocks deny vegetation a foothold. One such place is named the Devil's Half Acre. If you are interested in exploring one of these boulder fields, which at present are not on public land, speak with a ranger.

At the next junction, keep left. You've now entered a different kind of forest than the one you've been hiking through, a tall cedar forest characteristic of the lowlands. You'll pass some old stoneworks here that may have served as a dam. Walk straight through the crossroads at post #9. Ahead is a section of trail that may be quite muddy during wet periods. As you approach the starting point of the hike you will again join with the other trails. Pay close attention now to markers and junctions. At post #10, turn right. Then walk to post #11, which is located at the lower end of the pipeline clearing you crossed earlier. Turn right at post #12 and walk out to the pond, keeping it to your right. Your car is across the field in front of you.

BCS

34

Delaware and Raritan Canal Towpath—Kingston to Griggstown

Total distance: 5 miles (or 10 miles using one car)

Hiking time: 2½ hours (or 5 hours)

Vertical rise: Minimal

Rating: Easy to moderate

Maps: USGS Monmouth Junction/Rocky Hill/Hightstown; DEP Delaware and Raritan Canal State Park

From its opening in 1834 to its closing 100 years later, the Delaware and Raritan Canal served as a major transportation link between Philadelphia and New York. From the northernmost point of navigation on the Delaware River at Bordentown to the head of navigation on the Raritan River at New Brunswick, the canal totaled 44 miles. A water supply for the canal was created by digging a 22-mile-long feeder canal to divert water from the Delaware River at Raven Rock to the main canal at Trenton. Both main and feeder canals had towpaths (walkways for the mules that pulled the barges along). Today, about 34 miles of the main canal and towpath are used by hikers, joggers, canoeists, and nature lovers. The Delaware and Raritan Canal State Park (625 Canal Road, Somerset, NJ 08873; 908-873-3050) is a green corridor through the center of the nation's most densely populated state, and even though it is never far from suburbia, it offers many miles of walking.

How to Get There

The park has many access points. For this hike, you will use a large parking area located on the south side of NJ 27 in Kingston where the highway passes over the canal and river. There is additional parking at the Flemer Preserve across the street. If you wish to hike the full 10 miles, park your car here and begin hiking. A car shuttle is necessary for a one-way hike of 5 miles. To leave a second car at the northern end of the hike, drive east on NJ 27 uphill to the second traffic light in the center of Kingston. Turn left here onto Laurel Avenue. Drive north past the quarry and through

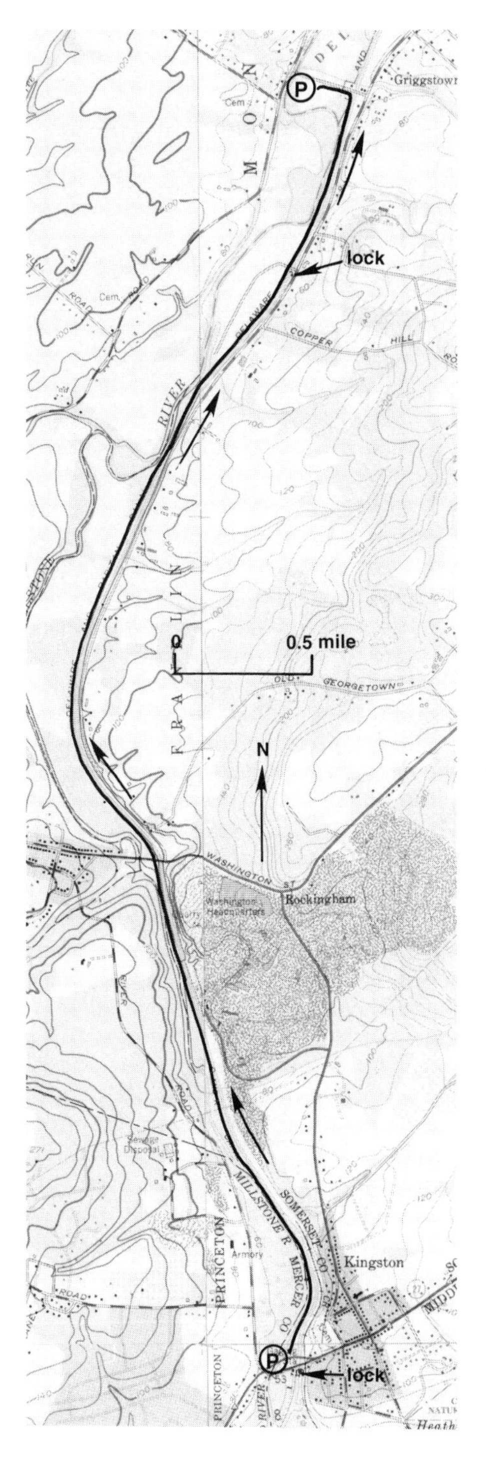

the traffic light onto Canal Road. Continue for another 3.4 miles to Griggstown Causeway Road. Make a left here, and leave your car at the large parking area about 0.2 mile ahead on the left. Return via the same route to the Kingston parking area in the other car.

The Trail

Take the paved path on the west side of the parking area through the tunnel underneath the highway. As you emerge, the Millstone River will be to the left and the canal to the right. This area is the Millstone River floodplain, the densely vegetated—though muddy—strip of land lying between the river and the canal. The path, which swings to the right and toward the canal towpath, is marked with occasional metal markers.

Once you reach the towpath, walk north on a well-used multipurpose recreational trail. The path is wide enough for a vehicle (though they are not allowed) and is used mostly by hikers, runners, bikers, horseback riders, and anglers. Throughout the hike, the canal will be on the right and the river below you on the left. A word of caution: Poison ivy abounds along the towpath. Frequently it is found as a vine climbing trees. Although the walkway is wide enough to avoid any contact with the plant, be sure you know how to identify it if you care to approach either the canal or the river more closely. For much of its length, the Delaware and Raritan Canal is paralleled by roads, though most of these are secondary country roads. In the section covered on this hike, a road follows the river for a while but then veers away, and with it the sounds of cars. You will get a feeling of isolation through this stretch. All kinds of wildflowers grow along the towpath here, including yarrow, wild carrot, pokeweed, and lobelia, as well as clusters of arrowroot in the water, a favorite food of Native Americans. The trees that line the towpath are mostly oak and maple with some horse chestnut, ash, and sumac. The great blue heron is also frequently seen along the canal.

After 1.5 miles you will reach the edge of a traprock quarry that borders the east bank of the canal. One of the largest and oldest quarries in the area, it supplies crushed basalt, called traprock, to road builders. The rock is quarried from what was once a large igneous intrusion, similar to and contemporary with the Watchungs and the Palisades. If you are hiking during the week, your solitude may be spoiled by the activities of this large operation. In recent years an exchange of land between the quarry and the state has taken place, and the section of the quarry nearest to the canal is now open to the public. It is quickly reverting to its natural state.

Look for a square concrete pillar with a tapered top, not unlike a fat 3-foot-high obelisk. This is a canal milepost, actually a replacement for the original stone markers. Notice that the number 23 is facing south and that on the other side, facing north, is the number 21. These figures indicate the number of miles from New Brunswick and Trenton, respectively. Adding the two gives the total mileage between these points. The markers, at least the ones that have survived, are found at every mile along the towpath. Just before you reach Rocky Hill Road, an inviting rock outcrop extends into the Millstone River on your left.

After about 40 minutes (just less than 2 miles) of walking, you reach paved Rocky Hill Road. There is a new parking area here on the other side of the canal where the trail on the opposite bank of the canal begins. If you wish to shorten your hike and don't want to retrace your steps, cross over the canal and find the footpath on the opposite bank. It will follow the canal back to Kingston and your car.

To continue the hike, cross the road and continue past the small dock and back onto the towpath. From here to Griggstown, Canal Road, a small country road, parallels the canal on the opposite bank. A number of old homes are located in this area, some of them well over 200 years old. In fact, George Washington himself gave his farewell address to the Continental Army in 1783 from a house originally located not far from the canal. Washington was said to have enjoyed his 3-month stay in this house on his way from Newburgh to Mount Vernon. It was here that he came to know of his great popularity, and history reports that he did much official entertaining. For a few months, this area was the social capital of the new nation. The house where Washington stayed, now called Rockingham, was relocated twice as the quarrying operation expanded. It is now about 0.75 mile from its original location. Within the next 5 years, it is due to be relocated again as per the state's agreement with Trap Rock, Inc. It will be moved closer to the east bank of the canal somewhere between Rocky Hill and Kingston.

Ahead on the towpath, pass mile marker 22/22, the halfway point between New Brunswick and Trenton. Beyond this marker is a small wooden bridge over the canal, a good spot for a rest or snack. Farther ahead on the left at milepost 23 is one end of a bridle trail that explores the Millstone River floodplain. It is called the Silver Maple Trail but is at present unmarked and unsigned. Just beyond the trailhead, notice that the towpath is lower than usual. This area is a spillway, which allows a swollen canal to shed water into the floodplain of the river. At the end of this section are stones placed to prevent erosion of the towpath. Just ahead is the Griggstown lock.

Canal locks on the Delaware and Raritan, which measure 220 by 24 feet, allowed boats to change water levels between sections of the canal. Though seven locks were necessary in the 6-mile stretch of canal from Bordentown to Trenton, only seven more were needed for the remaining 38 miles, a low route that follows the river valleys of the Millstone and Raritan. The house behind the lock is one of the old locktender houses found near every lock. Alongside the lock are some round concrete posts known as snubbing posts, which were used to secure boats making the passage. The turbulence of water rising or lowering in the lock required a tight line, but also one that could adjust as the water level changed. Such lines were also needed for braking purposes—the boat had to be stopped once it entered the lock. Aside from the technical problems of stabilizing a boat in the lock, the passage through was also a social event. Exchanges of news would take place between the locktender and the boatmen. Telegraph connections were in place and information, such as the arrival of boats, could be sent on to other locations. The locktender and his family would often trade with the canal boatmen who, like many of today's truckers, owned their own vehicles.

Returning to the towpath, find the other end of the Silver Maple Trail nearby. You may wish to walk a short distance on this trail down to the banks of the Millstone River. A large shagbark hickory tree grows on this well-watered spot.

Milepost 20/24 is found at a point where the canal and the river are very close to each other, though the river runs well below the level of the canal. Ahead is the paved Griggstown Causeway and several historic buildings. Notice a steel bridge on your left, located just before a house. Turn onto this to reach the parking areas without walking along the road. The bridge spans a millrace that once existed at this site, the nearby house being set on the old foundations of the old mill. Ahead of you, at the paved road, notice the long structure—built about 1800—of the Griggstown Barracks. This building was used to shelter the men who built and worked the canal. Today it serves in part as a small museum for the Griggstown Historical Society, which is open daily, weekdays 9–3 and weekends (if volunteers are available) 1–4. The bridgetender's house and station are on the other side of the canal; both were built around 1831. Griggstown Canoe Rental (908-359-5970) is also here; along with canoes, it also rents single-person kayaks.

If you haven't left a car in the parking area (to reach it, use the previously mentioned bridge), turn around and walk the 5 miles back to Kingston. At the Rocky Hill Road crossing, near the traffic lights, you may wish to walk the last section on the footpath across the canal.

BCS

35

Delaware and Raritan Canal—Weston to East Millstone

Total distance: 4.2 miles

Hiking time: 2 hours

Vertical rise: Minimal

Rating: Easy

Map: USGS Bound Brook

A century ago the Delaware and Raritan Canal—now the site of a state park (625 Canal Road, Somerset, NJ 08873; 908-873-3050)—was the scene of intense commercial activity. Hard coal was the most important item shipped on the canal, accounting for 80 percent of its total tonnage. Many of the canal boats used on the canal were of the "hinge-boat" variety; they measured about 90 by 10 feet and drew about 5 feet of water. Long strings of these canal boats loaded with coal were pulled by steam tugs, while other canal boats were towed by mules. Towing charges varied according to the service used. At one point steam tugs were charged a flat rate of $22.22, plus an extra $11.11 per barge for the trip to New York City. Mules and horses were available from barns at Bordentown, Griggstown, and New Brunswick. The open season on the canal was about 250 days a year, from early April to mid-December. Canal hours were from 6–6 daily, and the speed limit for canal boats was 4 miles per hour. When steam tugs began to be used on the canal, the wash began to undermine the banks in places. A stone lining called riprap was installed and can still be seen today in many places.

How to Get There

To locate this section of the Delaware and Raritan Canal State Park from I-287, take exit 7, Weston Canal Road. When you reach the end of the exit ramp, turn left (south) on Weston Canal Road, following signs to Manville. In 1.7 miles, pass Ten Mile Lock and the locktender's house on the right and, after that, the religious community of Zarepath. In 3 miles, the road will swing around and cross the canal. The parking area, created from a remnant of older pavement, is located on the right just before the road crosses the canal.

The Trail

Cross over the bridge and turn left onto the towpath, heading south. On the other side of the canal (the east bank) is the old bridgetender's house built circa 1831. Originally, a swing bridge spanned the canal here. If you are hiking in summer or early fall, notice the duckweed, the miniature lily pad plant that floats in clusters on the water. This plant tends to accumulate, sometimes covering the entire canal surface 10 or 15 miles before New Brunswick (the terminus of the waterway). The towpath, which receives an equal amount of sun and shade, is quite grassy here, though the actual walkway is worn to the dirt. The trees, mostly oak and maple, form an intermittent canopy over the towpath. Poison ivy is, unfortunately, abundant. On the other side of the canal is Weston Causeway Road, a country road with light traffic. On your right is the large Millstone River floodplain.

After a few minutes of walking, notice that the Millstone floodplain, undoubtedly very fertile, is being used as a cornfield. At about the point where the cornfield ends, Weston Canal Road turns away from the canal, and the towpath enters one of its very few sections not paralleled by a road. For the next 1.5 miles, the walking through this quiet and somewhat wild area—rare in densely populated central New Jersey—becomes very pleasant.

As the sounds of civilization fade out, the towpath takes on a wilder look. The Millstone River itself swings close to the canal, but 20 feet below it. The sounds of insects, fish jumping, and the hurried scrambling of turtles startled by your intrusion fill the void left by the sounds of traffic. If you are lucky, a great blue heron may wing its way down the canal. The only evidence of civilization is the boat dock

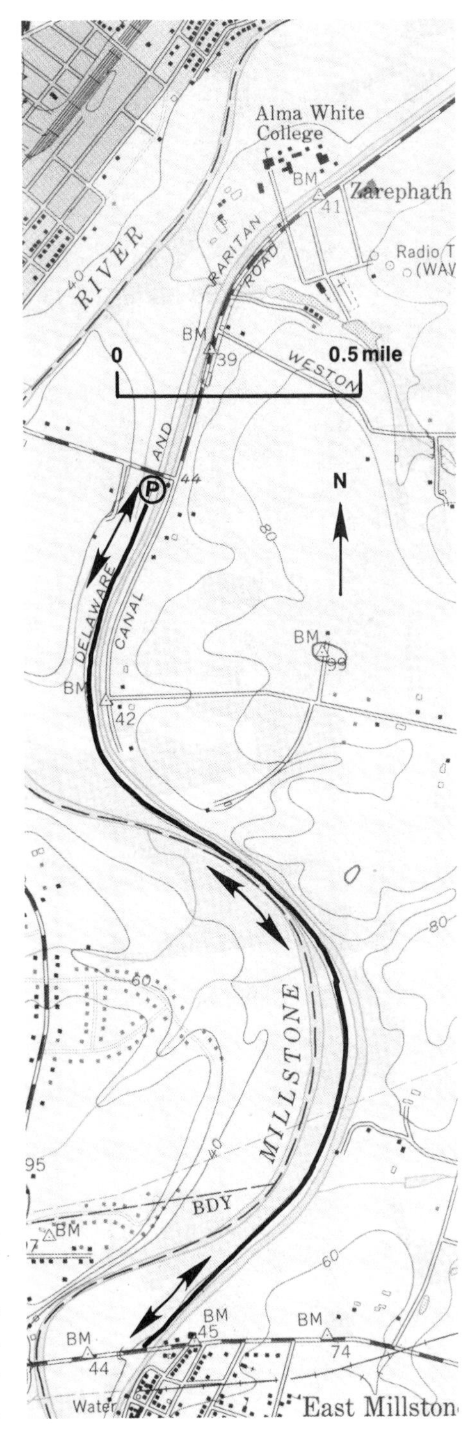

Stone mileage marker

for a day camp on the opposite bank of the canal.

Just before a spillway, come to milepost 31/13. This original canal artifact tells you that you are 13 miles from New Brunswick and 31 miles from Trenton. Ahead on the opposite bank is a cleared section of Colonial Park, which has a small dock. Next, pass over a culvert through which Spooky Brook runs, going under the canal on its way to the Millstone. This an example of one of the many streams that were channeled underneath the canal in order to keep its water level stable.

In another 0.5 mile, and all too soon, the quiet and privacy of this section of towpath come to an end. Ahead is a bridge and a parking area off Amwell Road in East Millstone. If you are interested, cross over the canal on Amwell Road and take a short walk into East Millstone, a small town that has changed very little over the years. The first road on the right leads to a small convenience store. On the way you'll pass a first-aid station, and in back of it, Turning Basin Park, a filled-in area where boats used to turn around. Today you'll find swings and other recreation for children. On the opposite side of the canal, but on the same side of the road as the parking area, is a bridgetender's house. Next to it is the historic Franklin Inn, its exterior refurbished and its interior now a nonprofit used bookstore run by volunteers of the Blackwells Mills Canal House Association.

After your visit to East Millstone, return to the towpath and retrace your steps to your car.

BCS

COASTAL PLAIN

36

Cheesequake State Park

Total distance: 4 miles

Hiking time: 2½ hours

Vertical rise: Approximately 200 feet

Rating: Easy to moderate

Maps: USGS South Amboy; DEP Cheesequake State Park

Located in the transition zone between New Jersey's distinctive northern and southern plant communities, 1274-acre Cheesequake State Park (Matawan, NJ 07747; 908-566-2161) may be of particular appeal to those interested in botany. There are a variety of habitats throughout the park, including salt- and freshwater marshes, northeastern hardwood forests, Pine Barrens, and a cedar swamp. Cheesequake is one of the oldest state parks in New Jersey, dating back to 1937 when acquisition of some farms, orchards, and salt marsh began. It was formally opened in 1940.

The area was occupied as early as 5000 years ago by Native Americans who hunted and fished here. The name Cheesequake was taken from a word in the language of the Lenni-Lenape tribe, which lived in New Jersey when the Dutch and English colonists first arrived. Some say the word means "upland people." During the 18th and 19th centuries, a fine-quality clay used to make stoneware pottery was mined in the area and shipped to pottery-making sites up and down the Atlantic Coast. Red clay was also mined to make bricks that some say were used extensively in the building of New York City. As late as the early 20th century, a steamboat dock existed on Cheesequake Creek, at the end of Old Dock Road; there products and produce were sent to markets.

There are several marked trails in the park (mostly footpaths) that are color coded. The recently improved markings in the shape of arrows will keep you on the trail and off the numerous unmarked side trails (also mostly footpaths) that could be misleading. This hike will use all three trails, especially the green trail, which begins after you walk a section of the red and yellow trails. The footpaths (and in some cases the sand roads) that the trail follows are soft and bouncy in places, covered by pine needles. There are many wet sections that have been covered by boardwalks or bridges; in a few places are rough stairs made of railroad ties. Rugged footwear is not required. Mountain bikes are not allowed (there is a special multiuse trail marked for them in another section of the park), but evidence of their trespass is widespread. Because of the proximity to swamps and marshes, it may be best to visit the park during the fall when both insect and human populations are at their lowest.

How to Get There

From the Garden State Parkway, take exit 120 and turn right (east) at the end of the ramp following the brown STATE PARK signs. Turn right at the gas station onto Cliffwood Avenue. Turn right again at the T-intersection onto Gordon Avenue, which in 1 mile will take you to the park entrance. Pass the park office and drive to the parking area on the left, about 0.2 mile ahead. A directory and map of the trails, as well as a fountain, are found here at the trailhead. A parking fee of

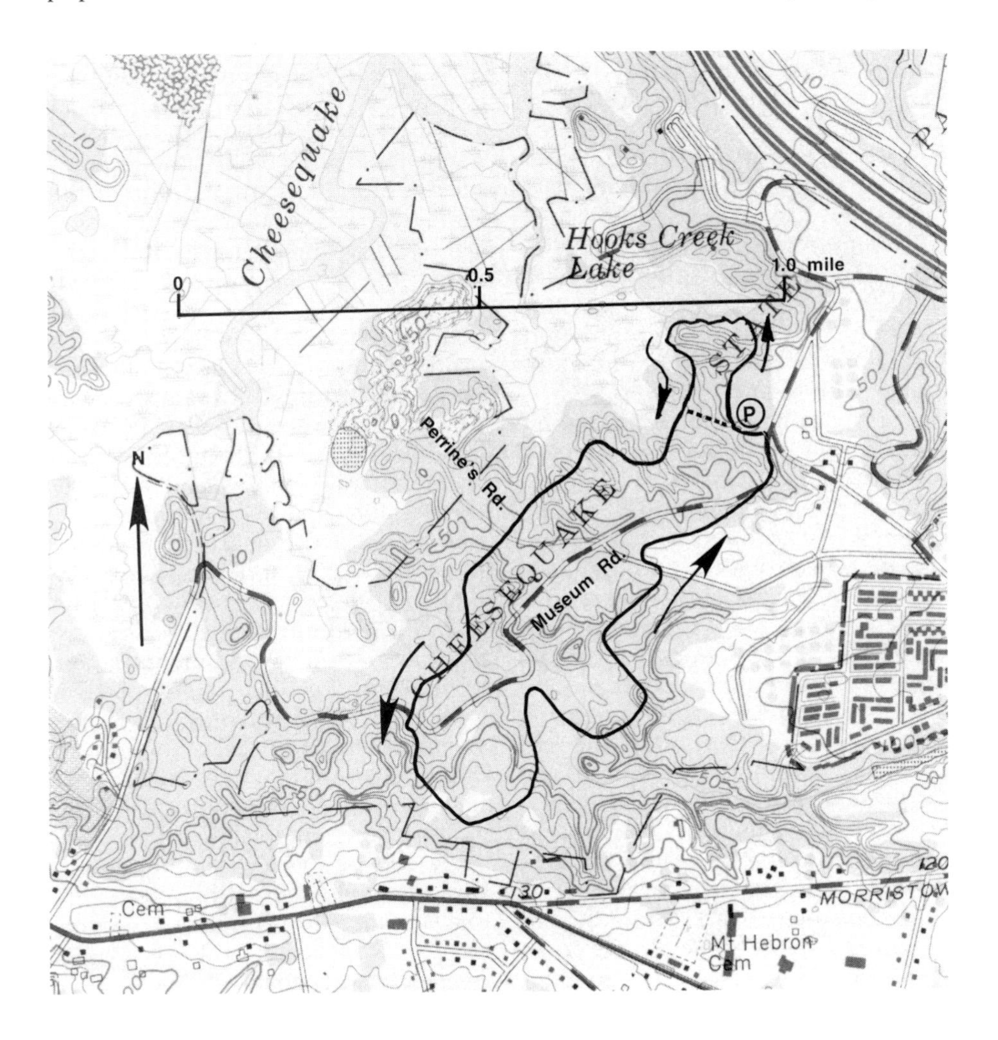

$5 daily, $7 weekends is in effect from Memorial Day through Labor Day.

The Trail

Begin your hike at the trailhead, just to the left of the directory. At the first fork, turn right onto the yellow trail and follow it to the Hooks Creek Lake. This section of the trail is noted for the many lady's slipper orchids that grow alongside the path. The trail follows the south shore of the lake on a narrow path, turns left at a junction, and then heads back through ferns to a junction with the red and green trails. From this junction, follow the red and green trails across a small brook (sign #6) on a new wooden bridge (the first of many). Pass (or visit) the Cheesequake Nature and Interpretive Center. One of the last major developments in the park was the building of this center. In it are exhibits illustrating the natural and cultural history of the park. You'll find a turtle display with live turtles in a tank, a model of a Lenni-Lenape village, both fresh- and saltwater aquariums, and rest rooms.

Continue on the trail through some sweet pepperbush, perhaps the most common plant along the trail. Pepperbush is related to mountain laurel and blueberry, also common in the park. During the spring, wild honeysuckle is in bloom here and in other sections of the trail. After leveling off, the trail passes a protected wet area on the right filled with tall ferns. Ahead is a view through the trees to the salt marsh below. The trail, still primarily marked with red, bears to the left here and heads downhill, crossing a muddy area. After crossing a few bridges, arrive at the base of an incline on which new wooden steps have been attached. At the top of the rise is a resting bench.

From the bench, the trail bears to the left, passing through a large stand of lowbush and highbush blueberries among some large pines (more typical of the Pine Barrens of southern New Jersey) mixed with the usual hardwoods. In this dry section are some large clusters of mountain laurel that bloom in June. After crossing a large bridge over a small brook, the trail comes out to a sand road (Perrine's Road) near a bench. It is here that the green trail splits from the red trail. Turn right, not onto the sand road but onto the green trail to the right of the bench.

Along this level section are many small sassafras trees, as well as some chokecherry, beech, maple, chestnut oak, and white oak. Through the trees on the right, you can see the now-closed Sayreville landfill about 2 miles away. Head downhill. At the bottom of the drop, the trail passes close to the tall sedges, rushes, and grasses of the saltwater marsh, which forms the western boundary of the park. After a short climb, proceed down a slope of badly eroded steps to a long boardwalk running over a freshwater swamp, heavily overgrown with arrowwood, elderberry, and buttonbush. In the middle of the walkway are two benches surrounding a red maple (sign #8). This quiet area, rich in plant and animal life, is a change from the woods and brush environments traversed so far.

At the end of the boardwalk, bear right at an unmarked junction, passing a bench, and out to another boardwalk (sign #9), this one in a cedar swamp. Here is an even cooler and darker environment than the freshwater swamp of a few minutes ago. The eastern white cedars (sign #10)—which grow out of black clay—dominate, shutting out light for other plants. The extreme moisture and the decomposing leaves make the soil very acidic, preserving any cedar logs that become

Cheesequake State Park

buried. In some similar areas of New Jersey, old cedar logs in good condition have been mined from the dense acidic soil. Great horned owls are known to frequent this swamp.

After leaving the swamp, keep to the right and follow the trail carefully through a muddy area. Come out to another sand road (Museum Road), which the trail crosses, and enter a woods dominated by huge white pines (sign #11). Because of their height and straightness, these trees were used by shipbuilders during colonial times—particularly during the Revolution—for masts. Overharvesting of the original white pines eventually forced the lumbering industry out of the state. These trees are estimated to be between 100 and 150 years old and are used as nesting sites by owls and hawks. The trail through this section is narrow and crowded in by pepperbush, mountain laurel, and rhododendron.

After climbing an interesting ladder/stairway on the trail, you will reach the highest elevation on the hike. The woods are dry here and composed mostly of oak, which provides food for the gypsy moth that has left evidence of its appetite in the form of standing dead trees. On the floor of the forest are large quantities of false Solomon's seal. At the junction, the trail bears to the left, leading to a stand of pitch pines typical of the Pine Barrens of south Jersey. Pitch pine grows in dry, sandy soil (as well as on rocky outcrops as it does in north Jersey) and can survive with few nutrients.

From this high area, the trail gradually descends. The trail, which skirts the southern boundary of the park (houses visible), is sandy here as it passes through a forest of hardwoods. After coming close to, but not touching, Museum Road, the trail continues along a path through a forest floor with numerous wildflowers such as the wild lily of the valley and the pink lady's slipper, both of which bloom in the spring. You can find violets, starflowers, and jack-in-the-pulpits here as well. Only plants that can tolerate frequent inundations survive here. Farther along, after sign #15, the trail swings around a small, stagnant pond that attracts wildlife. More boardwalk, built by Boy Scouts, keeps you dry and clean in this section of black mud, clear brooks, and wet swamps. Some of the boardwalks were damaged here in the winter floods of 1996. With luck the scouts will have repaired these sections by the time of your hike. After a rise, the trail comes again to Perrine's Road.

Turn left onto the road, following markers past Gordon Field, a camping area used by the scouts. Just ahead the trail swings back into the woods and once again merges with the red trail. There are many unmarked side trails in this section that head off to the left. Stay on the main trail, which follows the edge of the cleared area, until markers indicate a left turn leading downhill and onto Museum Road. Bear right here and follow the road, which in 0.2 mile leads to the trailhead and your car.

BCS

37

Hartshorne Woods

Total distance: 2.5 miles

Hiking time: 1½ hours

Vertical rise: 160 feet

Rating: Easy to moderate

Maps: USGS Sandy Hook; Monmouth County Park System Hartshorne Woods Park trail guide

Hartshorne Woods Park (Monmouth County Park System, Newman Springs Road, Lincroft, NJ 07738; 908-842-4000) contains several miles of marked and unmarked trails. The area, portions of which rise 245 feet above the Navesink River Bay, is surprisingly hilly for central New Jersey. The forest totally covers the 736 acres of the park and is primarily dry, upland, deciduous, and composed of oak, hickory, beech, and maple; however, the many ups and downs of the park's trails lead you through a variety of very healthy plant communities.

Hartshorne Woods was named for its original owner, Richard Hartshorne, who purchased the tract from Native Americans in the 1670s. Some of his descendants still live on part of the original family tract. The local pronunciation of Hartshorne is "harts horn," or horn of the hart, an old English word for deer.

As you will notice from the directory or map, there are several color-coded marked trails in the park. This hike uses the Laurel Ridge Trail, a loop trail that explores the Buttermilk Valley section of Hartshorne Woods. Be warned that most trails here are multiuse—expect mountain bikes.

In the late 1980s, Hartshorne Woods, formerly a relatively quiet woods for walkers, became extremely popular with mountain bikers (due in part to the closing of parks in nearby counties to bicycles). Trails in Hartshorne Woods quickly became degraded, forcing the Monmouth County Park Commission to find a solution to this problem. They launched a major trail rebuilding project and decided to go mostly multiuse—unlike other county and state agencies, which have chosen to keep bikers and hikers on separate trails where possible.

In 1991 the multiuse trail plan was devised and implemented with the help of some 40 volunteers. Worn and abused trails were covered and blocked with

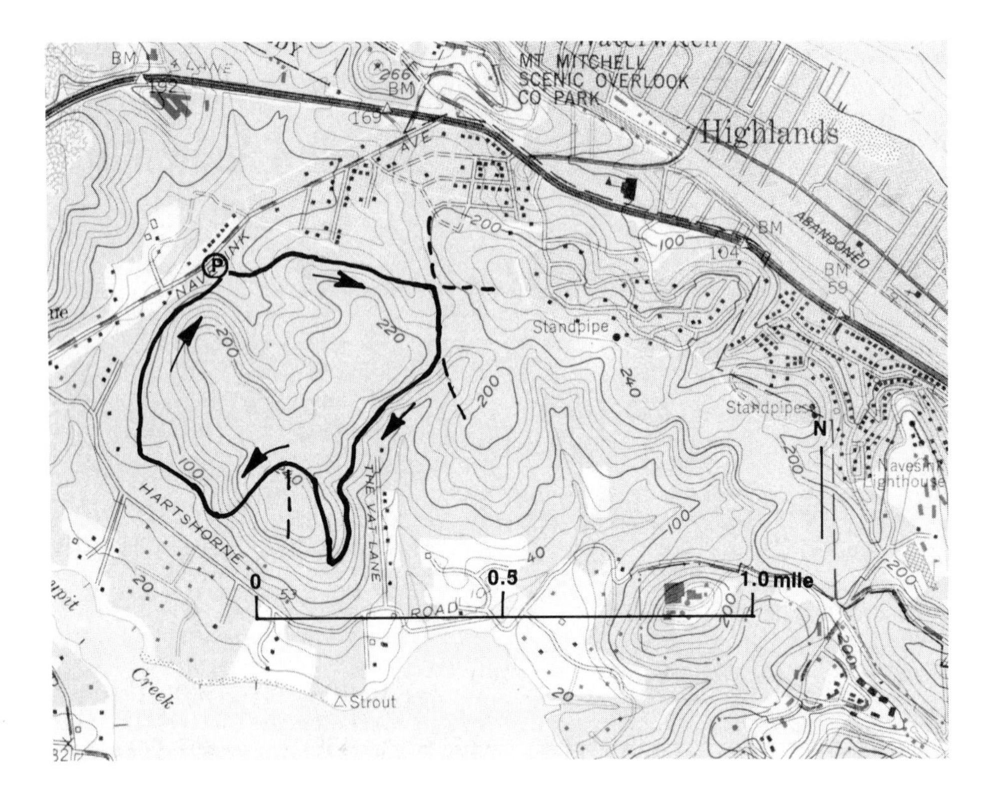

snow fence. New trails were cut and stabilized. Junctions were posted with signs and trails were color coded and labeled for differing degrees of difficulty. As with ski trails, a circle indicates an easy trail; a square one of moderate difficulty; and a diamond a challenging trail. A golden rule of this new trail system is posted and printed on the maps. It's shown in the form of a triangular logo with symbols of a bike, a hiker, and a horse. Arrows between each symbol show who yields to whom—bikers to hikers, and both bikers and hikers to horses. When I was last here it worked most of the time.

This hike is easy to follow and avoids areas more frequented by mountain bikes. You may wish to explore the Monmouth Hills section of the park on your own, perhaps during the week when usage is low. If you wish to avoid bikes entirely, two very short trails for foot traffic only begin at the main trailhead: 1.5-mile Candlestick Trail and 1.1-mile Kings Hollow Trail.

How to Get There

From eastbound NJ 36 in Atlantic Highlands, follow signs to SCENIC ROAD, a right turn off the highway. Take Navesink Avenue 0.5 mile to the large Buttermilk Valley Trailhead and Parking Lot on the left side of the road. A directory (which includes a large topographical map showing contours at 10-foot intervals) and a box of free hiking maps are located in the woods about 20 yards from the parking area.

The Trail

From the directory turn left onto the Laurel Ridge Trail, which is marked with blue blazes. This section of the trail is a wide and sandy service road that begins a gradual climb. Keep to the right at the first junction, then turn right onto Grand Tour Trail at the junction. A trail sign is posted here.

Still following blue markers, follow the path along the side of a slope through thickets of mountain laurel, an evergreen shrub. It is for this plant, abundant throughout the hike, that the trail is named. The trail meanders up and down as it swings around the slope passing a few holly trees, also green throughout the year. In a thickly vegetated section look for greenbrier, a vinelike plant with a green, smooth, and thorny stem. In this vicinity are also a few monster hickory and tulip trees. Smaller sassafras trees are scattered about, and in the understory are jack-in-the-pulpits.

The Laurel Ridge Trail climbs gradually, moving deeper into the flat summit of an elevated peninsula of land. You'll notice chunks of conglomerate rock (sand fused with pebbles) along the trail here and for the next 0.5 mile. This resistant rock has acted as a protective cap over softer sediments, creating highlands among sea-level plains. Another change you may note is in the vegetation itself. Oaks are now the predominant tree. As you climb higher up the slope, a view of water appears to your left, particularly when the leaves are off the trees. This is the Navesink River. Ahead, the trail winds back on itself and continues climbing, eventually reaching a junction with the path to the Claypit Creek overlook, the highest point on the hike (elevation 248 feet). Turn left onto this path and walk about 200 yards to the fenced overlook. From here is a view (somewhat obstructed in summer) of the Navesink River and bridge. This area makes a good rest stop. Return to the junction when you are ready to continue the hike.

Turn left at the junction and follow the blue markers down the other side of the hill. The descent is over soft dirt that in places may be torn up from mountain bike usage. The frequent passing of hikers or bikers seems to have no effect on the squirrel population in this section, though, and the abundance of oaks makes this a perfect place for these animals to harvest the year's acorn crop. If you are lucky, you may spot a deer or two.

As the Laurel Ridge Trail progresses around the hill, the trail bed widens. It passes through more patches of mountain laurel on the slope, then gradually descends to the directory. Just a few feet away is the parking area.

BCS

38

Gateway National Recreation Area—Sandy Hook Unit

Total distance: 4 miles with car shuttle; 8 miles without

Hiking time: 3 hours

Vertical rise: Minimal

Rating: Easy

Maps: USGS Sandy Hook; NPS map

Sandy Hook (Highlands, NJ 07732; 908-872-0115) is the only New Jersey unit in the Gateway National Recreation Area. The area is heavily used, so this hike is not recommended during the summer months when the parking lots are closed as soon as they are full—sometimes as early as 10 AM. In addition, beach areas may be closed at any time from March 15 through Labor Day to protect nesting shorebirds, such as black skimmers, least terns, and piping plovers. It is impossible to know where these endangered birds will nest, but in accordance with state and federal law, it is forbidden to enter those areas that are posted as closed. Areas are clearly marked in the effort to keep the young from being disturbed. Avoiding the closed area usually means you must use a paved road to complete the hike into Fort Hancock—another good reason to hike here out of season. Be aware also that the Gunnison Beach area is a clothing-optional beach.

Sandy Hook is a narrow, sandy spit 7 miles long, extending into the Atlantic Ocean and lower New York Bay. It is a barrier beach—the ocean on one side, a bay on the other. The beaches migrate because of littoral drift: The sand is slowly moved in the same direction as the near shore current. Every time a wave hits the beach, some sand is picked up; it is redeposited as the wave ebbs. At Sandy Hook, the littoral drift is from south to north, so the beaches at the Hook's northern tip are increasing in size and those to the south are decreasing. When the Sandy Hook lighthouse was built in 1764, it stood near the northern end of the spit, but now, as you will see during your walk, it is 1.5 miles south of the tip. There is some concern that Sandy Hook will again become an island, as it has been several

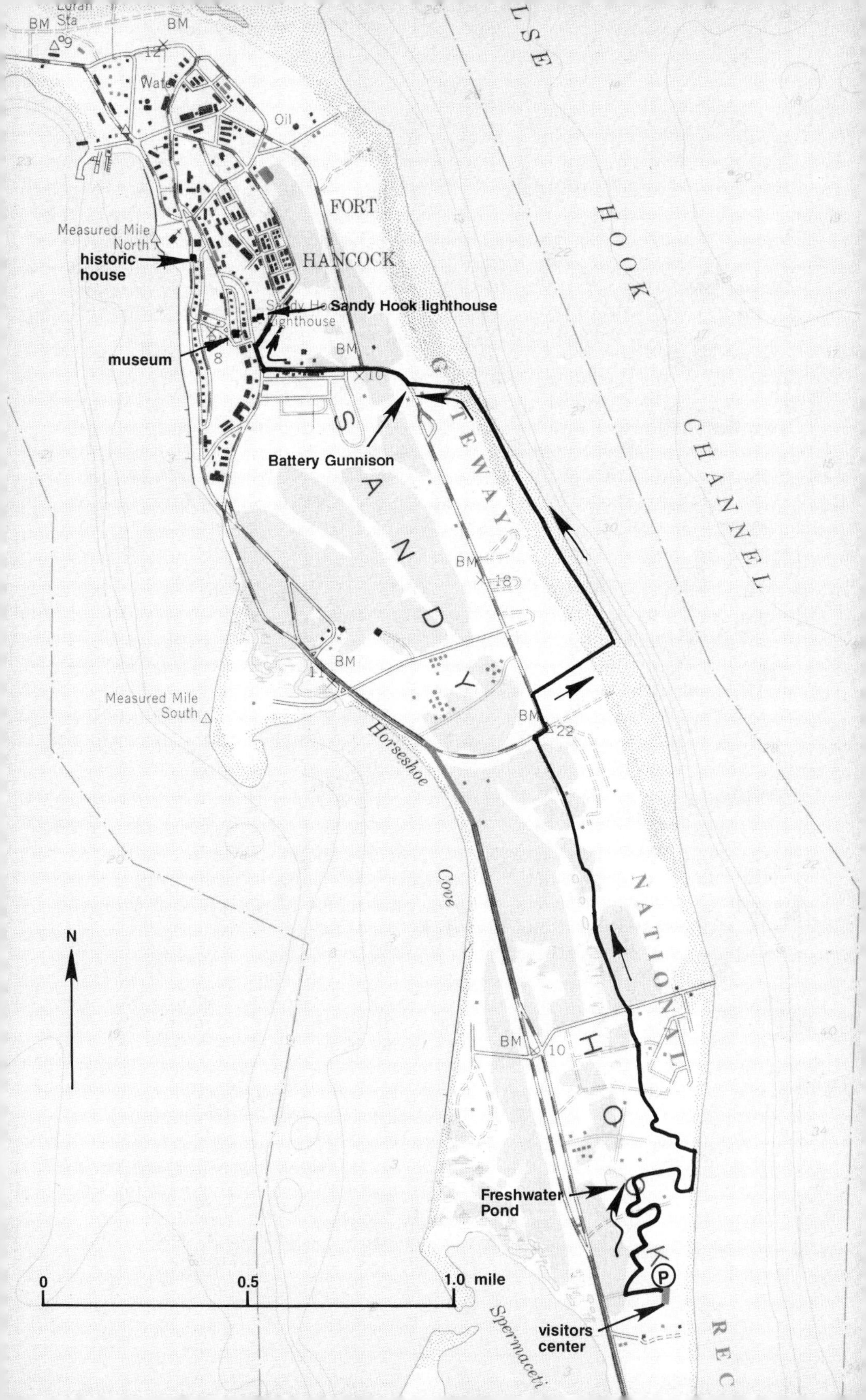
FORT
HANCOCK
historic house
Sandy Hook lighthouse
museum
Battery Gunnison
Measured Mile North
Measured Mile South
Horseshoe
Cove
Spermaceti
Freshwater Pond
visitors center
N
0
0.5
1.0 mile
SANDY HOOK
GATEWAY NATIONAL REC
HOOK CHANNEL

times in the past. In addition to the Hook's island history, this sandy spit has twice before been attached to the mainland at Atlantic Highlands.

Sandy Hook is a major bird migration route, and 300 species of birds have been seen in the area, attracted by the wide variety of environments ranging from fresh- to saltwater and from beach to grassland and forest. The osprey and the great blue heron nest here during the warmer months, and the area has a wintering population of robins. Just north of Spermaceti Cove on the bay side is the oldest known stand of hollies covering 280 acres. Some of the holly trunks measure 5 inches, indicating 300 years of growth. The area is closed to the public, except for occasional conducted tours.

There is a great deal of history associated with Sandy Hook. In 1524, Giovanni Verrazano supposedly landed on the spit; Henry Hudson also stopped here. Some of Captain Kidd's treasure is reputedly buried beneath a great pine tree on the Hook, though his booty remains undiscovered.

How to Get There

At exit 117 off the Garden State Parkway, take NJ 36 east, following signs to the villages of Atlantic Highlands and Highlands, and thence to Sandy Hook. Avid beachwalkers should only require one car for this hike, which can be left at the visitors center, approximately 2 miles into the spit. After exploring Fort Hancock, you can retrace your footsteps along either the beach or the main road back to the center. During the summer months there is a parking fee, but again, the low-use months—late fall through early spring—are the preferred months for your visit.

Alternatively, you can leave a car at one of the northern parking lots for use at the end of the hike.

The Trail

The visitors center building dates from 1894. Make a stop to look around the museum with its fish tank and slide program, shown on request. The center is housed at Spermaceti Cove, site of one of the first eight lifesaving stations built on the New Jersey coastline to provide rescue services following shipwrecks. One of the worst sea disasters occurred in January 1837. One hundred seventeen people died and whole families were found frozen in the rigging when, within sight of Sandy Hook, the American ship *Mexico,* full of English and Irish immigrants, was unable to sustain its anchorage in a tremendous gale and snowstorm and was swept aground off Long Island. Crews of these stations used the Lyle gun, which fired a rope to a ship in distress; when the rope was established, crew and passengers were pulled ashore. Regular practice sessions were held.

You can obtain a guide for the Old Dune Trail at the visitors center. Find the trailhead toward the bay side of Sandy Hook in the parking lot close to the handicapped parking places. Study the guide and stop at the numbered signs to read and learn about the area. The Old Dune Trail is only 1 mile in length and ends within sight of the visitors center.

As you walk, bear in mind that this area is under constant bombardment by salt and wind; plants have adapted to the harsh environment, but the area can still be easily destroyed by careless walking across the dunes. Please remain on the marked trail.

In season you will find many wildflowers here—apple blossom, honeysuckle, wild strawberry, rhodora. In the open area, beach heather and prickly pear eke out a precarious existence. To discourage competition for scarce resources, the roots of these two plants secrete a poison that inhibits the growth of neighboring plants. That this strategy is successful is apparent by the concentrations of beach heather. Another botanical oddity to be found on Sandy Hook is an import called dusty miller, with furry leaves that catch dew on their velvety surfaces.

Just after stop #5, the trail makes a right turn toward the parked cars, then turns left just prior to the blacktop. Some magnificent specimens of holly grow in this section. Walk across the paved parking lot entry road and up five wooden steps back into the holly grove. Just after stop #8 (you may spot an extra #8 nestling in a tree), the trail bends right and approaches a service station. Shortly, the trail becomes wider, and the increased breeze may tell you that you are walking toward the ocean. A sign will direct you to turn left. An arrow after a slight climb indicates another left turn (turning right would take you out to the beach). The trail then snakes through the dunes to an area where trees left as upright skeletons testify to the damage caused by salty winds.

After about 5 minutes the trail passes through chain-link fencing and comes to a stop at a wide sandy road leading to the beach. The trail then widens and reaches a wooden viewing stand on the left. Climb the small flight of wooden stairs for an unusual sight of a freshwater pond surrounded by a salty area. It is possible to get closer to the pond, supported on the left by a man-made stone wall, by walking for a few yards through tall phragmites down to the water's edge. Look closely along the shore, for a blue heron may be there.

Shortly after you leave the tranquil freshwater pond with its teeming wildlife, you will reach the remains of a Nike missile site, placed here to guard New York against air attack; the missiles could intercept and destroy aircraft long before they could pose much of a threat. Concepts of defense changed, however, and the missiles were removed in 1974. At the end of that year, the military installation at Sandy Hook, Fort Hancock, was officially discontinued. The site is now protected by a chain-link fence, and because garbage is the only thing to be seen behind the fence, walking down the path to the actual area is not suggested. Your trail turns right then immediately left to skirt the Nike site, becomes more open, and leads onto the beach. Walking the Old Dune Trail will probably take about 30 minutes.

Once out on the beach, stay close to the dunes and look for the unsigned entry to the South Beach Dune Trail, found just before a stunted tree and less than 100 yards from the end of the Old Dune Trail. Walk over the ridge of the dune on the left and, if you are in the correct place, you will see the wide and sandy trail with one wooden water bar. Turn left within a couple of minutes between two hiker signs. The arrows on the signs are a little confusing, but the path ahead is the wrong one; be sure to turn left. Within another few minutes, another hiker sign will direct you to the right, and herd paths will join from both sides. Stay on the main path, down two or three wooden steps, until you see a concrete building and a gunpost on the paved road to Area F.

Should you fail to find this section of the South Beach Dune Trail, continue along the beach from the Old Dune Trail until you reach Fishermans Parking Area F. There is a portajohn here. Turn left down the paved road until you arrive at the trail sign on the right, which indicates that the South Beach Dune Trail is 1.1 miles long. The parking lot is very small and full most weekends.

After crossing the paved road, the trail continues northward at quite some distance from the shore. The trees are taller and include oak and cedar as well as holly. Herd paths enter from both sides, but the main trail is wide and frequently marked. Toward its end the trail passes a marsh—where you can see signs of the range-finding units that were once established here—and emerges onto paved Atlantic Drive between two metal posts connected by wire. At present the South Beach Dune Trail ends here, though there are plans to continue it to connect with Parking Area L.

Turn right and follow the bend to the left until the road straightens, then continue for about 5 minutes to a wide sandy road on the right. Use this route to return to the shore, then turn left and continue northward.

If the beach and the road leading to it are closed to protect endangered birds, your only alternative is to walk Atlantic Drive north until it turns to hard-packed dirt and sand, passes the Resource Management Area, and arrives at Battery Gunnison. Although Atlantic is not the busiest road on Sandy Hook, walking the beach would obviously be preferable. Both paths lead to Battery Gunnison.

The width of the beach changes from time to time, and within a little while you get your first glimpse of Sandy Hook lighthouse. As you progress north, the backdrop of New York City becomes clearer, and the Verrazano Narrows Bridge comes into sight. The walk can be extended by proceeding as far north as you wish before turning inland to Fort Hancock.

As you walk along the beach, watch carefully on the left for a food and drink concession, a half-buried wooden breakwater, and perhaps even some equipment in the Resource Management Area. Walk left here to Battery Gunnison.

The gunnison was erected in 1904. Its 6-inch guns were intended to track and destroy small warships too speedy for Fort Hancock's huge coastal artillery. There are two separate gun emplacements, accessible by two small flights of cement stairs, and you also get an improved view of the ocean from this small elevation.

Leave Battery Gunnison and turn north onto Gunnison Road past the sign that says NORTH BEACH. Sandy Hook lighthouse will still be visible.

You will pass a large new parking area on the left, cross Atlantic Drive, pass by a smaller parking area on the right, and arrive at a T-junction with Magruder Road. The sign immediately ahead directs motorists to the park exit and NJ 36. The bay is visible through the houses of Fort Hancock.

Turn right to the lighthouse, passing the Marine Academy of Science and Technology and deserted houses, all numbered. At number 76, bear right again onto Hudson Drive for the best view yet of the lighthouse.

Sandy Hook is the oldest operating lighthouse in the United States. The white octagonal tower was often the first beacon seen by travelers arriving in New York because until 1907, the Sandy Hook channel was the only passageway for large ships to enter New York harbor. Built in 1764, it was among 12 lighthouses established by the original American colonies. It was occupied for a short time by British troops during the American Revolution and was fought over by British and rebel soldiers. The tower, visible 19 miles at sea, is 103 feet tall and still in use, though now unmanned and automatic.

Exploring Fort Hancock can take

considerable time. There are deserted batteries, a museum, and a historic house that all hold great interest for history lovers. Fort Hancock was established in the 1890s, but its buildings now stand empty and deteriorating, and there are apparently no plans for its rehabilitation. Close to the lighthouse is the mortar battery, which is open to visitors. Several mortars occupied a single pit here and were designed to fire simultaneously, lobbing 12-inch, 800-pound shells in high arcs to penetrate ships' lightly armored decks. However, these masonry forts proved to be no match for the new-style battleships, and the forts were abandoned in favor of individual gun batteries that were more easily concealed.

Search out the Rodman Gun close to the bay. After a large gun burst near Lieutenant Thomas Rodman in 1844, he committed himself to improving the technology of cannon manufacture and invented the casting process that made possible this one-piece smooth-bore barrel.

At the end of your exploration, you must either exit Fort Hancock at North Beach and retrace your steps south along the beach or return in the vehicle you previously parked at Fort Hancock.

SJG

39

Allaire State Park

Total distance: 4 miles

Hiking time: 2½ hours

Vertical rise: 120 feet

Rating: Easy to moderate

Maps: USGS Farmingdale, Asbury Park; DEP Allaire State Park

Allaire State Park (PO Box 220, Farmingdale, NJ 07727; 908-938-2371) was a 1941 gift to the people of the state of New Jersey from Arthur Brisbane, a prominent newspaper man. The original 1000-plus acres has now expanded to more than 3000 and includes a stream, narrow-gauge railroad, golf course, car camping area, and entire historical village dating from the boom days of the bog iron industry in the last two centuries. The park, located in one of the northernmost sections of the Pine Barrens, straddles the Manasquan River, which is popular with canoeists. The recent completion of I-195, which bisects the park, pollutes the park with sound, denying it the isolation it once had. On the other hand, the interstate also makes the park more accessible to the public.

Within Allaire's boundaries are a large number of sand and gravel roads and an abandoned railroad bed that are used for hiking, biking, and horseback riding. These trails are marked with colored tags and directional arrows. Because the park is essentially quartered by the river and the freeway, a complete tour is not possible, and we have chosen a route that takes you through some wooded areas as well as the park's main attraction, historic Allaire Village.

How to Get There

Take exit 31B off I-195 and head east on County Route 524 (CR 524). The park is well marked with signs, and you should have no problem finding the main entrance. The park is also accessible from the Garden State Parkway, exit 98; just follow the brown STATE PARK signs. This hike begins at an unmarked parking area on state land, 0.6 mile past (east of) the main entrance. By parking here you avoid both the fees and the crowds that visit the park only to see the historic village.

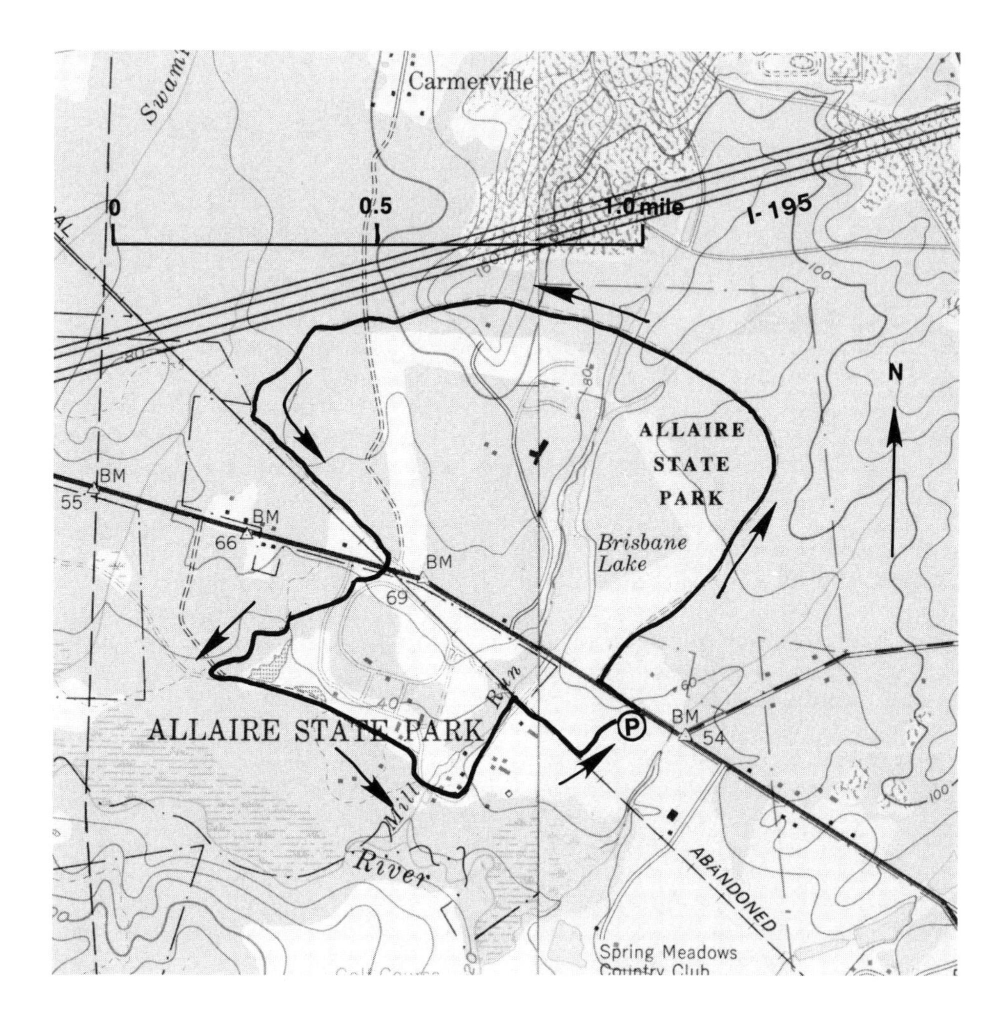

The Trail

Cross the road and head west back toward the main entrance. You'll be walking past a small horse ranch with a split-rail fence. At the end of the fence, look for a gate leading into a field. Just to the right of the gate is a post that marks the entrance to a lane running between the ranch and the field. Your route, marked with orange plastic disks, may be overgrown for the first 100 yards or so, but it soon widens and becomes more comfortable for walking. The lane—which is very straight because it is the border of a farmed field—is shadowed by tall sumac trees and vines. There are also a few patches of holly along the trail. As you leave the highway and the sound of traffic, the sounds of birds, plentiful in this area of field and woods, are heard.

After about 10 minutes, enter a typical south Jersey forest. The pathway widens into a sand and gravel road common to the Pine Barrens, and the walking becomes very pleasant. Ferns and blueberry bushes form the ground cover, and huge clusters of mountain laurel rise up from the forest floor. At first some oaks and maples appear; farther along come sassafras and the inevitable pitch pines. When the road comes to a fork, keep left.

This trail (or—more accurately—sand road) forms a large horseshoe, eventually returning to the county road you started on, though a little farther west. As it swings left and west, it parallels I-195 (always busy with cars heading to and from the Jersey shore) for about 0.5 mile. In this section is a short uphill climb to a gravel quarry and water tower, and then a long downhill when the trail comes within sight of the interstate. Stay on the main road/trail, now quite wide, which eventually swings away from the noisy highway and heads south toward the main park entrance and a quieter environment. The sounds of birds once again become more prominent. A wood thrush or two may resent your intrusion into their territory. In this section the trail parallels the bed of the former Freehold-Jamesburg Railroad, used in other sections of the park as a hiking and horse trail.

The trail will bring you to the main road at a gate similar to the one at the beginning of the hike. Cross the road here, bear somewhat to the left, and follow the narrow-gauge railroad tracks to the right toward where they enter the woods. Look for the orange trail markings and follow them—not the tracks—into the woods. After only a few yards, cross the park entrance road and reenter the woods, still on the orange trail. The trail next crosses a gravel maintenance road, zigs across another bridle path, and eventually comes to a T-intersection with a gravel road. Bear left here, cross a creek, and make a sharp left on a gravel road known in the park as the Raceway.

Follow the Raceway (marked both green and red) straight ahead, keeping the water to your left. After a short distance you should see a wooden bridge on your left. This bridge leads to the park nature center, which has some interesting displays and an accurate wall map of all the sand roads and trails in the park.

From the bridge, continue along the Raceway past the pond and through a large picnic area. This is the developed section of the park, and you should expect to see many people here, especially on summer weekends. After passing the large parking lot on the left, enter historic Allaire Village. Back in the 18th century, this village site was known as Monmouth Furnace and later as the Howell Works, after the first iron maker here. He leased the property to James P. Allaire of New York in 1822, who was already very much established as a brass worker. At the Howell Works, Allaire put together a community of more than 400 people to turn bog iron into pots, kettles, cauldrons, stovepipe, and other common items. The self-contained community included a wide variety of craftspersons to both run the industry and serve the population.

Bog iron, found in the Pine Barrens, is smelted from iron oxides leached from the sand and deposited in accumulations of decaying swamp vegetation. Interestingly, bog iron is a renewable resource as long as the vegetation decay cycle is not interfered with. The operation at Allaire's village prospered until around 1850, when competition from products made of higher grade iron ore lowered profits. After its abandonment, the

Allaire community was used for a time by the Boy Scouts as a headquarters; in 1941, it was deeded to the state. Today, the village of Allaire is remarkably well preserved and nearly intact from its heyday a century ago.

The visitors center, a long brick building, is on your left and offers a number of interesting displays about the park and the village. A map and guide to the village can be obtained here. A seasonal food concession is located in this area also. From here, continue straight ahead to the end of the visitors center, make a right, and follow the main road that heads downhill to the left and out to the main buildings of the village. Follow this main road as it swings to the left at the general store and heads north, eventually leaving the village area through a gate.

Follow the gravel road (which ultimately leads to CR 524) away from the village. To avoid walking back to your car on CR 524, bear right on a wide pathway that crosses the lane. This is actually an abandoned Freehold-Jamesburg Railroad bed. After only a few minutes, you'll find a narrow trail coming in on the left that will lead you through a field to the parking area and your car. This trail, which skirts a swampy area, may occasionally be too muddy to walk. If so, retrace your steps along the old railbed and walk out to CR 524. Turn right back to your car.

HNZ/BCS

40

Cattus Island

Total distance: 3 miles

Hiking time: 2 hours

Vertical rise: Minimal

Rating: Easy

Maps: USGS Toms River/Seaside Park; Cattus Island Ocean County Park map

Cattus Island Park (1170 Cattus Island Boulevard, Toms River, NJ 08753; 908-270-6960) preserves a small portion of the salt marshes and pine forests (now steadily being developed) on Barnegat Bay. Located in the midst of New Jersey's most popular summer vacation area, Cattus Island offers the hiker a variety of environments to explore, including pinelands, open marshes, holly forests, and bay beaches. The excellent views over vast marshes, across inlets, and out over the bay, plus the variety of wildlife found in the park, are further reasons to walk the trails in this 500-acre Ocean County park. Be advised that wood and deer ticks are found on the island. Take the usual precautions: Tuck pants into socks, spray with tick repellent, and check for ticks after the hike. Staying on the trails is also very important.

Cattus Island was first settled by the Page family, who moved here in 1763. Timothy Page, born on the island during that year, served in the local militia during the American Revolution. Most probably he was a privateer, essentially a pirate licensed by the Continental Congress. During the war, British ships were lured into Barnegat Bay through Cranberry Inlet only to be attacked and their cargoes sold for profit. Cranberry Inlet, an opening to the Atlantic near present-day Ortley Beach, existed between 1750 and 1812. It was opened and closed by strong storms.

After the death of Timothy Page, the family house burned down, and the property was sold to Lewis Applegate. He moved there in 1842 and developed the southeastern section of the island, now named for him. He built a sawmill and a port for lumber boats. The island was sold again in 1867 and was slated to be developed as a resort, but the 1873 depression canceled the project.

In 1895 the island was purchased by John V.A. Cattus, an importer and

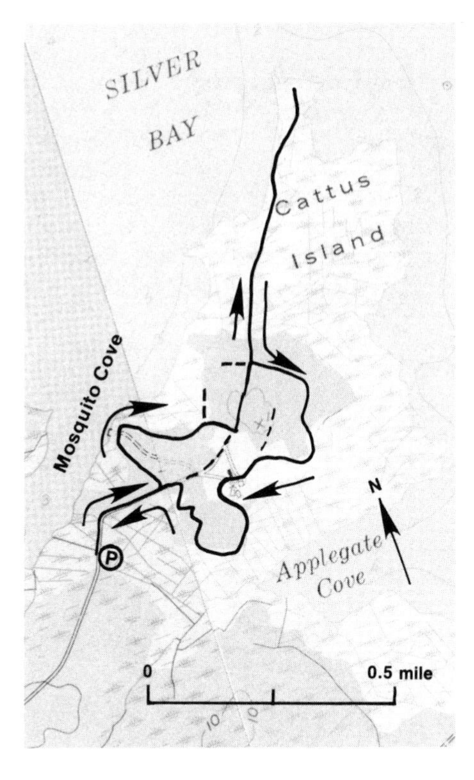

Olympic-class athlete. He used the island and its buildings for weekend vacations, not as a full-time residence. Cattus loved boating, owned many boats, and built a hunting lodge on the island. After he died, the land was sold in 1964 by his sons to developers. New state laws passed in the early 1970s that limited development in wetlands and along the coast discouraged the developers, and they sold the land to Ocean County in 1973. The property was acquired with county tax dollars and state Green Acres funds. In 1976 the park opened to the public, and the following year trail development began.

Before beginning the hike, follow the asphalt path to the nature center. Sign in, take a look around, and pick up a map of the park that shows both trails and terrain. The nature center has a number of displays and maps that pertain to Ocean County. The center is staffed by naturalists and a large number of volunteers, both young and old.

How to Get There

From the Garden State Parkway exit 82 (Toms River/NJ 37), take NJ 37 east 4.4 miles to Fisher Boulevard. Travel north on Fisher Boulevard for exactly 2 miles and turn right onto Cattus Island Boulevard (just after the Bellcrest shopping plaza). The park entrance road is 0.1 mile ahead on the left. Another 0.5 mile will bring you to the large parking area near the Cooper Environmental Center.

The Trail

After a visit to the center, walk around it past the directory and bear to the right. Pass through a wooden gate and onto a sand road marked sporadically with white. This road, more like a causeway, penetrates the salt marsh that surrounds the slightly higher and drier land ahead. Cattus Island is not an island in the true sense, but if it weren't for this road, access would be very difficult. The body of water to the left is Mosquito Cove. The sand road leads straight ahead into the woods and eventually out to the tip of the island, which extends well into Barnegat Bay.

Make a left turn onto a red-blazed footpath just after leaving the marsh. This path winds through a pine forest, makes a small loop out to the shoreline, then swings out again to the grassy shore of Mosquito Cove at the old Boathouse Landing. Here, rising from the water, are the last remains of the old boathouse and a dock.

Leave the dock area and continue following red markers through a forest of oak, pines, and enormous thickets of greenbrier. The walking through this aromatic woods is very pleasant. Pass near the gnarled trunk of an old cedar and enter a holly forest, green in all seasons. Notice that the red berries do not occur on all the holly trees—only the female trees bear fruit. These bright red berries are found on the tree year-round and well supply the bird population with food. Not far ahead, the red trail meets the sand road, blazed white, again. Turn left here, heading northeast.

Walk the white-blazed sand road causeway, bordered by salt marsh on the right and wet lowland forest on the left. Here are stands of pitch pine, red cedar, and other water-loving plants. Towering over the marsh to the right is an osprey nesting site. Other water birds, such as the great egret, may be feeding in this area. After 10 to 15 minutes the road ends at the narrow, sandy beach that forms the northern tip of Cattus Island. You may wish to walk along this narrow strip of sand to the final point of the island. After this short exploration, return to the sand road and retrace your steps to its junction with a yellow trail. Bear left.

The yellow trail again penetrates the drier woods of Cattus Island. It winds through a forest of holly and some rather large oaks. You will pass two large, twisted, gnarled, and quite dead cedar trees on the right. Deer are plentiful in this area, their footprints in the sand a common sight. After penetrating a dense pine forest, you will reach an extensive vista of black, muddy salt marsh, sliced by drainage ditches, and the forest beyond. From this vista, the trail swings to the right and ends at a junction with a blue trail.

Turn left onto the blue trail and follow it to an open area lined with bayberry bushes. The large clearing and the park benches under tall cedars mark the site where the island's former residents lived. Leave the blue trail here, turning left onto the red trail.

From the clearing, follow red markers back into the woods on a curving forest road. The trail makes a series of tight turns through holly trees, only to reemerge near the edge of the salt marsh. From here you will see Applegate Cove on the left and, to the right, the Cooper Environmental Center. After many small turns, the trail emerges onto the white-blazed sand road again. Make a left here, walk down the straight lane through the marsh, and journey back to the nature center and parking area.

BCS

Phragmites on Cattus Island

41

Island Beach State Park

Total distance: 3.5 miles

Hiking time: 2½ hours

Vertical rise: Minimal

Rating: Easy

Maps: USGS Barnegat Light; DEP Island Beach State Park

Along the 127-mile boundary between New Jersey and the Atlantic Ocean are a number of long, thin barrier islands. Separated from the mainland by large bays, these islands are part of a chain that runs from New England to the Gulf Coast of Mexico. The constant movement of sand pushed by the ocean waves, called littoral drift, both maintains and changes these relatively fragile land forms. Severe storms often open or close inlets, wash out beaches, and even extend barrier islands, creating new land. With the exception of Island Beach State Park (Seaside Park, NJ 08752; 908-793-0506), most of these islands have been developed with row after row of summer beach homes, boardwalks, and restaurants. If it were not for this park, many New Jerseyites would have no idea of what the shoreline in its natural state would look like.

Island Beach State Park occupies the southern end of a long spit that is joined to the mainland near Point Pleasant. This section of the spit was an island at one time; an inlet connecting the ocean and Barnegat Bay was once located near present-day Ortley Beach. This inlet, known as Cranberry Inlet, was created and destroyed overnight by storms in 1750 and 1812. More recently, in 1935, a storm opened up an inlet just south of the present park entrance. Local rum runners wanted it to remain open, but the owners of the tract at the time had it closed.

Originally, Island Beach was owned by Lord Stirling, owner of vast acreages in New Jersey during the 17th century (see Hike 29). During this period, the island was called Lord Stirling's Isle. Not much happened here during the next 100 years. These beaches were remote from industrial areas and were occupied only by squatters who lived in part from materials

Back dunes at Island Beach State Park

washed ashore. In 1926 Henry Phipps purchased the island with a shore resort in mind. He was able to build three large homes (one of which, mentioned earlier, is used by the governor of New Jersey as a summer residence) before his project was halted by the stock market crash and Depression. During World War II, Island Beach was used by the army for rocket experiments and, as such, was restricted to the public. The squatters and leaseholders who lived on the island were forced to leave, though they were allowed to return after the war. In 1953, after much talk about preserving the area, the state purchased the land from the Phipps estate and opened the park in 1959. The island residents who held leases were allowed to live there as long as they were alive. Of the original 90 leases, only 6 remain.

The 3002 acres of the park are divided into three sections, the northernmost and southernmost being natural areas, the central section public beaches and concessions. Located 1.2 miles south of the entrance are the park office and a nature center. A short, circular, self-guiding nature trail, which begins at the Aeolium (the nature center) is a good introduction to the park's vegetation. Farther ahead on the left is one of the original homes built in the 1920s as part of a planned development; it's now used as a summer residence for New Jersey's governor. Beyond this house are the two large beach areas with their huge parking lots.

How to Get There

From exit 82 on the Garden State Parkway, take NJ 37 east through Toms River and over the Barnegat Bay Bridge. The entrance to the park is 2.5 miles south of the bridge at the southern end of NJ 35. There are many signs directing you to the park along the way. You will find that a fee is charged at the entrance gate. In 1996 this was $6 weekdays or $7 weekends from Memorial Day through Labor Day; $4 daily the rest of the year. You should also know that although a large number of parking spaces are spread along the 8-mile road in the park, they often fill up quickly during peak season, and late arrivals are turned away at the gate. In fact, use of the area is so high that computer signs on the Garden State Parkway advise of the park's opening or closing. The best time to explore Island Beach State Park on foot is definitely during the off-season, especially during the week.

To begin the hike, drive the full 8 miles south from the park entrance to parking area A-23, the last one on the paved road. This area is very popular and may be filled on sunny days, even during the off-season. If so, park at area A-22 or A-21 and walk the extra distance along the road. (The area between A-19 and A-20 is a bird observation area).

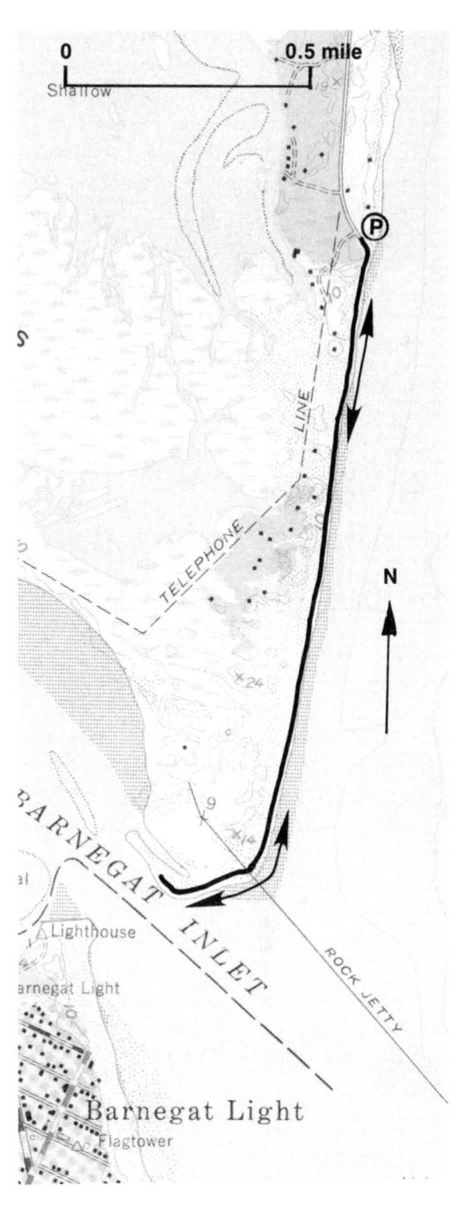

The Trail

From parking area A-23, walk through the gate toward the shoreline. You will be walking in a southerly direction toward the Barnegat Inlet and Lighthouse. You can walk either on the beach buggy tracks or along the water's edge, both far easier to walk on than the soft sand. The compacted sand along the water is probably the most interesting choice because it offers a fascinating variety of ocean debris that is constantly being reorganized by the tides and waves. Here are shells, dead fish, crabs, and driftwood. You will also encounter seagulls and fishermen with their beach buggies and campers. You will never be bored walking along what you may first think a monotonous stretch of beach.

After about 1.5 miles, you will reach the southern tip of Island Beach. This is Barnegat Inlet, where the Atlantic Ocean meets Barnegat Bay. Barnegat Lighthouse, built in 1858, stands across the inlet at the northern tip of Long Beach Island. In Barnegat Inlet, the ocean currents are steadily moving sand southward toward Long Beach Island. The accumulation of sand from this drift is awesome when you consider that the end of the road, more than a mile back, was once much closer to the end of the island. The Army Corps of Engineers struggles to keep this inlet, which is constantly filling with sand, open to navigation. It was hoped that the inlet would be stabilized by the two jetties, but even these structures don't prevent the sand from filling the inlet. During low tide, a sandbar or breaking waves are often visible between the two.

Walk west along the jetty toward Barnegat Bay. To your right is a protected bird nesting area and, beyond that, the dunes. The stability of the entire state park depends on these dunes, which are in turn stabilized by dune grass and other plants such as seaside goldenrod and Hudsonia or beach heather. These plants are very tolerant of the salty sea spray, which kills other species. Continue walking westward until you are nearly opposite the lighthouse. Comparing the present topography with that of the geological survey map reveals the incredible changes constantly taking place here. To your right are the Sedge Islands, a large area of salt marsh inhabited by countless birds. Also to the right are the higher backdunes, separating the foredunes and the bay, which support a thick barrier of holly, bayberry, and other shrubs that cannot tolerate salt spray. You can also see a residence from here, one of several at the southern end of the park.

A small promontory made of jetty stone juts into the inlet, usually a private spot for lunch or simply for viewing the bay, ocean, and inlet all at once. To the south, the lighthouse and a steady parade of fishing and pleasure boats are a sharp contrast to the wild, inaccessible Sedge Islands to the northwest. When you are ready, retrace your steps from this spot to the ocean shoreline and then to the parking area. The first large gap in the dune fence that parallels the shore is your access to parking area A-23.

BCS

42

Wells Mills County Park

Total distance: 4.5 miles

Hiking Time: 2 hours

Vertical rise: Approximately 200 feet

Rating: Moderate

Maps: USGS Brookville; Ocean County Parks & Recreation Wells Mills Trail Map

Wells Mills County Park (Box 905, Wells Mills Road, Waretown, NJ 08758; 609-971-3085) is located at the site of the former town of Wells Mills. Here, sometime in the late 1700s, James Wells established a sawmill. He created the lake, which drove the mill, by damming Oyster Creek. Others settled in the area and over the years the ownership of the mill was passed along, each owner benefiting from the local abundance of Atlantic white, or "swamp," cedar. This wood is not only strong but also extremely rot resistant and was used to build ships. Shingles and housebuilding lumber were other products of the mill.

During the 1870s Christopher Estlow and his sons operated two mills in the area, which explains why the name of the town, and now the park, is plural. In addition to the sawmill business, Estlow's son Tilden mined clay, which was sent to Trenton to be made into pottery. In 1936 the property was sold to Charles M. Conrad and his son Grove. A year later they began constructing the cabin that stands today on the shore of the lake at the boat docks. By 1979 the Conrad family found a buyer for all of their 200 acres in the New Jersey Conservation Foundation. This private organization moves quickly to purchase land that might otherwise be developed. Later the land is sold to public agencies, in this case Ocean County. Additional acquisitions by the county have increased the size of the park to about 900 acres.

The staff of the Ocean County Park System has created an excellent trail system. Several color-coded paths explore the park, one of which totals 7.7 miles. The first section of this long trail, the Penn's Hill Trail, will be used in this hike. The park system has wisely kept hiking trails and multiuse trails (on which mountain

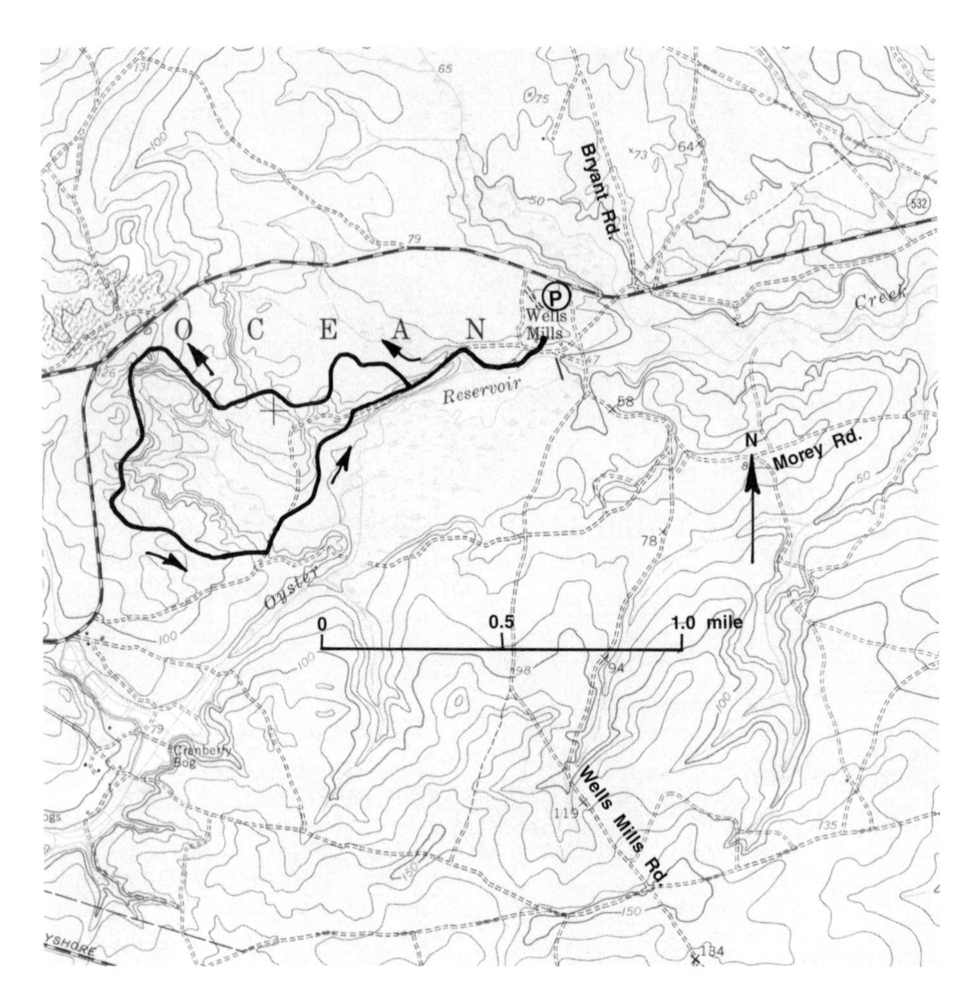

bikes are permitted) mostly separate. One of the surprises you will find here is the frequent ups and downs. Most of the New Jersey pinelands are flat. Here, and also just to the north in the Forked River Mountains (privately owned), the flatness is broken by small hills.

Expect to encounter ticks here—mostly wood ticks but also deer ticks. They are worse in summer, less of a problem in cooler weather. Take the following precautions: Wear light-colored pants and socks, tuck the pants into the socks, and then spray your legs and feet with industrial-strength (containing DEET) tick repellent. If you stay on the trail, chances are you may not pick up even one tick. If you bushwhack off the trail, you may collect quite a few. After your hike, de-tick yourself thoroughly.

How to Get There

Wells Mills County Park is on the eastern edge of the Pine Barrens, not far from the Garden State Parkway. Coming from the north, take parkway exit 74 (Forked River/Waretown) and drive east for 2 miles to US 9. Drive south on US 9 for 3 miles and then turn right (east) onto County Road 532 (CR 532). In 2 miles you'll cross under the parkway; in another 2.5 miles you will find the entrance to Wells Mills County Park on your left. If coming from the south, take parkway exit 69 and drive 2.2 miles east on CR 532 to the park entrance. Follow the entrance drive past the maintenance building to the large parking lot.

The Trail

Walk toward the rest rooms and fountain, then follow the paved path to the nature center. Be sure to sign in at the directory just past the rest rooms, and be sure to stop in at the nature center to see the displays illustrating the natural and human history of Wells Mills.

When you are ready to start hiking, leave the center and face the lake; you should see a tree with three white paint markers to your right. This is the Penn's Hill Trail (trail #4), which first follows the shoreline of Wells Mills Lake and then circles through a remote and hilly section of the park. Mountain bikes are permitted on the Penn's Hill Trail only where it follows sand roads.

Follow the white markers of the trail (which shares its route for a while with a yellow-blazed trail), keeping left and close to the shoreline. Notice that the marking system in this park uses one blaze to indicate that you are on the trail and three markers for a turn, with one of the upper markers indicating the direction of the turn. Walk between the cabin and the lake; you can get a good view of the lake from the floating docks. After you pass the cabin, the white markers lead you first under some holly trees, then through a deep woods of cedar and laurel. Here the trail turns away from the lake on a wood-chip bed, passing a junction with a red trail on the right, a fire ditch, and then a junction with a blue trail. Turn left here onto the sand road. This is Ridge Road, and it is open to mountain bikes. You'll cross over a small creek on a stone-lined bridge, and then pass a side trail on the left that leads out to an observation blind on the lake. Not far past this junction, the white markers of the Penn's Hill Trail turn right onto a footpath, leaving Ridge Road.

From here the trail winds through a forest of pitch pines and scrub oak with an understory of mountain and sheep laurel, crossing several fire ditches along the way. The well-maintained trail snakes its way deeper and deeper into the pineland forest, crossing over wet areas on "narrow-gauge" bridges. About 20 minutes into the hike, the trail reaches the top of a small rise called Raccoon Ridge. This is the 1-mile point, as noted by a sign. From here the trail alternately rises and falls, a highly unusual pattern for the Pine Barrens. In some sections you will find sweet pepperbush growing alongside the trail, in others highbush blueberry.

After a short climb, the trail attains a small ridge. This is Penn's Hill, which is about 150 feet above sea level and about 100 feet higher than the surface of Wells Mills Lake. Although this relief seems inconsequential when compared with the mountains of northern New Jersey, it is unusual in the Pine Barrens. As you come down the hill with a swamp on the left, you'll pass the 2-mile marker. Just ahead the trail crosses an arm of the swamp on boardwalk. Although this section of the hike is actually near a road, it feels quite wild and remote.

Over the next mile the trail climbs Laurel Hill, descends, and then walks along what is called Laurel Ridge. Like Penn's Hill, neither of these high points is much more than 50 feet above the surrounding woods, but they do require some effort. Along the way you'll walk through a small clearing, use some wooden stairways, and straddle a few wet sections made worse by trespassing mountain bikes. At the 3-mile point you should arrive at a major junction. Turn left here, leaving the white markers, onto a sand road that is open to mountain bikes.

Follow the sand road, marked with the green blazes of the Estlow Trail, in a northerly direction. Almost immediately you'll enter a cedar swamp. The narrow, perfectly vertical cedars and the dark waters of the brook are a sharp contrast with your last 2 miles of hiking. After you cross the brook on a small bridge, turn right onto a footpath following the green markers. This path slabs the side of a rise for about 0.5 mile, then reaches a junction with a wider sand lane. Turn left here, walk 100 feet to a much larger sand road, and turn right. You have now rejoined Ridge Road.

Follow the white markers past the trail to the observation blind and over the stone-lined bridge. Immediately after crossing, turn right, still following white markers back through the cedar swamp, past the cabin, and back to the visitors center.

BCS

43

Lebanon State Forest

Total distance: 8.5 miles

Hiking time: 5 hours

Vertical rise: 50 feet

Rating: Moderately strenuous

Maps: USGS Browns Mills; DEP Lebanon State Forest; DEP Batona Trail

Utilizing a section of the Batona Trail and the gravel and sand roads that crisscross the Pine Barrens, this hike takes in much of what Lebanon State Forest (Box 215, Route 72, New Lisbon, NJ 08064; 609-726-1191) has to offer. You will visit Pakim Pond, a good spot for lunch; cross a large cedar swamp twice; and follow the shores of reservoirs and cranberry bogs. In this latter section your navigational skills may be challenged. Though long in mileage, this hike is not especially strenuous because the land is so flat; however, hot weather and biting deer flies could make it seem difficult, and, like most long hikes in the Pine Barrens, it should probably be hiked in cooler weather.

Lebanon State Forest is named after the Lebanon Glass Works, manufacturers of window glass and bottles, located here during the middle of the last century. The availability of sand and wood for charcoal supported the glassmaking industry until about 1867 when the wood supply became exhausted. About 150 men worked here, and a small town of 60 homes, a few shops, and a post office was established but later abandoned. In 1908 the state began to acquire land in the area. Also part of Lebanon State Forest is deserted Whitesbog Village, the birthplace of the commercial blueberry and at one time the state's largest cranberry farm. The historic village is now being restored, and the abandoned cranberry bogs are appealing to walkers.

Cranberries are still harvested in some sections of Lebanon State Forest by farmers who lease the land from the state. The reservoirs are used to flood the bogs in the early fall for harvesting. Machines are run through the bogs to shake the berries off the vines. The berries, which float, are scooped up and loaded, via conveyor belts, onto trucks that take them to processing plants.

How to Get There

The main entrance to Lebanon State Forest is on NJ 72, 1 mile east of the traffic circle where it intersects NJ 70. The entrance is on the north side of the road and is well marked with a large sign. Proceed 0.3 mile on this entrance road and bear right at the first intersection. The park office is just ahead on the left. Park here.

The Trail

Take the blue access trail to the Batona Trail found south of the parking area. This trail, which is closed to mountain bikes, is labeled BATONA TRAIL. After a short walk, you will meet the true Batona Trail, marked with pink paint blazes. Bear left here, heading east. You'll be walking through a mixed pine and oak forest on a well-used footpath. The walking is pleasant and the trail surface, mostly sand, is soft and comfortable. After a short distance, the trail crosses a sand road and reenters the woods, continuing in an easterly direction. Here stands of scrub oak, sassafras, pink and white mountain laurel, and blueberry bushes close in on the trail. Tall ferns line the trail in darker places. Farther along, the Batona Trail crosses another sand road, this one larger, and reenters the woods on a small sand road. Gradually the trail climbs to its highest elevation, about 150 feet above sea level. The land is dry here, and blackjack oak, scrub oak, and pitch pine dominate.

About 2 miles into the hike the trail veers to the north and crosses paved Shinns Road. Continue following the pink markers of the Batona Trail and enter a swampy area utilizing a corduroy log footpath and boardwalks in some places. You are now on the edge of the Cedar Swamp Natural Area, a dense jungle of Atlantic white cedars surrounded by the pitch pine forest. The cedar wood, which is soft but durable, is used in boatbuilding, for some kinds of furniture, and for shingles and stakes. The management of this tree is an important project in the forest. Below the tall cedars, the vegetation is dense and the lighting is dark. Plant life includes rare orchids, curly grass ferns, pitcher plants, and sundews. After leaving the swamp, you'll come to a junction with a gravel road—follow the markers and bear right through an area where cedars have been harvested. This gravel road is also marked with red, it being part of a trail for the disabled. After you pass a few sand roads leading off to the right, the road swings left and meets an even larger gravel road, Coopers Road. Turn right and follow the pink and red markers into the Pakim Pond area.

Pakim Pond takes its name from the Native American word for cranberry. Its water is the reddish brown, acidic water typical of the Pine Barrens. Known as cedar water, it picks up its color and acidity as it moves very slowly through thick cedar swamps. Next to the pond is a swamp, a former cranberry bog. When the bog was actively cultivated, Pakim Pond was used as a reservoir to store water for the fall flooding of the bog. At Pakim Pond are rest rooms and picnic tables, but swimming is no longer allowed.

If you have time, you may wish to take the 1-mile nature trail located here, which explores both the pond and the swamp. This trail begins just off the Batona Trail at the southern part of the dam. A guidebook, which explains the points of interest located by numbered posts, is available at the park office. Carnivorous plants can be found here, including the pitcher plant and at least two types of sundew. The pitcher plant has funnel-like leaves that are filled with water. Insects are attracted to the leaves by their odor and color and, should they fall in, are drowned and digested by the plant. The sundew is very small

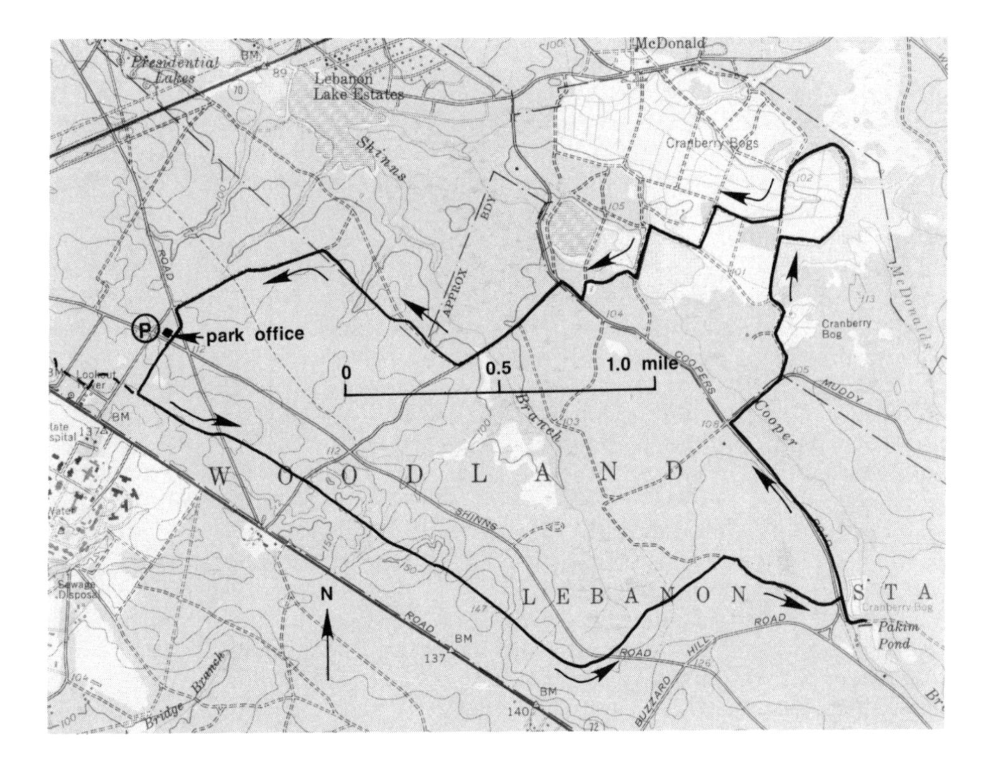

and grows in clumps in very wet but sunny areas. Its leaves, round or stemlike, have numerous sticky hairs that trap insects and then digest them. All three of these plants can be found along the northeastern shore of the pond just off the Batona Trail.

After either exploring or resting at Pakim Pond, leave the way you came in and return to the gravel road. Do not turn left on the Batona Trail at the junction, though; stay on Coopers Road. From now on you will be following sand and gravel roads and will need to pay attention to the text and map.

Coopers Road, like most of the gravel and sand roads in the Pine Barrens, is straight, flat, and lined with pines. It can be very hot here and very buggy during the summer. After about 15 minutes (0.7 mile), you'll come to a crossroads. Turn right here, onto a smaller gravel road known as Muddy Road, marked with white. Along the side of the road are rhododendron, pepperbush, spicebush, and various species of blueberry. You will pass through a cedar swamp with towering Atlantic white cedars, densely packed, looking down on you from both sides of the road. After another 0.2 mile, just where the road begins to swing to the right, follow the white markers that lead left onto a sand road. This road has some soft "sugar-sand" sections, and the going may be slow in places.

Farther along, you'll pass an open area that is, in fact, a former cranberry bog in various stages of regrowth. Follow the white markers and the road as it swings around the bog and heads north (ignore the road going off to the left); then head west again where it ends at a T-intersection. Bear right here and head north toward the reservoir, which, like Pakim Pond, was used to flood cranberry fields. The scenery as you walk along the dam is beautiful with the backdrop of pines and the green shades of water lilies and other aquatic vegetation. Wildflowers, not found in the shady woods, thrive in this sunny and well-watered environment. When you come to the corner of the reservoir, bear right, leaving the white markers. Now follow the reservoir's perimeter. The walkway heads east, then swings to the north, eventually leaving the reservoir with its dark cedar water, standing dead trees, and elusive pickerel. The sand road now winds through a quiet and remote pine woods with a forest carpeting of pine needles.

When you come to a junction with another sand road, keep left. Stay on this sand road, which is the white trail again, heading south for about 250 yards, then make a right turn on a sand road heading west. (From this junction, the edge of the first reservoir is visible.) An overgrown bog will be on your right and an open swamp, possibly with some waterfowl activity, on your left. From this point you will be working your way back to Coopers Road through a maze of old cranberry bogs, reservoirs, and sand roads. Don't be surprised if some large military aircraft fly by as well—these bogs are not far from Fort Dix and McGuire Air Force Base.

Take the second left turn at a T-intersection, and head south out to another reservoir. This was drained when we were here once and presented an awesome sight of blackish mud and gray tree stumps. At this junction, another T-intersection, bear right, heading west along the shore of the reservoir. Next bear left at the end of the reservoir and head south along the dam.

At the next T-junction, turn right onto a sand road that first swings to the left and then comes to a fork. Take the left fork and walk through an area where sand has been excavated, staying on the main path which swings left and soon arrives at Coopers Road. Turn right on Coopers Road, then turn left on another gravel road only 200 yards ahead.

After a few more minutes, you'll pass a junction on the left with the red trail. (From this point on you can follow red markers back to your car.) Once again, you will cross a cedar swamp. Here the cedars are particularly tall and completely shade the road. Just after you leave the swamp, follow the red markers right onto a sand road that heads west. After about 250 yards on soft sand, the markers lead to a small sand road on the left. Take this road south for about 200 feet, then bear right and west again on a very straight sand road that marks the boundary of Lebanon State Forest. You are still following red markers. This road is shady, surrounded by pine forest with an undercover of blueberries. Pass over a small mossy bog and then, after another 10 minutes or so, reach an intersection with a somewhat larger sand road. Bear left here, heading south with the red markers. Another 10 or 15 minutes of walking will bring you to a paved road. Make a left here, walk about 150 yards, and arrive at the park office and your car on the right.

BCS

44

Batona to Ong's Hat

Total distance: 9-plus miles

Hiking time: 5 hours

Vertical rise: Minimal

Rating: Moderately strenuous

Maps: USGS Browns Mills; DEP Lebanon State Forest; DEP Batona Trail

This hike uses 5 miles of the 50-mile Batona Trail, which was established in 1961 by the Batona (BAck TO NAture) Hiking Club. The trail is jointly maintained by the club and the New Jersey State Park Service. It was planned and is now maintained as a wilderness trail open to foot traffic only. No vehicles or horses are allowed, though there is some evidence of illegal ATV and mountain bike activity on many sections. You can shorten this hike to the most interesting 5 miles (rating reduced to moderate) if you leave a second car at the trailhead parking area in Ong's Hat.

How to Get There

This hike, like the previous Lebanon State Forest hike, begins from the ranger's office (609-726-1191), which has a large parking area. To find the office from NJ 72, 1 mile east of its intersection with NJ 70, take the forest entrance road 0.3 mile north and bear right at the first intersection.

The Trail

Take the blue-marked trail directly across the road from the ranger's office. A sign reading BATONA TRAIL marks the path. Head south for only 0.1 mile to the junction with the actual Batona Trail, which is marked with pink blazes. Look around you and try to remember this junction so you don't miss it at the end of the hike.

Turn right (west) here. You'll cross over two paved roads before you reach the Lebanon fire tower, about 100 yards in front of you. Only from the highest reaches of this fire tower do you get a bird's-eye view of the terrain through which you will be walking for the next few hours. The green of the pines extends in all directions, unbroken to the horizon except for a few man-made objects. In the distance to the northwest, the low hill is Mount Holly, a remnant of the original sea floor, which, after uplifting, has survived millions of years of erosion.

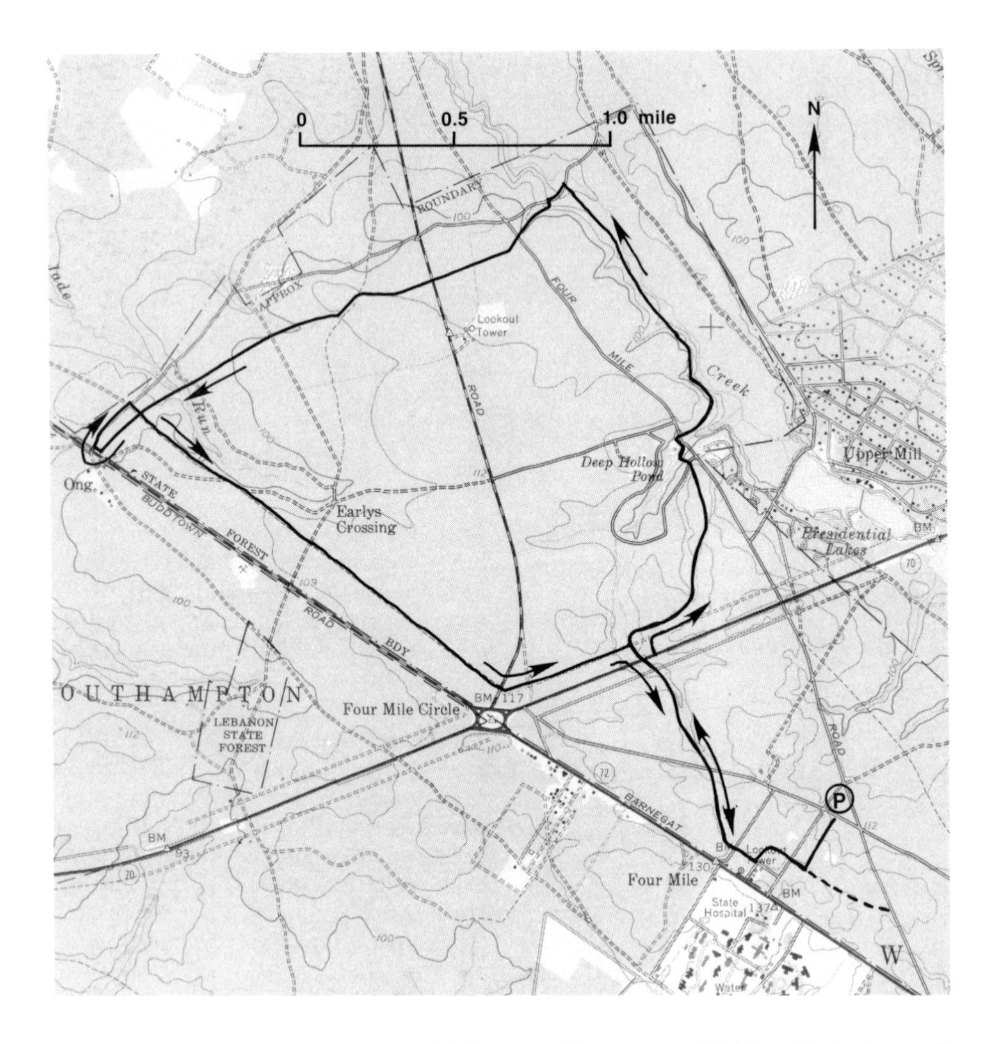

Return to the Batona Trail, which follows a paved road for a short distance until it reenters the woods at a T-junction with a sand road in poor condition. This section of pine and oak forest is particularly beautiful. The trail—a white, sandy ribbon bordered by soft green moss—enters a forest penetrated by the sounds of cicadas and distant motor traffic. After crossing two more sand roads, pay careful attention to the markers because the trail, which has been relocated, is obscure. Immediately after this section you'll come to NJ 70, which the trail crosses to reenter the woods on the other side.

The walkway in this section is wider, probably because of off-road vehicle abuse, and composed of loose sand, which makes for some extra work. Where the trail splits, follow the pink blazes onto a footpath. This will lead you to a small paved road, then to Deep Hollow. To the left are the remains of what was once Deep Hollow Pond, the recreational centerpiece of an early public campground in the state forest.

Deep Hollow Pond

The trail leads over the drainage of the pond on the road and then immediately reenters the woods on the right by a large cut tree stump. For the next mile or so, the Batona Trail parallels the course of Bisphams Mill Creek. Beginning in a mixed oak forest, it then descends a few feet into a forest dominated by pitch pines. It never comes within sight of the stream but grazes the edge of the swampy wetland that surrounds it. Where the trail closely approaches the wetter areas, which are dominated by ferns, you can feel the temperature drop. After about a mile along the streambank, the Batona Trail heads for higher ground. There are some new relocations in this section, so keep an eye out for the blazes. The trail reaches a sand road and turns left, following it, for 20 yards; then it reenters the woods.

Now, back in a drier forest, the Batona Trail crosses gravel Four Mile Road and enters an area where, during the late 1970s, the trees were cut and sold for lumber. The regrowth of both pine and oak gives you an idea of how fast these forests can recover from such a cutting. After crossing a few small sand roads, you'll walk through young pitch pines and, not long after, cross paved New Lisbon Road. After a brief woods section, the trail bears left onto an open and sunny sand road for 200 yards or so, then turns off to the right on a footpath. This turn may not be clearly marked.

You'll find yourself in a particularly beautiful pine forest. The trail makes a left turn onto a sand road then, after only 100 yards, another left back into the woods. Now on the final stretch to its terminus at Ong's Hat, the Batona Trail snakes its way through some cleared areas, crosses a sand road, and emerges on NJ 72 near a market and a restaurant. After about 5 miles you will have reached Ong's Hat.

Here at the northern terminus of

the Batona Trail is a convenient place to fill your stomach or just get a drink. It makes good sense to locate a major trailhead near a food source. Anapa's Family Restaurant and Diner even has an outdoor counter from which you can buy soft ice cream and sodas. If you don't care to buy your lunch or eat it in civilization, simply follow the pink blazes down a gravel road opposite the restaurant a few feet to the Batona parking area, which is grassy and has a few places to sit.

But what, you must be asking, is Ong's Hat? It's the name of this very, very small town (town?) facing you. The story begins in the early 1700s, when Jacob Ong built a tavern here. He was a Quaker from Pennsylvania who apparently strayed from the steady course and took a liking to dancing and flirting. The tavern, which made an excellent halfway stop for stagecoaches traveling between Philadelphia and the Jersey shore, soon became the scene of some wild goings-on, and in 1715 the history-making event occurred. Jacob got into a fight with one of his girlfriends. In a jealous rage, she grabbed the hat off his head and threw it high into a huge oak tree beside the tavern. For years the hat remained caught in the high branches, and passersby would frequently say, "Look, there's Ong's hat." It took a while, but in 1828 the town got recognition on official New Jersey maps. It is also shown on the USGS Browns Mills quad. As for the tree, well, it was cut down in 1978 by the county highway department. The present restaurant and the market next door mark the spot where all this action took place.

After your stop, follow the pink markers to the Batona Trail parking area, directly across from Ong's Hat on the sand road. Continue past the parking area for a short distance until you come to a junction with a sand road paralleling NJ 72. Turn right here, heading east on a very straight, soft sand road lined with pines. In just a short distance, you will pass the Batona Trail. Farther on, you come to a fork; continue straight ahead. A large cleared area will appear on your left. During 1986 and '87 this area was cleared by a commercial lumber company that bought the wood, mostly oaks, from the state. As you can see, it doesn't take long for the forest to begin regeneration. One of the advantages of periodically cutting the forest and creating open areas, which occurs naturally in nature with forest fires, is that habitats for certain animals are created. Deer love to browse in cleared areas, and birds, such as red-headed and red-bellied woodpeckers, summer tanagers, and bluebirds, thrive here also. Bluebirds are quite rare in New Jersey these days but make homes here—aided in part by the placement of nesting boxes by the forest service.

At the end of the sand road, cross Four Mile–New Lisbon Road and follow the asphalt paved path as it swings to the left and then down a lane lined with utility poles. Highway department maintenance sheds are on your left. The walkway is sandy and heads gradually downhill. Immediately after crossing a low (sometimes wet) area, look for the pink markers of the Batona Trail. Turn right here and retrace your steps to the state forest office. Remember, after you pass the area of the fire tower, to be alert for the junction with the blue-marked access trail to the office. This junction is indicated by signs for Pakim Pond on a tree. Be sure to turn left toward the park office—not toward Pakim Pond.

HNZ/BCS

45

Carranza to Apple Pie Hill

Total distance: 8.2 miles (or 5.2 with car shuttle)

Hiking time: 4½ hours

Vertical rise: 166 feet

Rating: Moderately strenuous

Maps: USGS Chatsworth, Indian Mills; WB #19; DEP Batona Trail; DEP Wharton State Forest

Walking uphill in the Pine Barrens is unusual. The entire region is just above sea level, and the very few "hills" are usually only 25 or 30 feet above everything else. There are a few exceptions, however, and this hike leads to the highest elevation in the Pines, a dizzying 205 feet above sea level and about 125 feet above the land around it. This is Apple Pie Hill, on which a fire tower is located. En route the hike will take you over another hill, 139 feet above sea level, as a warm-up for the big climb.

The Carranza Memorial, where this hike begins, commemorates the tragic crash and death of Mexican pilot Emilio Carranza. Carranza, only 23 at the time of his death, had been a Mexican hero for 5 years, his fame resting on both his aviation and military accomplishments. On June 11, 1928, he took off from Mexico in a Ryan monoplane, the same as Lindbergh's, and attempted a nonstop flight to Washington. He was grounded by fog in North Carolina but was still received with speeches and parades in both Washington and New York. Carranza was on the return leg of this goodwill flight when he flew into a thunderstorm over this remote section of the Pines and crashed. The local American Legion holds an annual observance of this event the first Saturday after the Fourth of July. Each year on this day wreaths are placed around the memorial, a stone marker made in Mexico that portrays a diving Aztec eagle.

How to Get There

To reach the parking area at the memorial in Wharton State Forest, turn left (east) off US 206 just south of its junction with NJ 70. The sign here directs you to the town of Tabernacle and the Carranza Memorial. You'll

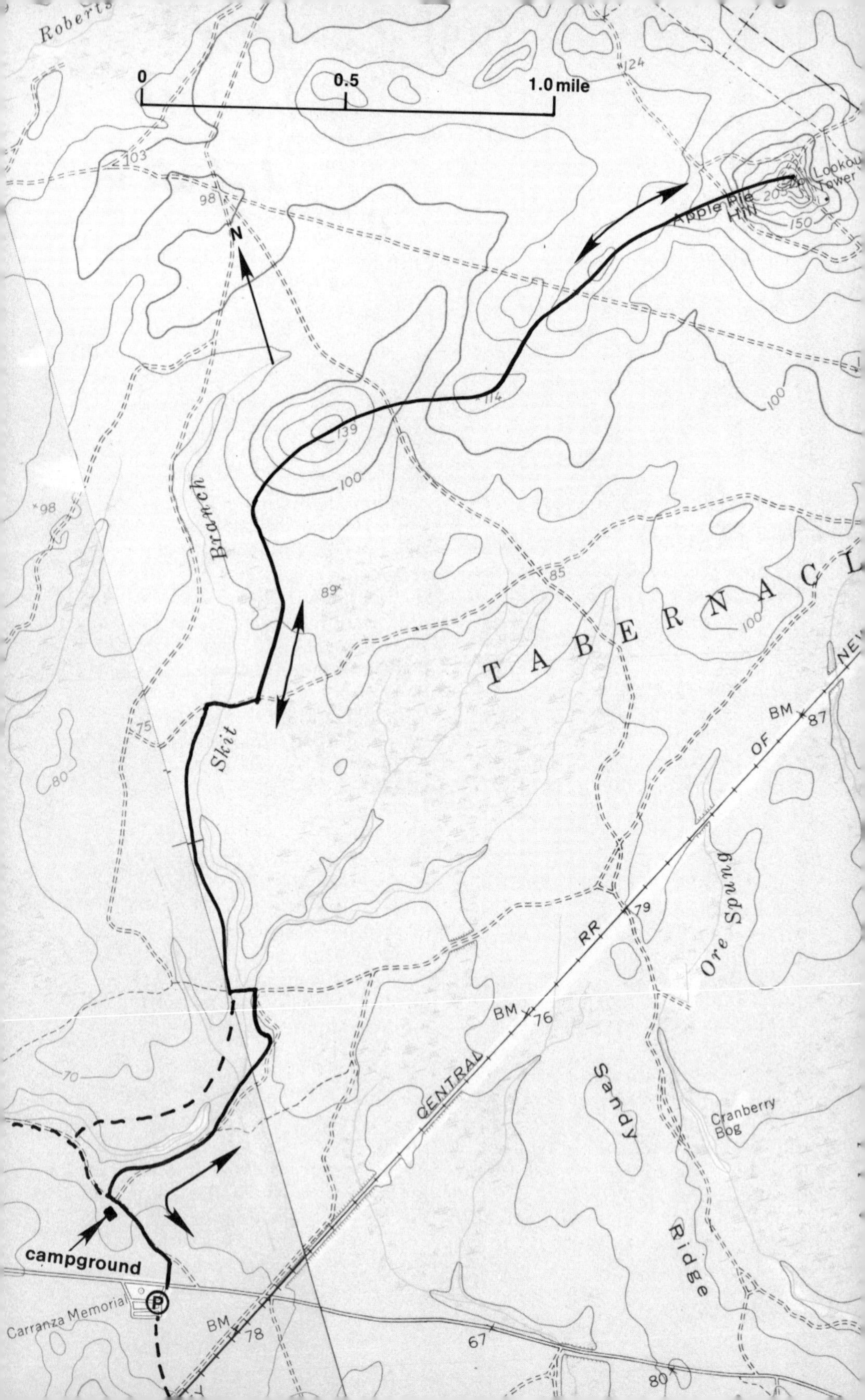

Roberts
0
0.5
1.0 mile
N
124
103
98
Apple Pie Hill
Lookout Tower
205
150
114
139
100
Branch
98
89
85
T A B E R N A C L
100
NEW
BM
87
OF
Skit
75
80
RR
79
Ore Spung
BM
76
CENTRAL
70
Sandy
Cranberry Bog
Ridge
campground
Carranza Memorial
P
BM
78
67
80

reach the little town of Tabernacle and cross County Road 532 (CR 532) in 2.3 miles. Continue straight ahead through farms and a residential area into Wharton State Forest (Atsion Office, RD #2, Route 206, Vincentown, NJ 08088; 609-268-0444). Seven miles from Tabernacle you will find the Carranza Memorial, which has ample parking, on the right. (If you wish to do the hike as a one-way trip of 5.2 miles, leave a car on CR 532 where the Batona Trail crosses it about 7 miles east of Tabernacle and 3 miles west of Chatsworth.)

The Trail

Cross the paved road and head north into the Batona Camp. A sign here indicates the campsite. After about 200 yards, you'll meet the pink-blazed Batona Trail, which connects with the camp access road from the right. From here to Apple Pie Hill and back you'll be following these pink markers. The 50-mile Batona Trail, begun in 1961 by the BAck TO NAture Hiking Club, is a foot trail only. Mountain bikes are not permitted on it. A map of the entire trail is available from the New Jersey Department of Environmental Protection, as well as at the Atsion and Batsto state forest offices.

Batona Camp is one of several primitive camping areas located in Wharton State Forest. The site is accessible by car and offers numerous spaces to pitch a tent, also providing a water pump and several pit toilets. If you wish to camp here, you'll need a permit, available from the Atsion Ranger Headquarters farther south on US 206 or from the office in Batsto. In 1996 the camping fee was $8 per night for one to six people. Pets are not permitted in the campsite for overnight camping.

When you reach the end of the camping area, the Batona trail veers to the right past a toilet and enters the woods on a footpath. Immediately, the typical flora of the Pinelands surrounds you. Highbush blueberries, which are found along the trail over much of this hike, make their first appearance. Blackjack oak and, of course, pitch pine surround you. Within a few hundred feet, the trail emerges onto a wide sand road, which it follows for a short distance. For the next 0.5 mile, the trail parallels this road, playing tag by using it for short stretches then cutting back into the woods on a footpath.

After a section that skirts the edge of a cedar swamp, the Batona trail emerges onto the road for a final time to use its bridge. The brook you are crossing is the Skit Branch of the Batsto River. Like all Pine Barrens water, it is tea colored from the cedarwood that grows in it. From the bridge is a good view of the swampy brook and its plant life. If you look closely at the clumps of grasses growing in and around the water, you'll see hundreds of tiny sundew plants. If you look even closer, you may find a few miniature pitcher plants as well. These plants survive in this nutrient-poor environment by digesting insects that get trapped in their sticky leaves or no-exit entrances.

After crossing the bridge, the trail turns right and back into the woods on a footpath, this time for good. For the next 0.5 mile, Skit Branch and its white cedar swamp will be on the right. The many dead cedars, still standing tall in the water, were killed by fire. Unlike pitch pines and shortleaf pines, Atlantic white cedars do not regenerate after a burn; only the water protects them from fire. In this section, the trail crosses a wet area on loose logs. Be careful, or you may sink into deep black mud. The next crossing is of the stream itself, again on logs and, once more, potentially perilous for your shoes.

The Batona Trail now leaves the wet area surrounding Skit Branch and heads into drier and higher territory. About 2 miles from the start of the hike the first climb begins. The ascent is first noticeable by the change from soft white sand as a walkway to a harder gravel path. After a "climb" of about 40 feet, you'll reach the tablelike summit of this unnamed hill and, before you know it, begin heading downhill. Pay close attention ahead as the trail veers left off the path, crosses a sand road, and then reenters the woods.

One of the creatures of the Pines you may encounter on this hike, particularly in the drier areas, is the aptly named fence swift lizard. You may see a blur and hear the rustle of leaves, yet not get a look at this speedster unless you catch him sunning on a piece of dead wood. This rather attractive lizard has a gray-brown body and some very jagged scales along his head and back. The males have a dark marking under their lower jaws.

After crossing three more sand roads, the Batona begins another climb, this one more serious. Some views out to the horizon in the south appear between the trees. The trail winds along the hill until the summit and its fire tower appear. This rise is Apple Pie Hill, and at 205 feet it's the highest summit in the Pine Barrens.

Although the hill, which is accessible by car or truck, is the scene of many a wild party, the view from its tower is spectacular. To the south, a wilderness of green pines extends as far as the eye can see. To the west in the distance is the slight rise of Mount Holly. To the north are pines and, far in the distance, a water tower and a few other protrusions of civilization. In the east is a cranberry field—and more pines. To the southeast, a sand road runs from the hill in a perfectly straight line. For the most part, the view is one of vastness and wilderness that gives you an idea of the magnitude of the Pine Barrens.

Fire towers, which are frequently manned, play an important role in controlling the frequent fires (about 400 a year) in the Pine Barrens. The soil in the Pinelands drains the water so well that the oil- and resin-rich pine needles and dead branches are nearly always dry as tinder. There are no earthworms or bacteria to digest the dead materials on the forest floor, so the tinder accumulates year after year until it burns. The shortleaf pine and the pitch pine, the most common pines here, are two of only three pines in the United States that can sprout from buds lying deep within their trunks or large limbs, thereby assuring their quick recovery following a fire. The persistence of fires in the Pine Barrens, many of them started by arsonists, has ensured the dominance of these two pines in the forest. Ecologists believe that without regular fires, oaks would probably make up the bulk of a climax forest.

Because it is somewhat abused and there is much broken glass, Apple Pie Hill may not be the best place for a rest or lunch. We suggest that you find a resting place nearer to the first hill you climbed, which shows little sign of use other than from hikers. If you parked at the Carranza Memorial, this will be on your way back. If you left a car on CR 532, it is 1.1 miles ahead on the Batona Trail. Please note that this section of the trail is not on public land. Respect the landowners by staying on the trail.

BCS

46

Penn State Forest

Total distance: 8.5 miles

Hiking time: 5 hours

Vertical rise: 125 feet

Rating: Moderately strenuous

Maps: USGS Woodmansie/Oswego Lake; DEP Penn State Forest

Penn State Forest (c/o Bass River State Forest, PO Box 118, New Gretna, NJ 08224; 609-296-1114), located northeast of the huge Wharton tract, contains a number of sand roads, a beautiful lake, and even a hill with a view. The forest is for the present undeveloped, though it is administered through Bass River State Forest just to the south. There are no designated hiking trails here, but the sand roads, as elsewhere in the Pinelands, make for good hiking. They also make for good biking. You may meet people using mountain bikes on this route, though the width of the roads will make for comfortable encounters. Unlike the other state forests located within the general region known as the Pine Barrens, the acreage in Penn State Forest includes an area of dwarf pines called the Plains.

How to Get There

From County Road 563 (CR 563), turn east onto Chatsworth–New Gretna Road and proceed 3.2 miles to Lake Oswego. This turnoff is located 0.4 mile north of Mick's Canoe Rental and 1.4 miles north of the junction with CR 679. The parking area is on the right, just over the bridge. The forest rangers suggest that hikers do not leave valuables in their motor vehicles. Also, swimming is not permitted in Lake Oswego.

The Trail

Walk east for a few hundred feet from the parking area, then bear left onto a sand road. At the first fork, bear left on what is known as Lost Lane Road. Follow the lane through an open forest of small- to medium-height pitch pines. After about a mile of walking, a sand road called Penn Place will turn off on the right. Ignore this turn and continue straight ahead on Lost Lane Road.

Just past the junction with Penn Place, Lost Lane enters a swampy area

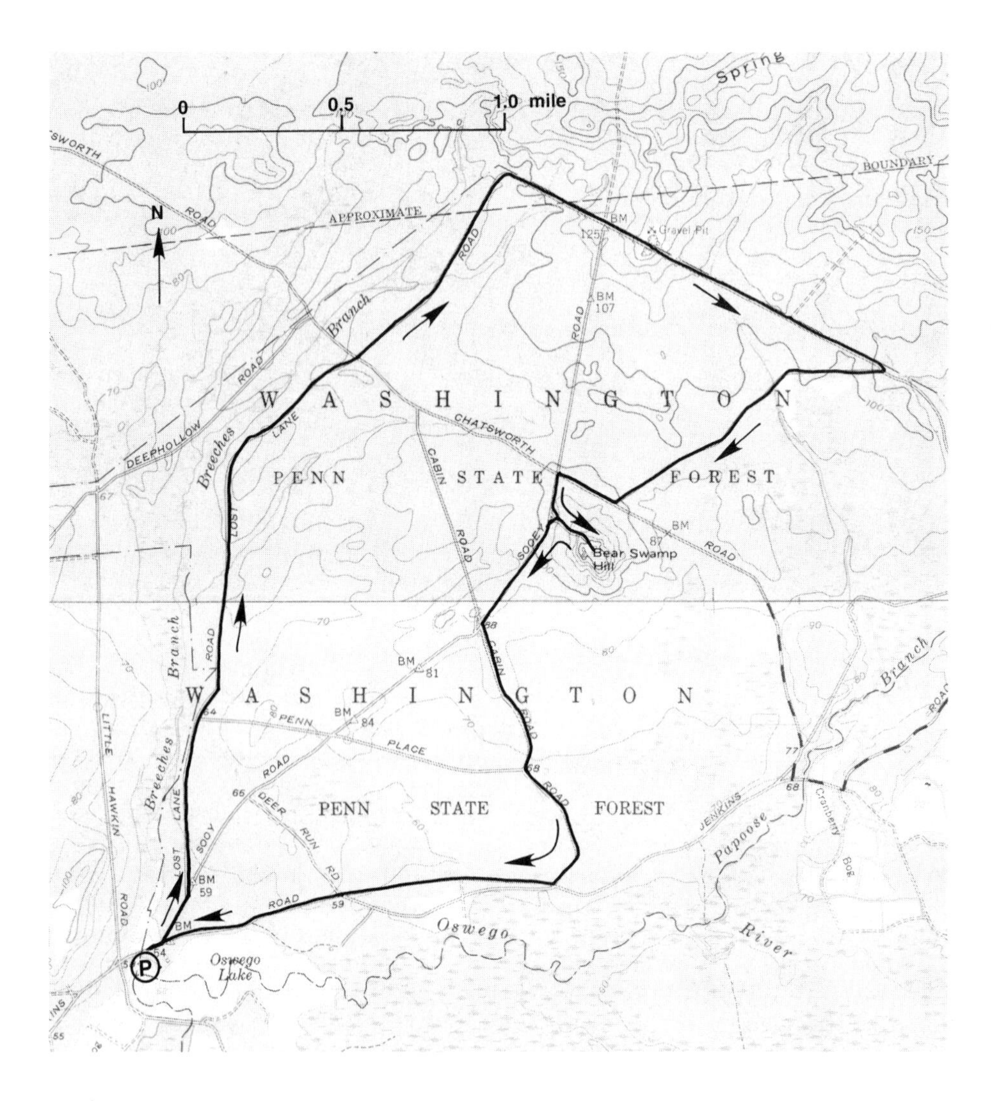

that is quite picturesque. Tall cedars line the road, which is high and dry in most places. Farther on, Lost Lane, which is fairly solid, easy to walk on, and remarkably white, continues to penetrate the pine forest, gradually swinging around to the right. On a clear, bright day, the contrast of white sand road, green pines, and blue sky is magnificent.

Two miles into the hike you will meet Chatsworth Road, once paved but now mostly sand and gravel mixed with some chunks of asphalt. Cross Chatsworth and continue on Lost Lane, heading northeast. After about 15 more minutes, enter another swampy area containing many dead cedars. As vistas open up, the terrain becomes stranger and wilder. The expansiveness of these relatively open areas is a prelude to what is ahead. With the exception of an occasional military transport plane taking off from

McGuire Air Force Base to the north, this section of the forest is about as remote as you get in the Pine Barrens. You may spot deer or, more likely, the common fence swift lizard skirting its way across the road.

Less than a mile from its junction with Chatsworth Road, Lost Lane makes a sharp right and begins a straight course, heading southeast along the boundary of Penn State Forest. After passing Sooey Road, which turns off to the right, Lost Lane climbs a small hill and then descends, flanked by some beautiful specimens of pitch pine and scrub oak. Notice that the bark of the trees is charred; fires occur here fairly regularly. Just ahead are the Plains.

Nothing in New Jersey compares with the incredibly expansive vistas created by 5-foot-tall stunted pine trees. The chaparral-like combination of white sand and clumps of green is reminiscent of both the high southwest deserts and the Cape Cod dunes. Many explanations have been offered for the dwarfed size of the pines in the Plains. One theory states that aluminum in the sand stunts the trees, though aluminum is found in other areas where normal trees are found. Another theory holds that the trees are stunted by strong winds that blow on the generally high ground of the area. This theory fails because equally strong winds blow elsewhere and, even at the highest elevations such as at Apple Pie Hill, those trees are of normal height. Other explanations include poor soil, shallow soil, and pine-eating moths, none of which have held up when tested.

The only explanation for the dwarf pines that has consistently held up amid all the debate is simply the frequency of fires in the area. On average, a major fire occurs in the Plains every 7 years. Once burned, the pine roots tend to spread horizontally, forming a ground mat that can extend up to 30 feet from the original taproot. It is still not known exactly how the fires cause stunting, however. One other interesting aspect of the stunted pines is relevant here and supports the fire theory. The pitch pine tree is capable of producing both closed and open pinecones. Closed pinecones can survive fires—in fact, they need fire to open up. In the Plains, which extend from here up to and across NJ 72 just east of Lebanon State Forest, the pitch pines tend to produce closed cones, though in other sections of the Pine Barrens the open type is more prevalent.

Continue walking through the Plains on Lost Lane, passing a road turning off to the left, until you reach a triangular junction with Stave Road. Turn right here, heading southwest. You are still in the Plains, about 4.5 miles from Oswego Lake. In another mile you will leave the Plains behind and reach paved Chatsworth Road. Bear right here, but only for 0.2 mile. Next make a left on Sooey Road, which was once paved. You should be heading southwest again.

In just 0.1 mile look for a paved turnoff on the left that leads to Bear Swamp Hill. After a short climb of 50 feet, something rare in the Pine Barrens, come to a parking area and, to the right, the site of a former fire tower. There is a partial view to the west that gives you a feeling for the vastness of the area. Bear Swamp Hill abounds in mountain laurel, beautiful when blooming in late spring. The wooden structure off to the left of the parking area housed rest rooms when the area was maintained. After your visit, retrace your steps downhill and bear left on Sooey Road, now a sand and gravel road.

After about 10 minutes, come to an intersection with Cabin Road and turn left, heading southeast. This road is narrow and receives less use than those traveled so far. The road will widen after a distance and swing around to the right. At a T-junction, bear left on Penn Place Road. More than a mile from Bear Swamp Hill you will reach a junction with paved Jenkins Road, one of the main roads through the forest. A sand road on the right parallels Jenkins Road. This road, which avoids motor traffic and has better footing and scenery to offer, is the preferred walkway. The gravel and sand on this road is particularly reddish, probably because of its high iron content.

After a walk of just more than 0.5 mile, the sand road will reconnect with paved Jenkins Road. Do not take the sand road heading off to the right. Walk straight ahead on the pavement—or, more accurately, on what's left of the pavement—to the parking area about 0.5 mile ahead. En route are some excellent views of Lake Oswego on the left.

BCS

47

Mullica River Wilderness

Total distance: 8 miles (from Batsto; 6 miles from trailhead)

Hiking time: 5 hours

Vertical rise: Minimal

Rating: Moderately strenuous

Maps: USGS Atsion; DEP Wharton State Forest

Backpacking in the Pine Barrens is a unique experience for those more familiar with mountainous areas. The pines are not so dense or tall that they shut out a good view of a starlit sky. In fact, the effect is sometimes more like camping in a desert than in a forest. The pine needle cover on the sandy ground also makes for a comfortable bed. From Batsto, in the heart of the Pinelands, a 4-mile walk leads to the Mullica Wilderness Campsite, a good choice for such an experience. This primitive camping area, which is monitored by the rangers, is expansive enough for private folks, is alongside the Mullica River, and has a water pump and pit toilet. You'll have to get a permit from the office in Batsto to camp here. In 1996 the cost was $8 per night for one to six people. Pets are not allowed.

Batsto was the site of an iron forge that produced kettles, stoves, cannon, pipes, and other iron products during the latter part of the 18th and the early 19th centuries. Like Allaire Village in the northern extremes of the Pine Barrens, the iron was made from bog iron—accumulations of iron oxides leached from the sand by water and deposited in decaying vegetation. During the Revolutionary War, Batsto was a major source of military iron, and its workers were exempt from military service.

At its peak, the village that developed around the furnace had a population of nearly 1000. When the iron industry declined, a glassmaking factory was built, and the town produced window panes and other flat glass products for a few years. In 1876, after a major fire in the village, Joseph Wharton bought the property as part of his plan to own the Pine Barrens and sell its water to the city of Philadelphia. The state of New Jersey responded by passing a law prohibiting

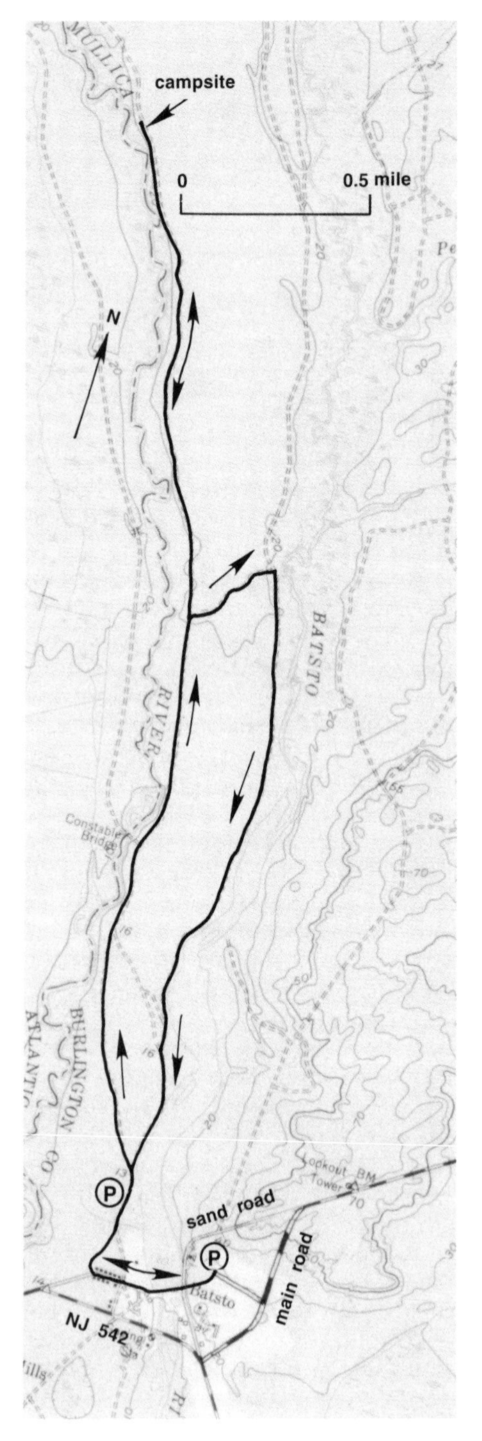

the export of water, effectively halting this project. Eventually the Wharton holdings were acquired by the state, forming the present-day Wharton State Forest.

How to Get There

Batsto, which is on NJ 542, is easy to find—signs directing you to it (it is a major historical site) are strategically placed within a radius of 20 miles. If you plan to backpack and spend the night at the Mullica Wilderness campsite, it is advisable to leave your car overnight at the parking area behind the state forest office in Batsto. After registering and picking up your permit, walk east on the main walkway through Batsto Village, across the dam on Batsto Lake, and turn right onto a footpath found just past the last building on your right. This path will take you to the gravel road onto which you should turn right. A walk of about 0.2 mile will bring you to where the road divides.

If you plan to day-hike the area, you should probably park your car at the end of a gravel road found 0.6 mile east of the main entrance to Batsto on NJ 542. Drive north on this road for about 0.4 mile and park near the lake on the left, just before the road divides.

The Trail

The entire hike is on sand roads that are unmarked and perhaps confusing in places; however, because the entire hike is on the land between the Mullica and Batsto Rivers, getting lost would be very difficult. Until you reach the actual Mullica Wilderness Area, these sand roads are open to motor vehicles. Don't be surprised if a huge four-wheeler or a truck towing canoes passes you. Because of all this traffic, sections of the sand roads are very soft, with poor traction. Wear appropriate shoes.

At the fork, take the sand road on the left and enter the Pinelands. Where the sand road swings sharply to the left and enters a maze of trails to the Mullica, keep to the right to stay on course. After about a mile, you'll come to Constable Bridge over the Mullica River. If you're hiking on a busy summer weekend, expect regular deliveries of canoes to this popular boat-launching point.

The Mullica, along with the Batsto, Wading, Great Egg Harbour, and Rancocas, is one of the major rivers draining the vast water reserves lying just below the sands and forests of the Pine Barrens. Though the river widens considerably farther downstream, the Mullica here in the forest is typical of other rivers in the Pines. There are no rapids, but the current is strong. The river is not wide, but it can be very deep. The fact that it runs all year along and through droughts at a constant water level indicates the extent of the aquifer underlying the Pine Barrens.

Continue hiking north on the main sand road (do not cross the bridge). The walking gets easier, for this section suffers less abuse from motor vehicles. After another mile you will reach the entrance to the wilderness area, a section of the forest where no vehicles (except the ranger's) are allowed. A sign here marks the boundary.

Almost immediately after entering the wilderness area, the forest becomes cleaner, the sand road harder, and the insects (in summer) more aggressive. Wildlife, including deer and flying squirrels, becomes more abundant. You may spot the red wasp, which looks like a giant ant, alongside the trail. In another 0.5 mile, the sand road swings close to the Mullica River, offering another view of its dark and narrow passageway through the tall cedars and pines. As you continue farther north, these encounters with the river become more frequent. This section of the Mullica has been designated a wild and scenic river by the state of New Jersey.

About a mile from the beginning of the wilderness area is the Mullica River Wilderness Campsite, a good place for lunch—or for the night. There's a pump for good water here and plenty of campsites within the limits posted and marked by a ditch. Along the banks of the Mullica are several beachlike areas.

The water of the Pine Barrens is dark, the color of tea. "Cedar water" is the usual name for it. The color comes in part from the tannins in the cedar trees that grow in the water and in part from the iron in the ground water. Because the water in the Pine Barrens tends to stay fresher longer, sea captains used to sail up the rivers that drain the Pinelands and take on barrels of what they called "sweet water."

The water table in the Pinelands is shallow, but the reserve of water is vast. As an aquifer, there is no equal to the Pinelands in the northeastern United States. Because the water lies so close to the surface and because the sand, which takes in the rain that falls on it, is not a good filter, the Pine Barrens aquifer is extremely vulnerable to pollution. For this reason, development, which constantly threatens this area, has been kept at bay.

After a lunch, rest, or possibly an overnight, leave the campsite area and walk south, retracing your steps to the sign marking the entrance to the wilderness area. At this point, make a left onto a sand road that heads northeast and leads in about 0.25 mile to a sand road running north–south along the

Batsto River. Make a right (south) on this road and begin the 2.5-mile walk back to your car. The sand is very soft in places, necessitating walking on the shoulder or on lesser-used trails parallel to the main sand road. Though it may not be immediately apparent to you, the Batsto River, on the left, is not far away. Perhaps the sound of paddles banging on the sides of aluminum canoes will alert you to its presence. Along the banks of the Batsto are tall cedars and highbush blueberries, ripe in August. Soon the northern end of Batsto Lake, which is mostly a large swamp, appears. Where the road swings to the right, you are finally rewarded with a wide panorama of the entire lake, right down to the village at its far end. When you come to another maze of sand roads, keep to the left and continue heading south. In this area you may encounter vehicular traffic, especially if you are hiking on a beautiful summer weekend.

After about an hour of walking along the western banks of Batsto River and Batsto Lake, you should arrive at the junction where you originally turned left toward the Mullica. If you day-hiked, your car is just ahead. If you backpacked, continue along the gravel road to the small opening in the split-rail fence. A left turn here will lead you through the village and back to the ranger's office and the parking area.

BCS

48

Parvin State Park

Total distance: 5 miles

Hiking time: 3 hours

Vertical rise: Minimal

Rating: Easy to moderate

Maps: USGS Elmer; DEP Parvin State Park

In 1930, the New Jersey legislature began the acquisition of Parvin State Park with an appropriation of just less than $74,000. Nine years later, following 19 separate transactions, Parvin entered the state park system. During the Depression, a Civilian Conservation Corps (CCC) branch was established in the park. The men hacked out trails through the dense forest, using the wood to build bridges across the swamps. They cleared the main beach and picnic area and constructed the cabins (each with its own boat landing) along the shore of Thundergust Lake.

A German prisoner-of-war camp was located in a section of the park in 1942. When the European hostilities ended, the camp was converted for use by interned Japanese Americans from the West Coast. The year 1952 saw the last nontraditional use of Parvin. Six years earlier, Stalin had the Kalmyck people and some other Tartar groups transported to Siberia in retaliation for their revolt against the Communist government. Only about a quarter of the 400,000 people involved survived the ordeal, some of whom escaped to the United States. They came to Parvin in three groups but stayed only a few months. Some are now settled in the Philadelphia area and in Howell Township in New Jersey.

This hike starts on the Parvin Lake Trail and uses the Long Trail for the rest of its route. All the trails in the park, even those in the natural area, are open to bike and horse use. If you live in the area, volunteers are needed to help maintain the trail system. Please contact the park administration.

How to Get There

Parvin State Park is located in southern Salem County along the Cumberland County border. The park entrance is on County Route 540 (CR 540), slightly more than 1 mile east of Centerton or 6 miles west of Vineland. The surrounding area has many road signs to point you in the right direction. The office (701 Almond Road, Pittsgrove, NJ 08318; 609-358-8616) is located in one end of the park bathhouse, with a large parking lot across CR 540. In-season, there is a parking fee. Stop in the office for a free map booklet (worthwhile). The trails are named on the park map, but, as there are no signs, the names exist only on the map.

The Trail

Your hike starts just outside the park office. Facing Parvin Lake and the bathhouse, walk to the right (west) along a brown dirt path, through and then beside a green chain-link fence, and then beside a long split-rail one. The trail is over flat terrain, and the walking is easy. It travels between the highway and the lake, passing a children's area and some picnic tables, and is marked with occasional green paint blazes. Holly trees and mountain laurel abound.

A few minutes after crossing a small brook on a tiny stone bridge, you will reach a small open clearing. Avoid both the trail to the left (which soon fades out) and the overgrown trail to the right. Instead, continue straight as the route swings closer to both the road and a few houses seen through the woods. Large pitch pines with their distinctive, thick shingle bark are much in evidence. Ground pine moss abounds on the forest floor.

You may notice a short side trail leading left down to the edge of Muddy Run. Continue straight ahead, also avoiding the trail to the right. Shortly afterward, there is another path to the water's edge. Muddy Run is a typical slow-moving stream of south Jersey. A tributary of the Maurice River, its water eventually empties into Delaware Bay. In the 1880s, small ponds were formed by damming to provide power for gristmills and sawmills. One of these was owned by a family named Parvin.

Proceed ahead, crossing a series of small plank bridges to meet a paved crossroad. This road forms the main boundary between the developed area and the designated natural area of Parvin State Park—the latter to be left in a "forever wild" condition. A short walk left (suggested) along this road leads to both Muddy Run and an interesting jagged bridge designed to discourage illegal motor bikes. Back on the main trail, continue straight ahead as the path gets a little sandier. In a few minutes you will reach an area known as Second Landing. Uphill to the right is a picnic area with a rain shelter and rest rooms. The shore of Muddy Run is just to the left. Because the trail now enters the heart of the designated natural area, the trail is basically unmaintained and less obvious. There are some blowdowns to climb under and over, and the footway may be wet in spots—a minor price to pay for the peace, solitude, and natural dignity here.

The League for Conservation Legislation, the New Jersey Chapter of the Sierra Club, and Assemblyman (later Governor) Thomas Kean can take credit for the 1976 passage of the Natural Areas System Act. This landmark legislation, which followed in the footsteps of the Forest Preserve article of the New York State Constitution, allows the designation of areas to be left forever in their natural state. Except for trails, they remain fundamentally undeveloped, and the trees remain uncut.

Continuing ahead, avoid the nature trail forking to the right and proceed over two small wooden bridges

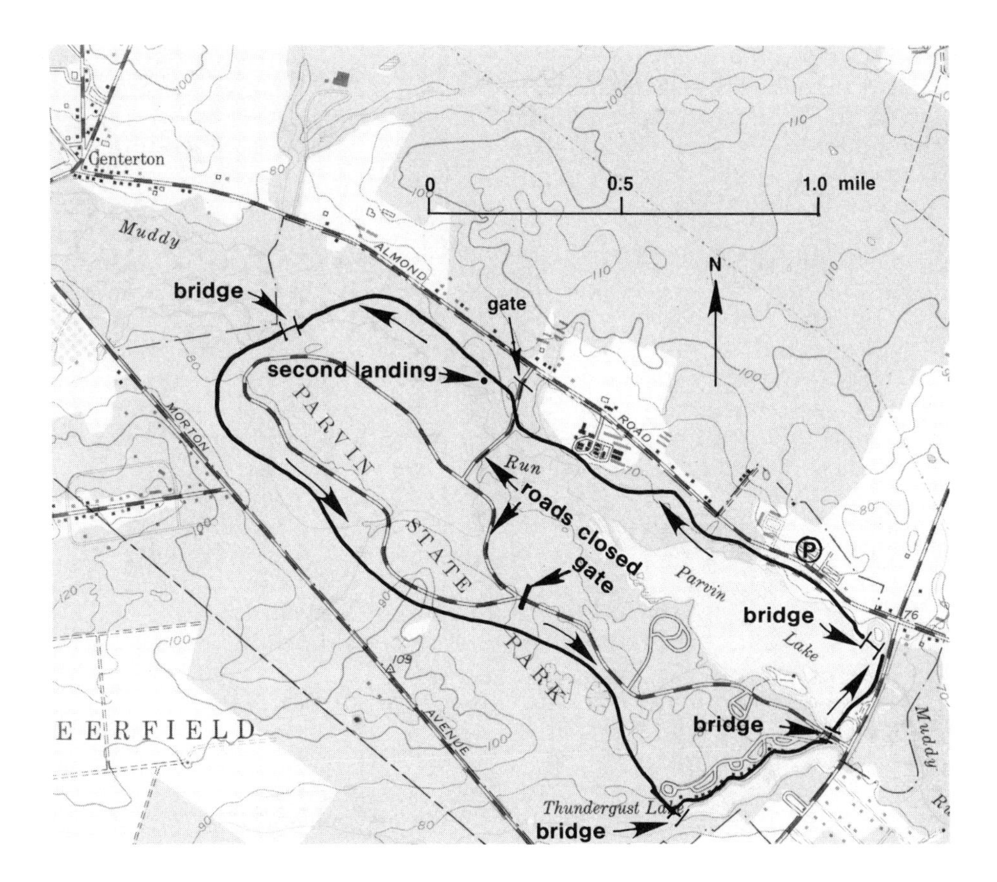

onto the footway, now on land slightly raised from the surrounding marsh. This part of the trail has many small plank bridges but has otherwise not been maintained in many years. This path, and most of those in Parvin, were built during the 1930s by the CCC. Considering that more than 50 years have passed, it is easy to admire their fine, long-lasting workmanship.

The route through the natural area is obvious, even though indistinct in a spot or two. Don't worry, you can retrace your steps easily; but it is much more likely that after just brief hunting and pecking, you will regain the path. In one wet, open area, the trail does bend somewhat to the right, but otherwise it is mostly straight with gentle curves. The wooden posts seen occasionally along the route are long neglected mile markers, which may even date back to CCC days.

Cross three or four small feeder inlets as the trail winds out and bends slowly left toward Muddy Run. Be sure to take time to observe the forest around you. Left alone by humanity, it has developed a distinct wild feel. Birds seem to like the area—you will hear many, see few. In about 20 minutes you will reach a substantial bridge over Muddy Run. Shortly after crossing it, and just as the main trail takes a distinctive turn to the left (red arrow), watch for and take the fainter path on the right (orange arrow). If you miss this spot, you'll soon climb gently to a paved interior road of the park—just retrace your steps, find the correct path, and resume the hike. This junction, by the way, is incorrectly located on the park map.

Going ahead on the fainter trail (much improved of late), almost immediately you will spot a conspicuous downed tree with exposed roots. It's interesting to observe the complex web of the root system and large ground hole left by its fall. Many times we have seen these otherwise unexplained dips in the forest floor after the tree has rotted or been carried away.

The trail continues as before with many two- and three-plank bridges. It soon comes to and parallels a small inlet creek flowing through the dense brush and forest. Cross a woods road. The trees begin to open up a little, and the trail resumes the wide, groomed look it had in the beginning of the hike. Through the trees to the right are glimpses of some houses as the trail nears the southern border of the park.

This part of New Jersey is known to have a considerable tick population. As you hike here, especially during the warmer months (June through September), be alert for the little monsters. The introduction to this book provides some basic advice on ticks and Lyme disease, which are widespread in New Jersey.

The footway becomes more distinct again, and the walking very easy. The plant community resumes the character it had early in the hike. The large pitch pines attest to the years the area has been undisturbed by logging. Young white pine trees add to the gentle feel, with their long, light green needles. Holly trees canopy the now-wide trail at one point. The holly is an evergreen tree that, like mountain laurel, keeps its leaves throughout the year. The trees can be either male or female, and both sexes are needed before berries develop.

When the trail comes to a T-junction, go right, crossing over a sandy road after a minute or so. Continuing ahead, you will pass some indistinct trails, one on the right and one just beyond it on the left. About 15 minutes past the T, at another junction, take a 90-degree right turn over a small mound of dirt. Should you miss this turn, you'll shortly be at a paved road and can retrace your steps.

The path is again raised from the surrounding forest floor. Crossing yet another trail, continue straight as the path gets a little narrower. In less than 5 minutes, the main trail swings sharply to the left, while a fainter trail goes straight. Take the latter. Off to the left, through the woods, you can see some of the cabins in the Thundergust Lake area. You will quickly arrive at a nice wooden footbridge over Thundergust Brook, a pleasurable place to pause as the hike draws to a close. The 15-plus rental cabins are available from April through October. Each is well equipped with a fridge, stove, toilet, shower, and electric lights. They sleep four but can accommodate six if you're willing to bring the extra cots.

This route does not cross the bridge, though. Take a left onto the trail along the near shore of Thundergust Lake, passing the cabins and sandy boat-launch beach. Stay between the lake and service road, passing a wooden fishing platform and small brick structure. As the trail approaches the main highway, you'll notice a dam (with a wrought-iron railing) on your right and the campground entrance road on your left. Walk on the road into the park past the 20 MPH sign. Shortly afterward, in a split-rail fence area, turn right onto a footbridge over a small section of Parvin Lake. The park office and bathhouse, where your hike began, are now visible.

From here, no formal directions are required. Just continue through the more developed part of the park, always remaining close to the shoreline. The outlet dam of Parvin Lake is especially interesting with its art deco lines and unusual curved spillway. Two bridges, one concrete and the other wooden, cross what appear to be streams, but they actually take you on and off Flag Island.

You will be back to your car before long. Stop at the office (nice rest rooms!) and tell the staff there of your excursion through the outer areas of Parvin. They don't get all that many hikers in the area and may enjoy hearing your anecdotes.

HNZ

49

Belleplain State Forest—East Creek Trail

Total distance: 7.2 miles

Hiking time: 4½ hours

Vertical rise: Minimal

Rating: Moderate

Maps: USGS Woodbine/Heislerville; DEP Belleplain State Forest

Located in the southern tip of the Pinelands, Belleplain State Forest (PO Box 450, Woodbine, NJ 08270; 609-861-2404) is a popular camping spot containing a few hundred family camping sites, 14 all-season cabins, two group campsites (which can each accommodate 75 people), a group cabin (up to 30), hot showers, and flush toilets. Belleplain has, in fact, more campsites than any state forest in New Jersey. Central to the camping areas in this recently enlarged 14,000-acre forest—90 percent of which is part of the Pinelands National Reserve—is Lake Nummy, a transformed cranberry bog with white sand beaches. It was named in honor of King Nummy, chief of the Kechemeche tribe and the last to rule in the Cape May area. For hikers, Belleplain offers many short trails in the camping area along with the East Creek Trail, a white-blazed footpath that will be used in this hike. Most trails in the forest are multiuse; there are even some ATV–dirt bike trails.

The East Creek Trail is a 7.2-mile circular trail, which you will hike clockwise. Marked with white paint on trees and new brown carsonite directional posts, the trail was refurbished in 1996. Cut for nearly its entire length, it encircles the area drained by Savages Run between Lake Nummy and East Creek Pond. It generally traverses dry, oak-pine forests but frequently descends into deep, dark cedar brooks and swamps—more characteristic of the Pine Barrens to the north. Unlike the Pine Barrens, shore vegetation—particularly greenbriers and holly trees—is found throughout the forest, revealing the transitional nature of the region.

Be warned that the forest abounds in mosquitoes, ticks, and deer lice. Strong insect repellents may prevent unnecessary problems (see the Introduction). At the time of this writing, the East Creek Trail was fairly well marked but not that well maintained. Some footbridges were slippery, and a few areas very overgrown. However, an extensive refurbishing program should be finished before you read this. Most of the hike is easy walking. Its moderate rating comes from the length.

How to Get There

Take exit 17 (Woodbine/Sea Isle City) off the Garden State Parkway. Bear right following signs for Woodbine; turn right onto NJ 9 and go 0.6 mile; then turn left onto County Route 550 (CR 550). After 6.3 miles, you reach the town of Woodbine (historically a sanctuary for European and Russian Jews), where CR 550 makes a left, then a right. Stay on it. From Woodbine, it is 1.4 miles to the state forest. Turn left at the entrance (there is a new park office), pass the entry station (fee collected seasonally), and drive 0.5 mile to an intersection. A right turn here will lead in another 0.5 mile

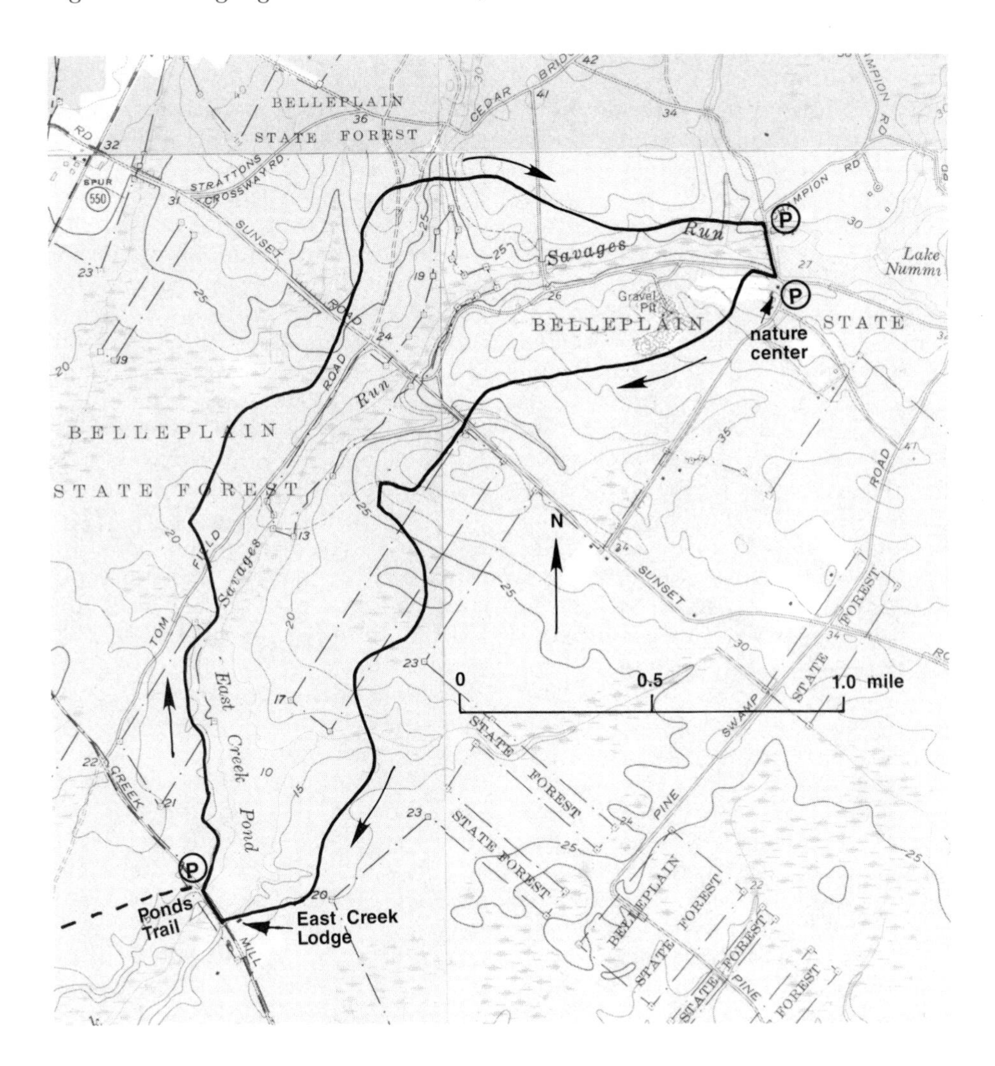

to Lake Nummy on the right and the nature center on the left. Park at the nature center. If you are hiking during the summer peak season, you may need to continue on to the beach (refreshment stand), where there is also a large parking area.

The Trail

From the nature center, follow signs and white blazes to a dirt road about 100 yards west of the center and just to the left of the main road. A post with two white markers is found at its entrance, and a sign that says HIKING TRAIL is just beyond.

Still following the white markers, begin hiking southward. The trail, a moss-covered footpath, penetrates first an open forest of young oaks, then a pitch pine forest reminiscent of the Pine Barrens. Where the trail parallels a fire ditch, the first of many along the trail, be alert for a sudden right turn where the ditch swings left. Clumps of mountain laurel, small pine trees, and, in places, bracken ferns form the ground cover seen here and all along the trail. About a mile into the hike, it crosses a creek in the dark shadows of tall cedars. Here are the first of many holly groves and tangles of greenbrier that threaten to overwhelm the trail. After crossing the small brook, reach and cross paved Sunset Road.

The trail now follows the perimeter of an abandoned field filled with wildflowers in season. The transition from field to forest is evident here, and wildlife, including deer and game birds, is abundant. After reentering the woods, the trail joins an old sand road, following it through a pine forest for only 100 yards or so before turning sharply left. Here is an old boardwalk, the first of many that will aid you through the wet sections ahead. The narrow trail now penetrates an older, deeper, and darker forest; some of the pines are very large. In the wetter areas, huge holly trees are found.

Beyond this low and wet area, the trail crosses another stream on planks at the edge of a dense stand of cedars. Then it recrosses where the same stream is wider, the cedars denser. The trees seem to be standing on their roots to keep out of the wet, green earth. Be careful while crossing on the planks, which were moss covered and slippery—although they may have been replaced.

The next section of trail is very green, dominated by pine, holly, and laurel. This forest must be quite striking with a snow cover. After traversing two more sections of boardwalk, the trail winds through an open section of trees killed by the gypsy moth. Follow an old woods road through a forest of young pines before you reach an open area. Walk straight ahead, following markers, toward the building at the southern end of East Creek Pond. This is the rebuilt East Creek Lodge, available from the state forest for group use. The front of the lodge has a dock and many picnic tables; if not already in use, this makes a good spot for a snack or lunch. This is the halfway point of the hike—about 3 miles from the start.

Nowadays, the view over East Creek Pond is a calm one—blue water lined with tall, green pines. If anything, the pond is underused, yet it is regarded as an excellent pickerel lake and does attract some anglers. A hundred years ago, however, this area was the scene of much activity; a lumber and gristmill were located here.

When ready to continue, walk to the other side of the lake along the paved road (it is busy), following white markers. The new parking area here was built to accommodate users of the new multiuse Ponds Trail to Pickle Brook Lake; it was dedicated on National Trails Day in June 1995. Still following the white markers, reenter the woods, heading north. The trail parallels the lake for a distance before it actually arrives at the shoreline near an inlet. Here is a wilderness vista of the lake. With the possible exception of anglers in boats, the entire panorama is of water and forest. From this point the trail turns left, skirts a wet section, then heads toward higher ground.

You now traverse a forest of young pines on both cut trail and woods road. As the trail nears the northern end of East Creek Pond, it meanders through a very dense cedar forest and, farther on, crosses a swamp on planks. At the swampy northern end of the lake, the trail makes a sharp left and meets, in 100 feet, a woods road. You will use this road for only a short distance, then bear left at the fork (a right would lead to a last look at the pond) and almost immediately turn left again, off the road and cutting back into the woods on a footpath. After a short walk, arrive at gravel Tom Field Road, which is open to vehicles.

After crossing the road, the trail heads back into the woods, making a sharp right turn after about 200 yards. For the next 0.5 mile, it penetrates some very dense growth in a low area and in some places uses fire ditches. Eventually you will see Tom Field Road on the right; cross paved Sunset Road for the second time in the hike. North of Sunset Road, the trail traverses some higher and more open land, making for easier hiking. After about 0.25 mile, the trail, now heading northeast, descends and crosses Tom Field Road, then a smaller sand road.

From here the trail once again enters a cedar swamp, crossing a brook on a wooden bridge and a wet area on a boardwalk. After a grassy road, the trail travels through a mature white pine forest, where some large holly trees may be seen as well. Ahead, it makes a final road crossing and heads toward Lake Nummy. This last section begins on fairly high ground but descends toward a large cedar stand. In the heart of this river of cedars lies Savages Run, the stream that drains Lake Nummy and feeds East Creek Pond. After keeping its distance from the cedars, the trail finally enters what may be the darkest and wettest of all the cedar brooks on the trail so far. Be careful here, for the trail can be slippery and very muddy in places. After emerging from the cedars, the trail bears left then right on a utility-line cut; in a short distance it meets the paved road that crosses Lake Nummy's dam. If you parked at the main parking area, bear left and then right on paved roads. If you parked at the nature center, turn right, then left.

HNZ/BCS

50

Cape May Point State Park

Total distance: 2 miles

Hiking time: 1 hour

Vertical rise: Minimal

Rating: Easy

Maps: USGS Cape May; DEP Cap May Point State Park

The land that makes up this 190-acre state park was once used by the navy to defend Delaware Bay. In 1942, huge bunkers (containing large guns) were erected here and across the bay in Delaware. At the time, these bunkers were located about 900 feet from the water's edge, but today, because of beach erosion, one bunker stands precariously just offshore. The lighthouse located here was built in 1859, constructed well to the north of the two earlier lights. It stands 157 feet tall and was recently (1994) painted. Cape May Point State Park (Box 107, Cape May Point, NJ 08212; 609-884-2159), which came into being in 1974, preserves both the military and natural history of the area and is especially popular with birders. Hikers may wish to visit the park's visitors center, which houses a museum where exhibits on the natural and historical features of the park are on display.

Cape May is located on the Atlantic Flyway, the main path for birds migrating from north to south. Many birds that summer in the Northeast migrate to Central and even South America for the winter via New Jersey. The birds, which utilize the New Jersey coast as a guide in this migration, converge on Cape May Point before the relatively long flight over the waters of Delaware Bay. Fall is considered the best time to observe birds in the park, particularly the hawks that migrate south in large numbers from September to November each year.

Cape May Point State Park, although very small, offers about 2 miles of trail through a variety of habitats where both northern and southern species of plants exist together. A total of 153 acres of the park is a designated natural area called Cape May Point Natural Area. Portions of the pathways throughout the park are covered with boardwalk, and there is even a trail for wheelchairs. Three trails are color coded and marked with large arrows. This hike uses the entire blue trail,

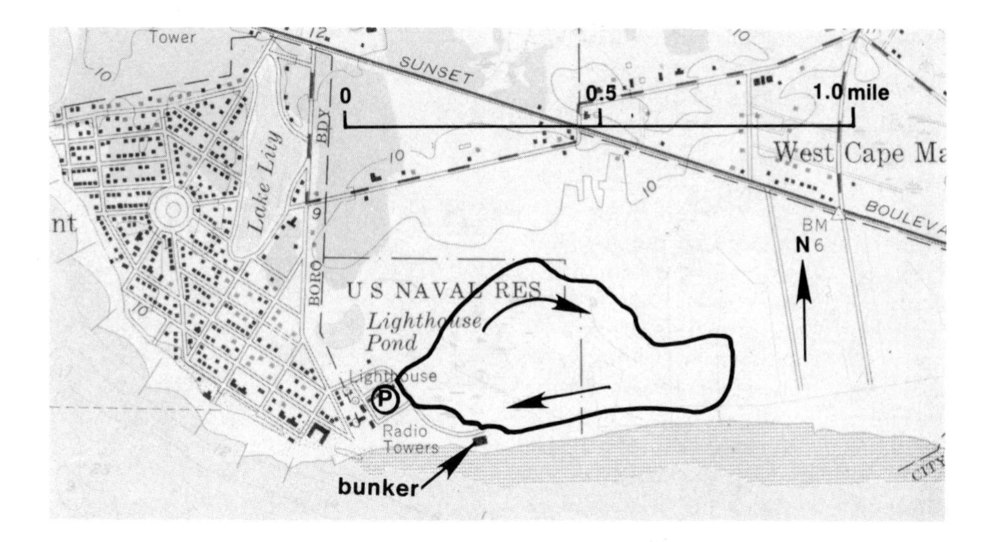

with a return walk via the beach. The trailhead is located near a directory at the far end of the parking area and begins on a boardwalk. There is a sign here indicating the entrance to the nature area. Pets are not permitted on these trails, though they are permitted on the beach. You won't encounter any bicycles in Cape May Point State Park; all trails are for pedestrian use only.

How to Get There

Take the Garden State Parkway to its terminus just before the town of Cape May and follow signs to Center City. Make a right at the T-junction, Sunset Boulevard (CR 606), following signs to Cape May Point. After 2.2 miles, make a left onto CR 629 and travel 0.7 mile to the park entrance, which is on the left. Park toward the far end of the large parking area, near the covered picnic area if possible.

The Trail

Begin hiking on the boardwalk, over which rise tall red cedars and phragmites. Phragmites, the common marsh reeds seen all over New Jersey, originated in the Old World but have now taken over the habitats formerly filled by the native cattails. The red cedar is the source of the aromatic cedarwood used to make cedar chests. Almost immediately, the boardwalk divides. To the left is the red trail, suitable for wheelchairs, which leads to a freshwater pond. There is one observation platform and one birdblind here, and those interested in birds may wish to take this side trail, which reconnects with the blue (and yellow) trail about 0.1 mile ahead. To the right, the blue (and yellow) trail crosses a wet area on a well-constructed bridge, goes through a wooded area, and soon meets the red trail coming in from the left.

Continue along the trail in the direction indicated by occasional blue and yellow arrows, now a narrow footpath meandering through a tangle of greenbrier, holly, and other shore vegetation. The scenery changes to phragmites again where the trail enters a marsh but soon returns to woodland. After crossing another marsh on a straight causeway, the trail comes to a junction where a left turn will lead to an observation platform overlooking Al's Pond, a habitat for muskrat and a food source for migrating birds. Return to the main trail where, just ahead, the yellow and blue trails separate. Bear to the left on the blue trail, which crosses over water on a wooden bridge and winds its way through a cedar and shadbush swamp. Ahead, the trail passes along the edge of a marsh where tall phragmites are growing. After reentering a particularly viney woods, the trail bears to the right, climbs a dune, and meets the ocean.

On the beach, turn right and head back toward the lighthouse in the distance. Foredunes stabilized by dune grass protect the marshes and woods traversed by the trails from the encroaching sea. As you walk along the beach, look for the small, clear, and very polished pebbles known locally as Cape May Diamonds. These pebbles, pieces of clear quartz, have been tumbled by the waters of the ocean and bay for countless years. The original source of this quartz was probably northern New Jersey, New York, or Pennsylvania, the material being washed down to the Cape May area by the ancient Delaware River. The largest Cape May diamonds ever found were reported to weigh about a pound, though most are much smaller than these. The museum at the visitors center has a display on this unique geological feature.

Just before reaching the lighthouse area, a huge concrete bunker stands on wooden pilings in shallow water.

Cape May Lighthouse

Built during World War II to protect Delaware Bay, the bunker has turrets that once held 6-inch guns and 155-mm coast artillery guns. Originally located far from the ocean, the bunker was covered over with earth. The amount of erosion in just over 50 years is staggering, and it seems inevitable that this heavy construction will soon topple from its wooden perch.

Just past the bunker, a path leads through the dune fence. A right turn here will lead past a bird observation platform overlooking Shallow Pond and on to the parking area.

BCS